The Biography Of Phil Spector

Printed and bound in Great Britain by MPG Books, Bodmin

Distributed in the US by Publishers Group West

Published in the UK by Sanctuary Publishing Limited, Sanctuary House, 45–53 Sinclair Road, London W14 0NS, United Kingdom

www.sanctuarypublishing.com

ISBN: 1-86074-543-1

The Biography Of Phil Spector

Dave Thompson
Sanctuary

Contents

Acknowledgements

At a time when Phil Spector is making headlines for all the wrong reasons, it feels strange to be completing a book that celebrates him for what, outside of the tabloid gratuities that pass for news these days, seem to be the right ones.

In the months since police were called to his home in the Los Angeles suburb of Alhambra, there to discover the body of actress Lana Clarkson, more articles and discussions on Phil Spector have been published and republished than appeared in the 20 years before that, an astonishing deluge which, frankly, makes one wonder what there could possibly be left to talk about.

Certainly a considerable number of the friends, associates and former colleagues whom I approached for interviews as this book took shape felt that way. While several key names declined to speak to me at all, a number of others agreed to talk only on condition of anonymity, or else submitted prepared commentaries drawn from interviews granted elsewhere, earlier. Others still agreed to contribute strictly 'off the record', to either verify or deny incidents and stories to which other sources claim they were witness, and it was these conversations, perhaps surprisingly, that turned out to be the most illuminating. On more than one occasion, I entered an interview expecting to emerge with 'Wall Of Sound Babylon', only to leave with 'The Little Multi-Track On The Prairie'; this was not because the information I was given in any way whitewashed the truth, but because, as indicated by subsequent researches, it simply *was* the truth.

Phil Spector is the subject of more urban legends than anybody else I have ever written about. Why that should be is, on reflection, obvious. Although society requires its idols and icons to seem glamorous, it also demands that they are accessible, in words and pictures if nothing else. Remove that accessibility and first imagination, then invention, will replace the daily updates from the entertainment pages.

Phil Spector, by the very nature of his chosen career, has never been accessible. So much of what he does takes place behind closed and sometimes secretively locked doors that he transformed his very existence into a mystery – when the real mystery would have been his ability to live any kind of 'conventional' superstar life while making those records. A record producer does not tour, does not make public appearances, does not appear on *Top Of The Pops* and rarely even gives interviews. He simply makes records and then goes home until it's time to make the next one. Let the artist deal with all the other stuff.

To many people, however, those who admired the records and were responsible for the manner in which Spector's name became synonymous with the groups he recorded, the producer himself was the artist and the artists were simply the tools he used, no more or less important than the tape machines, the echo chambers, and the guy who played castanets on the B-side. But Spector would not play the whole game. He allowed the public to fete him, he accepted the superstardom. But he still went home once the record was finished. And so, to his admirers, he became a recluse. Then the recluse became an eccentric, the eccentric became a crazy man and the crazy man became an even greater legend than Spector was in the first place.

He could have stopped that cycle at any time, of course; by wildly clubbing in front of the cameras, by throwing vast parties and inviting the world; by hiring a publicist to let the fan club know every time he went out and bought a fresh pair of socks. But, again, that wasn't what he entered the music industry to do. Performers performed, producers produced.

So the legend grew and, in doing so, it caused such a blurring of realities that, as I started this book, one of my own dearest friends (who himself appears several times in these pages) counselled me to be very careful about what I wrote, 'because the only way you'll know if you've told the story is, if the story itself surprises you.' He was right. With every interview I conducted, and every conclusion I drew, the surprises never stopped mounting up. And the biggest surprises of them all was, I'm glad it worked out that way.

There are two ways, after all, of looking at a celebrity's life. One is through the anecdotal testimony of the various firsthand witnesses to incidents that have since become a part of the public record – the time he waved a gun at this person, or set the dogs on that one, the day he built the barbed wire fence. The other is through the public record itself, laying down the incontrovertible facts, then fleshing the rest around it, to discover why he waved the gun, why he unleashed the dogs, why he built the fence. The problem with that approach is, often the anecdotes don't fit any longer, at least not in the manner one intended retelling them. He waved the gun because he was under attack, he unleashed the dogs because it was time for their walk and he built the fence so they didn't walk too far. And then what are you left with?

Well, let's start with the music. Nobody would deny that, across two bursts of activity that spanned the dawn of the 1960s, then the whole of the 1970s, Phil Spector was responsible for some of the most remarkable records ever made, and some of the most unexpected.

From The Teddy Bears to The Checkmates Ltd, from The Ronettes to the Righteous Brothers, through his collaborations with The Beatles, Leonard Cohen and the Ramones and onto his most recent work with Starsailor, Spector's achievements in the studio outweigh any of his misbehaviour out of it – and, even if they didn't, still the catalogue of calumnies to which he can lay claim owes its deafening amplification more to a 40-year game of Chinese Whispers than it does to any consistent record of madness, malice or mayhem. Again, people want to know what their idols are up to and, if the idol doesn't tell them, then someone else will. (And you'll never guess what I heard about *you*, by the way.)

There are, of course, incidents recounted here that cannot be explained away within the boundaries of 'acceptable' social behaviour. But many of them still fall within the looser confines of all that modern culture deems permissible, particularly within the rarified strata in which Spector has lived his entire adult life – even the most reluctant star will still behave like a star on occasion, for how else does he know how to behave? The one question mark that does remain, the truth behind the incidents of 3 February 2003, will itself be erased once the case itself reaches its conclusion – which, at the time of writing, with Clarkson's death now officially ruled a homicide, could be several years distant. Until that time, again one is advised to accept nothing and expect surprises.

Writing his autobiography in 2000, Andrew Loog Oldham – the nearest rock 'n' roll has ever come to replicating Phil Spector's genius – opened with a simple reminder: 'there is your truth, there is my truth and there is *the* truth'. This book, although it is undoubtedly drawn from all three of those truths, is an attempt to tell the story as Phil Spector himself would tell it – or, at least, as he might recall it.

It is a life seen through the context of his work, as opposed to the work seen through the context of a succession of gaudily lit snapshots, handed around by passing photographers who can scarcely remember when they took them. Of course, motives can only be guessed at; motivation can only be surmised and it is safe to say that for every hitherto unquestioned fact that is corrected here, another has been allowed to roam unchecked, or else distorted even further from reality. For those I apologise, both to the reader and Phil Spector.

Hearty thanks, on the other hand, are due to everybody who assisted me on my journey through the Wall of Sound, and whose hospitality, help and recollections contributed so much to this book. This includes the many people I spoke to in the years before I ever thought of writing it, but whose past associations with Spector arose in conversation regardless. Special thanks, however, must go to Sandy Beach, for pointing me in so many of the correct directions, and Amy Hanson for unearthing several more.

And finally, thanks to everyone else who was there as this book took shape: my agent Sherrill Chidiac; Iain MacGregor and all at Sanctuary; Anchorite Man, Bateerz and family, Blind Pew, Kevin Coral – Witch Hazel General and Spectorite Supreme; Barb East, Ella, Gaye and Tim, Jo-Ann Greene, the Gremlins who live in the furnace, K-Mart (not the store), Jane and Nathan and Jessica, Geoff Monmouth, Nutkin, the Schecklers Three, Snarleyyow, Sprocket, all the Thompsons, Neville Viking and, to Abyssinian Henry – sweet dreams.

1 He's (Not Yet) A Rebel

Berthe Spector was just six months old when she first saw the land that was to become her home. On 29 April 1912, the prize of the French Line's transatlantic steamer fleet, *La Touraine*, docked in New York harbour to offload the passengers who had travelled aboard her since leaving Le Havre, France, seven days before. With Berthe in one arm, and 4-year-old Dora toddling by her side, Clara Spector, the girls' 25-year-old mother, was already craning her neck to pick her husband George out of the vast crowds thronging the dockside.

He'd already been in America since November, just weeks after the arrival of his second daughter, sailing from Liverpool, England aboard the *Adriatic*. Since then, he'd done well for himself – well enough that he could afford to bring the rest of his family over to join him. He'd found them a home, comfortable rooms in the Soundview neighbourhood of the South Bronx; he found work. Just a few hours more, passing through the immigration office on Ellis Island, and the family would be ready to commence its new life.

The Spectors were Russians – George's immigration papers further note him as a 'Hebrew' – who had moved first to Paris, France, where Berthe was born, before deciding to move on to the New World. Theirs was not an unusual journey – all things French heavily influenced the Russian court of the time, and a number of families relocated to that country, some simply for a few years, others as the first stage in a far longer journey. Eastern European Jews already heavily populated Soundview itself, and the Spectors settled there gladly. In 1918 they had another child, a son they named Sam; soon enough after that they'd be weighing up prospective sons-in-law, as both Dora and Berthe – or Bertha, as she was now called – prepared to fly the nest.

Spector, or Spektor (spelling skills were not the highest requirement among immigration officials of the day), was not an uncommon name, either among Russian Jewry or among their neighbours in Soundview. Still it provoked a few laughs and light-hearted teasing ('I hope he's not a long lost cousin') when Bertha began dating Benjamin Spector, around the time of her 21st birthday.

His family also emigrated to the United States around the turn of the 1910s; Benjamin himself was just 7 when they arrived, and no more than 14 when America joined World War I in 1917. Swept up in the great rush of patriotism that accompanied the declaration of war, Benjamin volunteered to fight and would be overseas for much of the next two years. Now he had a steady job at one of the many steelworks that lay in and around the Bronx, and a secure enough income to offer Bertha a comfortable future as his wife.

The couple married in 1934, and moved into one half of an old brick house at 1024 Manor Avenue, one of the network of streets that, today, lay between the Bruckner Expressway and the Bronx River Parkway as both scythe through the Bronx on their way to brighter lights. Their first child, Shirley, was born the following year; five years later, on 26 December 1940, they had the son they named Harvey Philip – Phil.

Six-year-old Shirley doted upon the boy as much as her mother did. In later years, when outsiders commented upon the awkward turbulence of the adult Phil's relationships with the opposite sex, it was easy to ascribe many of his 'difficulties' to the effects of growing up so drenched in love that he could scarcely breathe. In fact, by the time he was five or six, breathing was one problem that the smiling, chubby little boy did have. Horribly asthmatic in a neighbourhood where the thick stench of industry clung to every fibre, it would have been unnatural if his mother and elder sister had not thrown a cloak of over-protection around him. Boys, after all, will be boys and left to his own devices, Phil would doubtless have been running with the wildest, right up until the moment he choked his asthmatic last in a deserted warehouse somewhere.

It was a rough area, in the way that only America's East Coast industrial enclaves can be, a land where the old world of pre-World War II America lived on in the minds of men who'd been too old to fight, even as the values of the post-war society took root in the hearts of those younger than them. Employment was high, but the wages were low – most children grew up in households where their father was a semi-mythical beast who returned home each evening encrusted in dirt, then spent the evening complaining about his job and endlessly worrying about the bills.

There were few distractions, although if you had to live in the South Bronx, Manor Avenue was as well placed as you could be. Just a couple of blocks down the road lay Soundview Park, with its riverfront picnic areas and its own network of lagoons. A few streets to the west, where the railway lines crossed over the river, there was no end of adventure and excitement for an imaginative mind to seek out and absorb. And, of course, there was the world-famous Bronx Zoo, where a few cents admission money could buy you an afternoon marvelling at one of the greatest wonders in all of America, the newly opened African Plains exhibit that brought a taste of the savannah to that grim inner city. Even Manhattan, the glittering, glimmering heartbeat of the country, lay just three miles distant to the south.

The most thrilling arena of them all, however, was the street, and when the young Phil could escape his womenfolk, his adventures there would be sufficient to fill his elder self with glowing nostalgia. In 1975, the 35-year-old Spector recorded an LP with fellow Bronx boy Dion DiMucci. An Italian-American, of course, DiMucci grew up around Belmont Avenue, just a couple of miles from Manor Avenue, and Spector reflected, '[We] grew up on the same streets. As kids, we probably threw rocks at the same gangs – or each other. We fought the same wretched battles rooted in boredom and bigotry. And it was the same music that kept us from (destroying) ourselves.'

Like DiMucci, Spector grew up surrounded by music. On the streets, black R&B pounded out of apartment windows, barbershop quartets serenaded passers-by while gospel and blues spilled out of the churches. At home, meanwhile, his mother, his sister and his aunt Dora all loved to sing, and the family radio always seemed to be switched on, pumping out its non-stop diet of light orchestral music and the latest 'popular' hits: Hoagy Carmichael, Perry Como, Harry James, Bing Crosby, Betty Hutton, Dinah Shore and the young Frank Sinatra. Years later, once more, Spector would turn again and again to the music of this halcyon age when he was searching for fresh inspiration.

Johnny Mercer's 'Zip-A-Dee-Doo-Dah', from Disney's *Song Of The South*, was rising up the chart when he celebrated his sixth birthday; Bing Crosby's 'The Bells Of St Mary's', Frank Chacksfield's 'Ebb Tide', Gordon Jenkins' 'My Foolish Heart', Kitty Kallen's 'Little Things Mean A Lot', Ben Bernie's 'Long Ago And Far Away', Georgia Gibbs' 'Seven Lonely Days' – so much of Phil Spector's later musical landscape, and great swathes of his first group's, The Teddy Bears, debut album was drawn from the days when 'rock and roll' still meant nothing more than something unmentionable in the crudest slang imaginable.

This idyll came to a brutal end on 20 April 1949, the day Phil's father committed suicide. A little after eight in the morning, Phil was still getting ready for school when his father left the house; in the background, the radio would have been whittling away at one of the biggest hits of the day, Mel Torme's 'Careless Hands', maybe, or one of several competing versions of 'Cruising Down The River'. Ben Spector set off in his usual direction, but then turned the car into Myrtle Avenue, into the forecourt of one of the deserted buildings that were, like the street itself, simply awaiting demolition. Then he ran a hose from the exhaust pipe into the vehicle. Half an hour after Ben left the house, a passer-by found his body. The engine was still running; the coroner described the cause of death as 'Carbon Monoxide Poisoning – Asphyxia; Suicidal'.

It has been said that Bertha never told her children what really happened; that, deep into his teens – and possibly even beyond – Phil believed his father had been felled by a heart attack. Neither, if she knew, did Bertha ever tell what drove her husband to such a final act. He had money worries, but so did everybody. He might have had daughter worries – Shirley was almost 16, and blossoming fast. But, again, every parent knows those fears. All that really mattered was that he did it; he was dead, and his family would have to live with the potentially traumatic consequences.

Ben Spector was buried two days later at Beth David Cemetery in Elmont, New York, about 20 miles from home. It was a long journey for Bertha and the children to take when they went to visit his grave, but it was a beautiful spot, marked with a simply engraved headstone: 'Ben Spector – Father Husband – to know him was to love him.'

For the next two or three years, it was Bertha's brother Sam, an aeronautical engineer working in Manhattan, who looked out for the widow and her two children. But Uncle Sam was not the only member of the family who rallied devotedly to Bertha's side. While she had settled in New York, other members of her family had continued westwards to Los Angeles, California, and, barely was Ben buried than they began calling upon her to join them. In 1952, three years after her husband's death, she agreed.

Home now was on South Spaulding Avenue, as it meandered through West Hollywood. Almost 19 years old now, sister Shirley was thrilled – her long-cherished dream of becoming a movie star had just been swept one massive step closer. Bertha found a job as a seamstress in downtown LA, and Phil was enrolled at the local elementary school, to finish out his final year. That September he moved on up to Junior High; two years later, in September 1954, he entered Hollywood's Fairfax High.

It's fashionable today to describe Fairfax, a huge stone monument on the corners of Fairfax and Melrose, as the original rock 'n' roll high school. Of course, there was still no such thing at all as rock 'n' roll when Spector arrived there, but the corridors echoed with the war cries of the revolution to come nevertheless. Jerry Leiber was a student there, long before he became one half of the duo (with Mike Stoller) that gave the world 'Yakety Yak' and 'Hound Dog'. So was Shel Talmy, the visionary American who relocated to London in the early 1960s, to guide The Who and The Kinks to sonic greatness. Herb Alpert, Jan and Dean (and, in years later, members of The Red Hot Chili Peppers and Guns N' Roses), they all called Fairfax home throughout the school year but when Phil Spector entered those halls of learning, he found that he had little to share with any of them.

Interviewed for CNN's *People In The News* magazine programme in 2003, Fairfax contemporary Bert Prelutsky insisted, 'he seemed to be just about the only student who wasn't on the academic track, so I figured he was taking Shop or was going to grow up to be a mechanic'. In fact, the young Spector was quite the opposite. Where other kids were riotous, he was studious. Where other kids learned to kiss 'French', he learned to speak it – entranced by his mother's Parisian birth, he developed an affinity and fascination with the country that she delightedly encouraged. He absorbed himself, too, in American history, lionising Abraham Lincoln. America's 16th president was assassinated at the theatre in 1865 and, years later, when he was forced to listen to somebody complaining about some trivial situation, one of Spector's favourite quips remained, 'yes, Mrs Lincoln – but how was the rest of the play?'

Skinny, spotty and insanely shy, Spector had just one thing in common with his more outgoing schoolfriends – an insatiable urge to play the guitar. Homesickness for the sounds of New York had awakened a love of music; in Hollywood that love became a passion, the only non-academic subject on which he would happily hold forth with anyone who dared broach it in his presence – dared, because he would happily talk their ears off once he got started. Bertha presented her son with his first guitar when he was 13, for his bar mitzvah present and, already, he was capable of picking out tunes immediately after he first heard them.

Marshall Lieb, the son of a local car dealer, was one of the first kids to discover these hidden depths in the new boy, first when they met in class then when they found themselves journeying weekly together to take jazz lessons from guitar teacher Burdell Mathis, at his apartment-come-studio across the street from Herb Wallach's Music City, one of the hottest instrument stores in town. The pair would take their lesson, then cross over the road to gaze covetously at the equipment lined up in the shop window, before making their way to Canter's deli, the famed high school hang-out where they planned the rest of their evening's entertainment.

High school teens doing high school stuff. They went bowling, they hung out at the Fairfax Social Club, they 'cruised the Strip'. A couple of nights were sacrosanct – they usually aimed to be in front of a TV at 8pm every Sunday night for the *Ed Sullivan Show*, simply because you never knew what was going to be on; Sullivan's weekly guests could range from a troupe of performing poodles to the latest pop singing sensation.

The Dorsey Brothers' *Stage Show* was worth catching as well, on a Saturday night; comedian Jackie Gleason was in charge of the show's booking, and he could usually turn up a surprise as well – like the night in January 1956, when an all-but-unknown Elvis Presley made his network TV debut, performing a song that wouldn't be released for two months, 'Heartbreak Hotel'. Later, when the record was No 1 and everyone knew Presley's name, there were serious bragging rights to be gained from knowing you'd heard it before all the fuss, and Spector – who devoured music television as though the MTV-era had already dawned – was among the few who could. Damn, he even knew what Sam Phillips, the man who *discovered* Presley in the first place, thought of it. 'He called it "a morbid mess".'

Spector was 14, nearing the end of his first year at Fairfax, when rock 'n' roll first hit America. Of course it had been percolating beneath the surface for years – in history's endless quest to discover the true 'first' rocking record ever, the clock has already been pushed back to the late 1940s. But it was with the advent of Bill Haley And The Comets and, more specifically, the rip-roaring stomp of 'Rock Around The Clock', that the music truly moved into the minds of mainstream America, to unleash a summer of madness. 'Rock Around The Clock' topped the charts for eight weeks that season; the movie of the same name ran at theatres all year.

The bug bit Spector hard. He and Marshall Lieb joined the Barons, the Fairfax music club, and stepped up their guitar lessons as well. Yet Spector's own deepest interests leaned towards jazz. Barely months into its lifespan, nobody knew whether rock 'n' roll was going to last a couple of years, a couple of months or even just a couple of records. Fads came and went, after all, and a bunch of kids fresh out of college making an exciting noise on guitars and drums was never going to push aside the hegemony of truly great musicians who currently ruled the roost.

Jazz, on the other hand, already had a history and a hierarchy. Spector had long since purchased a subscription to the Chicago-based *Down Beat* magazine, and he devoured each issue the day it arrived, noting down musicians he needed to investigate, marking off records he needed to hear. And when, on his 15th birthday, Bertha and Shirley surprised him with a night out at an Ella Fitzgerald concert, he could barely wait for the evening to end, so he could start calling his friends and telling them about it.

At home, it was just Phil and Bertha now. Shirley had shifted to an apartment of her own, and mother and son moved into a smaller flat at 726 North Haywood, just a block away from Fairfax. From all accounts, their relationship was fractious – a protective mother and a bridling teenager both had their own reasons for feeling insecure and possessive, and both had their own ways of showing it. For Bertha, it was a constant need to know exactly where her son was, and what he was doing. When he visited a friend's house, his mother was forever calling up, demanding to know when he'd be home. When he himself was on the phone, whomever he was talking with could hear Bertha loudly insisting that he hang up immediately.

What Spector himself did not seem to realise was that he shared many of those same traits himself. To the astonishment of many of the other kids, he had recently started dating one of his classmates, Donna Kass, and she quickly came to realise – as all his friends had realised – that, if she were not where he expected her to be when he wanted to talk to her, he would devote the rest of the day, if necessary, to tracking her down, then spend the night berating her for deserting him. An engaged telephone line could put him in a foul mood for hours, a forgotten appointment drove him to absolute distraction.

Only when things moved just as he planned them; when all his friends were precisely where he wanted them to be; when he had, as far as was possible in the turbulent world of teenaged hormones, placed everything exactly how he needed it to be placed...only then was he happy and, years later, Sonny Bono mused, 'I didn't know Phil as a kid, we met later on. But somebody was telling me what he was like back then, how obsessive he was about everything and everyone, and I was..."he hasn't changed a bit". Except it's not people he does it with now, it's music. That's exactly how he makes his records. The way he behaved with his friends was exactly the way he behaved with his music.'

Possessiveness or obsessiveness? Opinions shift depending upon who holds the opinion, but the schoolboy Spector certainly knew how he wanted his world to be ordered, and he lashed out at anything that threatened that scheme –

things like the interview that *Down Beat* magazine ran with Sal Salvador, guitarist with the Stan Kenton Band, in its 3 October 1956 issue. One of the questions led Salvador to namecheck some of his favourite rhythm guitar players – a generous list, but not generous enough. Spector's own favourite, Barney Kessel wasn't on it.

Spector discovered the Muskogee, Oklahoma-born Kessel in the band that backed Ella Fitzgerald on his birthday. Then 33 years old, Kessel started out playing in local blues bands, and the University of Oklahoma Dance Band. He moved to LA in 1942, where he recorded with Lester Young, then landed a gig with Chico Marx's band, a year of solid gigging that readily established his reputation as one of the hottest young guitarists on the jazz scene.

Returning to LA in 1943, Kessel combined studio, radio and club work in a career that brought him acclaimed appearances alongside the likes of Charlie Ventura, Roy Eldridge, Oscar Peterson and Artie Shaw, before he joined Norman Granz' Jazz at the Philharmonic in 1952. That, too, occupied him for just a year – back in LA in 1953, Kessel found himself elevated alongside the most in-demand session guitarists in the city, working with Paul Desmond and Art Tatum (among myriad others), as well as igniting his own solo recording career. His own *To Swing Or Not To Swing* album was fresh in the stores when he joined Ella Fitzgerald's band.

Listening to Spector talk afterwards, one could almost believe that he spent more time watching Kessel than he did the star of the show herself – which, being an aspiring guitarist himself, was quite natural. Since that show, Spector set himself to hearing everything else that Kessel had done, from his revolutionary interpretation of Bizet's opera *Carmen*, through to the album of Rodgers and Hart Broadway standards he cut with Fitzgerald earlier in 1956. Every new record sent the guitarist's work soaring in Spector's estimation. And Salvador didn't even mention him.

Pen, paper, stamp. Spector was generally forgiving about *Down Beat*'s editorial policy – under the inspired guidance of Nat Hentoff, after all, the magazine had led him to find gold in quite unexpected places... Liberace, Patti Page, Maurice Chevalier, even comedian Jerry Lewis (an unlikely patron of the big bands) had all graced the magazine's cover in recent months and, in reading the attendant interviews, Spector learned to appreciate the most unlikely talents.

But this was different. Just a few weeks before, fellow guitarist Laurindo Almeida had happily placed Kessel in a stratosphere far beyond his own strivings, while he would easily dominate *Down Beat*'s 1956 readers poll. Before he'd even finished reading it, Spector was formulating a letter to the editor and, six weeks later, when he opened the 14 November issue, it was to find his own name staring out at him from the letters page.

'Just finished reading your article…"Garrulous Sal"…and am a little disappointed that, when naming his favorite guitarists, Salvador left out the name of Barney Kessel, who in my opinion holds the title of the greatest guitarist.

'Salvador mentioned Howard Roberts, a very fine jazz guitarist from the West Coast, and also mentioned the state of California, where Kessel is most well-known. Yet he failed to say a word about the man whose style of guitar is copied so much, but never equalled, and is a favorite among jazz fans everywhere.

'This I cannot understand. Maybe you could ask Salvador, who I think is also a fine guitarist, just why Kessel does not rate. Sure wish you could ease my pain and have a story about Barney in one of your future issues.

'Phil Spector.'

Over the next few weeks, according to Kessel's son David, the guitarist was deluged with calls from the Spector women, as both Shirley and Bertha prevailed upon him to grant Phil an audience. Finally Kessel, who'd never imagined that this outspoken admirer was just 15 years old, agreed and, soon after, found himself setting up the meeting, at Dupar's coffeeshop on Vine Street.

Kessel imagined he would be spending a few hours with a fan. Instead he found himself all but pinned to his chair as Bertha took control of the meeting and began quizzing him on every aspect of life as a jazzman. Nothing, she impressed upon him, was too good or too expensive for her son, if it would help him pursue his dreams of making it in the music world. But she wanted to know all the pitfalls, all the disappointments, all the failures that he might expect to encounter, so she could be prepared to mop up his tears in their aftermath. Phil himself barely got a word in all afternoon. He listened, though, and he learned, especially once the guitarist began expounding upon the current state of jazz in America.

Rock and pop had taken over. In the year since Haley's Comets first flashed across the firmament, a veritable battalion of young guitar, mike and even piano-slingers had arisen – Chuck Berry, Jerry Lee Lewis, Little Richard…and now there was this new one, Elvis Presley, who'd scored eight hit singles in less than six months and was already making his first movie. Anybody who thought you could start earning a living from any kind of music other than rock 'n' roll was either already wealthy, or quite, quite mad.

So, Phil should become a rock 'n' roll star? Not quite. The music may have been new, but the music business was the same as it had ever been. And anyone who really intended making their way in the industry should place performing itself way behind them. The real secret to success lay in the back rooms – the songwriters, producers and publishers. Pop stars come and go. But the men – and women – behind them go on forever. One of Kessel's own personal credos was, 'I'm not interested in a marketable product: I'm interested in what I know from my life experience to be standards of excellence.' For a youngster just starting out, however, the opposite was true. Marketing first, excellence later. Phil was still digesting Kessel's advice when Shirley announced her own future plans – she, too, had been paying rapt attention to the jazzman's words. A friend of hers, an 18-year-old sax player named Steve Douglas Kreisman, had just formed a band. She was going to be their manager.

Her brother moved more slowly. Over at Marshall Lieb's house, he was painstakingly piecing together his first stabs at songwriting on the family's Hobart piano, but he was still keeping up with his guitar lessons and was always on the lookout for other musicians to play with. Bruce Johnston, the future Beach Boy, was one who entered his orbit, and even this early, he told rock historian and author Peter Doggett, 'Phil Spector…got sounds that haven't been invented.'

Spector chanced upon another vital collaborator one day in the music room at Fairfax. As he walked in, he heard another student, Michael Spencer, playing jazz at the piano – Spector, whose own guitar rarely left his side, joined in and soon the trio of Spector, Spencer and Lieb were rehearsing wherever they could.

Friday nights usually found them at the Spencers' house, jamming with whichever musicians they picked up *en route*; other times, they would gravitate to Donna Kass's garage – unusually for the time, her mother (Donna's father passed away shortly before she met Spector) seemed willing to tolerate a bunch of would-be musicians banging away in there. There, too, the trio was guaranteed an appreciative audience – Donna, of course, but also a friend of hers, a 16-year-old New Jersey transplant named Annette Kleinbard.

Herself an aspiring vocalist, Kleinbard packed a lovely soprano and, though Spector's own musical visions had little room for a girl singer, still he encouraged her to join in with the band's rehearsals, learning the lyrics and helping out with the harmonies.

The group's ambitions soared way beyond their abilities. Spencer's family was insatiably musical – their tastes ranged the spectrum from the lightest pop to the deepest classics, and Spector spent hours at their house simply pulling record albums off the shelf, to listen and learn and, if he could, incorporate ideas into his own music. It was a very hit-and-miss process; many of his earliest compositions would never even be introduced to the band. But Spector's self-confidence rose way above such frailties.

In conversation with other musicians, he spoke glowingly of his own group – unnamed though they were, he could reel off the successes they had scored on the local live circuit. He talked of how his songs were all attracting interest from various local publishing houses and, when he was feeling especially audacious, he fabricated wildly, telling his new acquaintances how he himself was already established as a record producer, sought after by studios all over Hollywood. There was, however, no point in anybody actually looking for his name on any of the records he'd worked on. 'Us producers never get our names on records,' he complained. 'I guess we just have to get used to it.'

Spector had not simply pulled the role of producer out of thin air. Still acting upon Barney Kessel's advice, he had made it his business to visit every recording studio in Hollywood, simply to hang out and watch the recording process – an unimaginable happenstance in the modern world, but common enough practice in those far-away days of rock's innocent youth. He found it fascinating; more than once, he had to stop himself from stepping forward and making his own suggestions as to a sound or an effect; and occasionally, who knows, he might even have done so.

He noticed everything, including the sheer dynamism with which a record producer actually did a job which many people weren't even aware existed…let alone knowing what it entailed. There had always been record producers, of course, men whose job was to marshal not only the talents of the artist, but also the capabilities of the recording equipment, and meld them into a solid whole. The actual mechanics of what they did, however, were often bound up within their other activities – Les Paul, one of the founding fathers of the profession, was a renowned guitar player; Sam Phillips, whose sharp ears brought Elvis Presley, Johnny Cash, Jerry Lee Lewis and Carl Perkins into the world, was better known as the owner of the fabled Sun Records label; George Goldner, the doyen of doo-wop and street-corner singing, headed up the Gee label.

Dig deeper into this mysterious world, however, and already a handful of names bestrode the profession like colossi: John Hammond, the veteran whose career travelled from pre-World War II jazz to folk and R&B at the end of the 1950s (and who would soon be bringing Bob Dylan to the world's attention);

Milton Gabler, who transformed Bill Haley's jobbing country and western group into the first rock 'n' roll band of them all and Owen Bradley, whose Bradley's Barn studio was machine-gunning the sounds of Nashville onto hot wax.

Each of these men brought an indefinable spark to the anonymous world of the record producer; each was a god to those music fans who cared to look behind the faces of the artists whose records they purchased. At 16, Spector dreamed that one day, he too would share that immortality – more than that, he dreamed he would epitomise it. 'When I started out,' he reminisced 20 years later, 'there was no such title as "record producer". I invented that word and I honestly believe that I did not know I was creating "a legend". I just did what I honestly felt was right and I will continue to do it until the very day that I die.'

Spector's painstaking exploration of the myriad studios that had grown up around Hollywood quickly taught him which were the most welcoming, and which would send him packing. There was no shortage, after all, of starry-eyed kids with dreams of pop stardom, and studio owners could afford to be choosy about who they let in – usually the ones that had the money for a couple of hours of recording time, and a couple of reels of tape.

The one studio where he was more or less guaranteed a welcome was Gold Star Sound on Santa Monica and Vine. Opened in 1950 by Dave Gold and a Fairfax old boy, Stan Ross, Gold Star was unique in that it possessed two echo chambers (one of which was the bathroom), ideal for capturing both the lush harmonies of the singing groups that were now springing up all over Los Angeles, and the harder-hitting rock 'n' roll that everyone seemed to be able to play. Unique, too, was the studio's equipment, most of which was designed and built by Gold himself. He personally hand-crafted the acoustic wall covering, with the stated aim of creating a studio – one of the first in the world – that was deliberately tailored towards creating a specific sound, rather than the more malleable atmospheres of larger, more conventional set-ups.

His innovations, coupled with the expertise that partner Ross had learned from his own apprenticeship with another studio pioneer, Bert B Gottschalk, quickly paid off. In 1956, the studio scored a Top 10 hit with Don Robertson's 'The Happy Whistler' – a number improvised on the spot, to try out a volume control technique that Ross had just developed. Two years later, Gold Star perfected flanging, or automatic double tracking, just in time for Ritchie Valens to use it on his hit 'Donna.' In 1959, Miss Toni Fisher's 'The Big Hurt' became the first hit record ever to employ electronic phasing; and 'Jungle Hop' by the

R&B duo Don And Dewey entered history as the first record to employ an electronically distorted guitar.

'What made Gold Star unique was the personality of the place,' another of the studio's engineers, Ross's cousin Larry Levine, enthused. 'We were having fun. It wasn't like a big studio where nobody gave a shit about the product.'

He continued, 'the control room…was the single greatest listening area that I've ever been in. Dave didn't have any formal audio qualifications *per se*, instead he designed the studio by feel. He would occasionally turn to reference books to discover some facts and figures on acoustics, but generally he used his own initiative, based on where he thought things ought to be. Consequently, that control room sounded like no other. [And] when a session was going well, it was the most thrilling sound imaginable.'

Although Levine would, in years to come, establish himself among Phil Spector's most trusted right-hand-men, it was Stan Ross who had the most time for the inquisitive teenager who seemed to spend all his free time hanging around the studio. But though the boy was persuasive, Ross would never grant him his greatest wish – free studio time – even after he'd heard the song that Spector wanted to record, even after he'd sat through countless explanations of the techniques Spector wanted to try. The going rate was $30 for two hours of studio time, $12 for a couple of reels of tape and, if Spector ever wanted to lay a hand on the studio's equipment, that was what he needed to raise. In the event, it would be a new year, 1958, before Spector was ready to take Ross up on even that offer. In the meantime, he simply sat, watched and learned.

Spector, Spencer and Lieb played out wherever they could. Most of their live gigs fell into the ubiquitous circuit of weddings, parties and bar mitzvahs that were the lot of so many aspiring bands of the age, hammering out a repertoire of seasoned instrumentals when they could get away with it, or roping in a singer from the Barons music club when they couldn't. And, after a fashion, they flourished. According to legend, one Saturday evening even found them opening for Johnny Otis at one of promoter Art Laboe's regular rock 'n' roll extravaganzas at the El Monte Legion Stadium, east of LA.

Not quite so prestigious, but important nonetheless, was the evening just before he graduated from school in June 1957, when a solo Spector took the Fairfax stage and won the school talent contest with a version of Lonnie Donegan's transplanted folk-blues 'Rock Island Line'. Skiffle, that peculiarly British response to rock 'n' roll, never took off in America. But Donegan's nasal approximation of the country's own musical heritage had its moment in the sun regardless, and Spector – whose own singing voice was no more conventional than Donegan's – mimicked it to perfection.

Shortly after this triumph, Spector and Lieb entered another contest, this time a late-night TV talent show sponsored by one of Lieb's father's auto salesman colleagues, Bob Yeakel, and hosted by his wife, Betty. The Yeakel Brothers dealership specialised in Oldsmobiles and Cadillacs – *Rocket To Stardom*, Saturday nights on station KTLA 5, was named for Oldsmobile's Rocket 88 model, and was broadcast from Yeakel's own showroom on Wilshire Boulevard and Western Avenue.

Rocket To Stardom was strictly amateur hour, and few of its stars ever truly caught that mythical rocket. Indeed, Yeakel himself might have been its biggest name, after he appeared as himself in the 1957 movie *Man On The Prowl*. (A legend in Southern California hot-rodding circles, Yeakel died several years later, when his private plane crashed alongside the San Bernardino Freeway.)

However Lenny Bruce, the extraordinarily risqué Jewish comedian who was already established as one of Spector's all-time favourite performers, made one of his earliest TV appearances on the show, in January 1956, and now Spector was to follow in those illustrious footsteps. He and Lieb performed a version of The Five Satins' recent hit 'In The Still Of The Night', won the competition and, for one whole week (until the next *Rocket* picked up another group of aspirants), they bathed in the accompanying limelight.

The fact that his musical dreams were already coming true left Spector with an awkward dilemma as he graduated high school. The next step, of course, would be college – Michael Spencer had already been accepted by the UCLA, Marshall Lieb was aiming for the LA City College, to major in political science. Spector knew that he ought to join him there, but he had no abiding academic interest in anything outside of pop music, and that certainly wasn't part of the proffered curriculum. Finally, he gravitated towards law, enrolling in a downtown business school and staking any calamitous future that might not involve music on stenography and court reporting – transcribing dialogue verbatim as it was uttered in the Halls of Justice. He was good at it as well, although only his friends knew precisely how diligently he practised, sitting in front of the television feverishly transcribing the newly (October 1957) launched show that was already established as America's hottest rocking TV programme, Dick Clark's *American Bandstand*.

By early spring 1958, the band and, more importantly, Spector himself were ready to take their first steps towards recording stardom. Throughout the winter they had diligently rehearsed a Spector composition called 'Don't You Worry, My Little Pet', a rocking guitar riff overlaid with an Everly Brothers-ish harmony vocal. Don and Phil Everly had emerged the previous spring with the hit 'Bye Bye Love', and a sound that crystallised many of Spector's own sonic imaginings. But, though he made no secret of his admiration for the duo's sound, still he was ever ready to point out where the Everlys went wrong – by utilising just the two single voices. What Spector wanted to hear, and what he intended to do, was the sound of two voices transformed into a choir.

By early April, Spector had raised the necessary cash to book two hours at Gold Star on 20 May 1958. Bertha contributed $10, Marshall Lieb raised another. Harvey Goldstein, a UCLA student who was one of the more regular singers in Spector's live band, pooled $10 more, and was promised a role in the recording; Donna's friend Annette Kleinbard threw in the rest – on condition that she could sing on the record as well. It wasn't the most ideal way of forming a band, Spector mused. But it would have to do.

Stan Ross sat in as engineer on the session, but Spector made no bones about who was actually in charge. Only when he was in the studio room himself, singing, playing guitar or piano, would Spector leave Ross alone at the controls – in fact, Ross later confessed that some of Spector's ideas were out of the range of even his experience. Having recorded the first set of vocals to his satisfaction, for example, Spector then announced he intended overdubbing further vocals onto a live playback of the original set, an effect that would create a sound far vaster than any previously caught on record.

It was not altogether successful. Listening to the playback, there was a distinct collapse in fidelity as the recording equipment tried to assimilate all the information being flung at it. But Ross cleaned up most of the obvious problems when he sat down to master the tape and, by the end of the two hour session, Spector was in possession of his very first acetate. Now he had to figure out what to do with it.

2 To Hear Him Is To Love Him

Era Records was one of the multitude of tiny LA labels that, in the flurry of madness and novelty that creased the mid-'50s American music scene, hit the ground running. Launched in mid-1955 by Lew Bedell, a former host for New York's WOR TV station, and his cousin, Herb Newman, a one-time partner in Liberty Records (another cousin, Si Waronker, was head of that company), Era specialised in country, pop and jazz and was just three singles, and as many months old, when singer Gogi Grant's 'Suddenly There's A Valley' brought the company its first Top 10 hit. Six months later, her version of one of Newman's own compositions, 'The Wayward Wind', went even further, sweeping to No 1 and knocking 'Heartbreak Hotel' off the top in the process. From nowhere to everywhere, Era was suddenly seen as one of the country's leading record labels.

The next couple of years saw Era effortlessly consolidate that position. Without ever changing its musical tastes to embrace the teenaged clatter of rock 'n' roll, Era scored national hits with *Your Hit Parade* TV regular Russell Arms, the immaculately named Arthur and Dotty Todd, and T-Bones Tony Savonne and Joe Saraceno, as well as regional smashes with Ronnie Deauville, David Andrews, Bob Florence, Doyle O'Dell and the Cass County Boys. By 1958, however, the label's momentum was beginning to fade, country and jazz were falling fast, and Era were looking for a new superstar.

They would find it, 40-year-old Bedell and Newman decided, in rock 'n' roll and, in mid-1958, the pair launched a new label, Doré – named for Bedell's son. An A&R department was set up, staffed by two thrusting young representatives of the incoming generation, Lou Adler and Herb Alpert. Their job would be to trawl the local youth clubs and concert halls in search of the rich, untapped talent that was supposedly exploding out from all over the city, and Doré was launched that summer with a single by the vocal group The Marketts, 'Summer Means Love'. The Whips' 'Yes Master' followed soon after.

But the greatest talent of them all would be delivered not by the A&R department, but by the kid who lived next door to Bedell – a lad named Donny, who couldn't stop raving about the record that some friends of his had made. Bedell agreed to give it a listen.

Spector wasn't sure what to expect from the meeting, although failure of any kind does not seem to have entered his head. He sat patiently while first Bedell, then Newman, played and replayed the 'Don't You Worry My Little Pet' acetate, not even wincing as every listen ground another few moments from the precious disc's life expectancy.

It was an exciting moment for all three of the men in the room. Bedell and Newman, of course, were old hands in the music business, so accustomed to exuding an almost weary seen-it-all, done-it-all confidence that they wore their experience like a second skin. But, as they listened to 'Don't Worry My Little Pet', they recognised something they'd never heard before, a rawness and enthusiasm that, despite its obvious clumsiness, bespoke an inventive musical ear that surpassed anything around at the time. Era itself already boasted a brilliant in-house producer, Buddy Bregman, but even he would have been hard-pressed to equal the sound that this scrawny little kid had wrung from his first-ever time in a studio.

Spector, in the meantime, was doing his best to keep his emotions in check as Bedell and Newman prepared to talk business. Yes, they were definitely interested in the song; more than that, they wanted to hear more. They offered Spector a deal for two singles, four songs, and the assurance that, if those singles did well, there was no reason why the group couldn't become full-time Doré recording artistes. It was, they told him, a very generous offer – but not, Spector decided, generous enough. Promising only to think about it, Spector headed straight over to Marshall Lieb's house, to talk to his father about it. Days later, with the Lieb family's lawyer having given the offered contract a sharp looking over, Spector was back at the Doré offices, looking to renegotiate the proffered royalty rate.

The new deal, according to what Marshall Lieb told Spector biographer Mark Ribowsky, wasn't much better, but it was an improvement. Each member of the group – Spector, Lieb, Goldstein and Kleinbard – would receive one-quarter of one-and-a-half cents for every record they sold, meaning they would need to shift 3,000 copies of one record, simply to make back their original $10 investment in the recording. Nevertheless they agreed, and Doré briefed its own lawyer to start drawing up the final contracts.

Under California law, all four of the group were considered minors – before the contracts could even be signed, the label first had to go to court to obtain approval, under the so-called Jackie Coogan law, named for the child movie star who made millions, only to discover that his parents had been spending it as fast as he earned it. The law states that the parent(s) of children who earn large sums of money can only spend, with the court's permission, as much money as was required to sustain a *normal* standard of living, with the remainder safely banked for the earner.

It was to prove a time consuming process – more than once, Bedell thought of just walking away from the entire situation and, once the case did get to court, his own instructions to the judge were simple. 'Ask them if they want to sign. If they say yes, fine. If they say no, forget it.' Everybody said yes.

'Don't You Worry My Little Pet' was scheduled as the quartet's first single, and Gold Star was booked for the following week, so that the group could cut the B-side, a Spector ballad called 'Wonderful Lovable You'. Another bridge was crossed when the band finally found a name – newly released in mid-June, Elvis Presley's latest single, 'Teddy Bear', was preparing to race up the chart. The name was already on everybody's lips – and imagine the fun that DJs could have, slipping from a song called 'Teddy Bear', to an actual record by The Teddy Bears. It was brilliant.

There was only one cloud on the newly named group's horizon. A few months earlier, Harvey Goldstein had volunteered for the Army Reserve, a term of service that would prevent him from being drafted into the US Military itself. No sooner had The Teddy Bears signed their recording contract, than Goldstein received his first orders from the Reserves, to report to Fort Ord, about five miles north of Monterey, for two weeks of basic combat training. The Teddy Bears' recording session, in July, fell smack in the middle of that fortnight.

In a way, Goldstein was better out of it. For two hours, the three remaining Teddy Bears struggled to create something...anything...from 'Wonderful Lovable You'. Spector and Lieb had determined that it would emerge at least as vast an epic as 'Don't You Worry My Little Pet' – an intention that Bedell and Newman, who themselves had expected to be producing the recording, simply couldn't understand. The song was a B-side, something to stick on the back of a potential hit, just to make the kids think they were getting something extra for their money. Nobody paid any attention to B-sides – not in the studio, not in the shops and especially not in the marketplace.

Spector, however, would hear none of it. Any record that he made would be the best record he could make and, when time ran out in the studio that afternoon, Bedell was left with no alternative but to reconvene the session for the following Monday. But matters were not improved by the break – indeed, Spector only complicated things further by announcing that he wanted to replace his earlier attempts at percussion, whacking a phone book with a drum brush, by overdubbing a real drummer, Sammy 'Sandy' Nelson, a member of Bruce Johnston's latest band, Kip Tyler And The Flips.

For the next hour, Spector worked to perfect the overdub. Then, when Bedell and Newman walked out in exasperation, he carried on for another hour. Finally, as the group's allotted two hour session drew to a close, Spector turned to Stan Ross and asked if there was time for the group to try a different song altogether. He gave them just half an hour. They came back with what proved to be an instant masterpiece.

Spector wrote 'To Know Him Is To Love Him' specifically to showcase Kleinbard's voice. He'd always enjoyed listening to her sing, and her performance on 'Don't You Worry My Little Pet', lost and buried in the murk though it was, confirmed his enthusiasm. In an interview for the *Spectropop* website in 2002, Kleinbard remembered Spector calling her up when he'd finished the song, and singing it down the telephone. 'It sounded awful! He may be the world's greatest producer, but he does not have the world's greatest voice! And he said, "Be here tomorrow, we have to rehearse it." I said, "But then I have to take a bus." He said, "Fine, then take a bus." So I took a bus. I think we rehearsed it in Marshall Lieb's garage, if I'm not mistaken, because Phil's mother…wouldn't allow us to rehearse at the house.'

It was no secret within the Spector family where he found the song's title – from the gentle sentiment engraved upon his father's tombstone, 'to know him was to love him'. But the simple change in tense that Spector enacted for the song transformed the words from elegy to eulogy, from pain to panegyric. From the moment he completed 'To Know Him Is To Love Him', he knew it was destined for greatness; and the first time he heard Annette Kleinbard sing it, he was convinced it could be even bigger than that.

From pushing towards the hugest sound they could possibly find on those other recordings, this time Spector went for minimalism. The recording itself was completed in just 20 minutes. Stan Ross had them play it once through so he could check the balance on the guitar and vocals; the next time through was the final cut.

The shortest possible intro and the briefest conceivable fade bookend two minutes and 24 seconds of absolute perfection. The simplest imaginable beat, the lightest touch, the purest voice – Kleinbard herself sounds absolutely angelic, every word crystalline, every nuance exquisitely positioned…two minutes in, with the song's end in sight, she places so much emphasis on one simple word, an almost thrown-away 'just', that hearts could break simply listening to it.

Indeed, the song's beauty barely disguises an inalienable melancholy, one whose impact lies far beyond anything suggested by the lyric, or the soft sway of the melody behind her. Portentously, a succession of observers have suggested that the song's delivery unerringly turns full circle back to the cold stone that inspired its title, as if Spector was exorcising his nightmares while exercising his dreams. And maybe he was. But he was also placing himself in the footsteps of every teen who has mourned for a love that, if not out of sight, is out of reach – and that, in turn, touched the heart of every teen who heard the record.

'To Know Him Is To Love Him' was not, as some histories have stated, the first innocent girl ballad of the time; or even, as others affirm, the first one to make the chart. The Chantels' 'Maybe', just as sad, just as yearning, had already broken the American Top 20 earlier in the year, and that certainly fired Spector's schemes for his own song.

Where 'To Know Him Is To Love Him' truly made history, then, was in confirming what The Chantels' hit had only suggested, that high school angst wasn't simply a marketable product, it was a saleable *lifestyle*. The first musical fires of rock 'n' roll were dying down now, but the teenaged armies marched on, hungry for anything that spoke to them of their own lives and loves. It was a world in which *American Graffiti*, *Archie* and *Grease* were lived for real, where Betty would always wear Jimmy's ring and every letter was sealed with a kiss. Amazingly, Doré came very close to letting it all slip away.

For the single's release in August 1958, Doré decided that 'Don't You Worry My Little Pet' should be the A-side. It was faster, it was hipper and early response to it was encouraging. Local radio spun it a few times, and The Teddy Bears were guests on DJ and promoter Art Laboe's local TV show. They performed both sides of the single, but there was no mistaking which one was the 'plug side'. They might even have managed some extra promotion, but the new school year was upon them; Kleinbard was just entering 12th grade at Fairfax, Lieb and the newly returned Harvey Goldstein were back at City College, and Spector was due back in court with his stenography machine. Little more than a month after release, 'Don't You Worry My Little Pet' was, effectively, finished.

Unwilling to admit defeat, Doré tried again, this time pushing 'To Know Him Is To Love Him' as the A-side. From all accounts, neither Bedell nor Newman was exactly head over heels with the song, but too many recent hit records had emerged from beneath the shadow of an ill-chosen A-side for them not to at least give it a go. But that, too, looked like a dead end. At a time when the sonic bar was being raised by every new release, where the likes of Norman Petty (producing Buddy Holly), Steve Sholes (Elvis Presley) and Leiber and Stoller (The Coasters) were conjuring ever new and dynamic sounds out of the studio, 'To Know Him Is To Love Him' simply sounded under-produced, under-performed. The girl had a nice enough voice, but where was the music, where was the 'ooomph'? You couldn't sell a record unless it had some 'ooomph'.

Not in Los Angeles, anyway. Although one or two courageous DJs had flipped the record over under their own steam, the city itself seemed content to leave The Teddy Bears on the shelf. Way out in Fargo, North Dakota, however, KFGO's Charlie Boone couldn't get enough of it. By the beginning of September, listeners to his daily *Boone In The Afternoon* show were hearing 'To Know Him is To Love Him' every day. (Boone himself would become an international name six months later, as host of the last ever Buddy Holly concert.) The first orders for the single began trickling in.

Days later, KDWB Minneapolis followed suit, only this time it was the station's programme director, Lou Riegert, who fell in love with the record, and made sure that all his DJs gave it a spin. More orders came in, a handful at first, then more and more. By the middle of the month, Doré had shipped out more than 20,000 singles and, on 22 September, 'To Know Him Is To Love Him' pushed into the *Billboard* chart at No 88, on mid-western sales alone. The problem was, that was the only place it was selling. As far as the rest of the country, LA included, was concerned, The Teddy Bears could get stuffed.

One of the names in Bedell's address book belonged to Dick Clark, host of *American Bandstand*. Although Doré's distribution was tied to Universal Distributors, a company with whom *American Bandstand* had a number of strong business ties, it wasn't a number he called very often. As both the frontman and the motivating force behind the country's top-rated music television show, Clark had grown understandably cautious of industry acquaintances just ringing up to say 'hi'. Bedell had a problem, however, and Clark was the only person he could think of, he said, who might be able to help him solve it. He had a monster hit single in the mid-west, and an absolute turkey in the rest of the country.

Clark promised to give the record a listen and, on 3 October 1958, 'To Know Him Is To Love Him' received its first national airing on *American Bandstand*. The following week, it leaped into the *Billboard* Top 40, and soon it was soaring. Within a fortnight, The Teddy Bears were poised on the edge of the *Billboard* Top 10 and, suddenly, it was Dick Clark's turn to call Lew Bedell. Midway through a hectic week of daily shows that would also see Gene Vincent and Buddy Holly headline the *Bandstand* stage, Clark wanted The Teddy Bears in Philadelphia on 29 October, to perform their hit in person.

That was the last push the record needed. 'To Know Him Is To Love Him' topped the Billboard chart on 1 December, for the first of three weeks. A fortnight later, it shoved the Kingston Trio's 'Tom Dooley' down to crown the rival *Cashbox* listing.

The invitation to appear on *American Bandstand* marked the end of the road for Spector's years of idle dreaming. It marked the end, too, for Harvey Goldstein's time as a Teddy Bear. He had not performed on the hit; it stood to reason, Spector argued, that he should not be a part of it, either. Not that Spector delivered the decision quite so abruptly; according to Goldstein, he spun some cock-and-bull story about Dick Clark not wanting to pay expenses to an artist who wasn't on the record. In fact, Clark didn't pay any artist expenses whatsoever, and Goldstein found himself in the historical position of being the first aggrieved artist ever to take legal action against Phil Spector. Of course he would not be the last. (The dispute, in which Goldstein claimed 25 per cent ownership of The Teddy Bears' name, was eventually settled out of court.)

Bedell and Newman, too, were approaching a crisis. When they signed The Teddy Bears to just two singles, they thought they were playing safe – giving the group the chance to make it, and cutting themselves free if that chance never came. Instead, they found themselves with one of the biggest hits of the year and a group – or, rather, a single artist, for there was little doubting who wore the trousers in The Teddy Bears family – who had no intention of remaining with the company. 'To Know Him Is To Love Him' was still climbing the chart when the first rival labels stepped in with offers for the band, and Spector made no secret of the fact that he was considering several of them.

Doré were outmanoeuvred every way they turned. Even the song that Spector offered up as the follow-up to the hit, the plaintive 'Oh Why', seemed deliberately crafted to fail, yet Bedell knew from the group's rehearsals that they had far stronger songs elsewhere in their repertoire. Doré would, in the end, wrest a more appropriate song from the reluctant star, as the group finally completed

'Wonderful Lovable You' to Spector's satisfaction, but by then it was too late. Imperial Records stepped in with both a long-term contract and a much higher royalty rate, and The Teddy Bears were away.

The new deal brought the group all manner of instant thrills. They were sharing a label with the multi-million selling Fats Domino, for a start; they were also billed alongside teen idol Ricky Nelson, whose backing band now included Spector's still-all-time favourite guitarist, Barney Kessel. Even more importantly, Imperial wanted the group to record an entire album, before they even began thinking about further singles.

The group were sequestered within Master Sound Recorders, just a block away from Fairfax High. Imperial artists were among the studio's most regular clients and, though the studio itself certainly had its limitations in terms of space and equipment, Spector quickly discovered the benefits of having a record company fully behind him. Bassist George 'Red' Callender and drummer Earl Palmer, regulars in Fats Domino's band, were loaned to the group as backing musicians, while the meagre two hour shifts at Gold Star suddenly seemed a lifetime away.

The downside to the session players' involvement, of course, was that they brought two more pairs of questioning eyes into a working environment that neither they, nor Imperial head Lew Chudd, nor even studio boss Bunny Robyne, had ever encountered before. LPs were seldom taken especially seriously back then – most were built around a couple of hits, their accompanying B-sides, and a handful more songs that would pass as filler.

The Teddy Bears were immediately at a disadvantage in that their only hit to date, 'To Know Him Is To Love Him', was still under license to Doré. They found themselves in further difficulties when, with the trio having spent a full week in the studio, Lew Chudd turned up to hear the completed LP – and discovered that they'd barely recorded two songs, as Spector instead insisted upon experimenting with the equipment, putting the studio through its full sonic paces and trying to replicate the Gold Star effect. He swore he'd almost finished his preparations and was ready to get down to work, but when Chudd returned the following week, the group had still completed just six numbers.

According to Kleinbard, Imperial head Lew Chudd 'wanted a record out there, Phil wanted perfection, and I was caught in the middle. I was going to school, so I would just go in and do my part, and then split. And then Phil, if I'm not mistaken, would go in and redo everything for a century, Lew Chudd would be screaming and I'd just be trying to get back to school!'

Spector asked for more time – a week, two weeks at the most. But Chudd had had enough. He gave the group just three more days in which to finish their album and, to make sure his orders were adhered to, he pulled Spector out of the control room and replaced him with Jimmie Haskell.

Now established as one of America's most in-demand arrangers, producers and composers, a three time 'Best Arrangement' Grammy winner with Simon And Garfunkel, Bobbie Gentry and Chicago, Haskell was himself just starting out in the music industry when he encountered The Teddy Bears – the previous summer, while working in Imperial's copyright department (transcribing Fats Domino recordings to paper), he convinced Chudd to let him try his hand at arranging and production. Chudd agreed and, that September, Haskell produced a single by the R&B band The Spiders. Another of Haskell's earliest productions for the label was his own *Count Down*, an truly imaginative album of space age music and effects inspired by the recent launch of the Sputnik space satellite. His most successful partnership, however, was with Ricky Nelson, with whom he rang up a staggering 20 hits in under three years between 1957 and 1960.

The Teddy Bears job was just that – a job. Haskell recalls banging out as many songs in three hours as had been completed in 14 days. Contrary to popular legend, however, he never banned Spector from playing guitar at the session, although 'I do recall that he did not play. I suspect that if he was banned from playing guitar, Chudd forbade him to play just so that all we professionals could squeeze six tunes within the [time] allotted to us by Chudd.'

Neither were The Teddy Bears to be allowed any input into the songs they were recording, as Chudd presented them with a clutch of standards ranging from 'Little Things Mean A Lot' to 'Tammy', and on to 'Unchained Melody', a song that both Fats Domino and Ricky Nelson had already recorded, and which the session players knew backwards.

With the album complete, but scarcely in any form he might have wished upon it, Spector could honestly say that only one worthwhile thing emerged from the first months of the New Year – an introduction to Lester Sill. Searching for a publisher for a handful of new songs he'd written, Spector turned up at the offices at 1610 Argyle, where Sill and partner Lee Hazlewood had just opened, knowing that he was encountering one of the 'best connected' names on the Los Angeles music scene.

Manager and co-producer (again with Hazlewood) of both The Coasters and Duane Eddy, Sill was also a partner in Jerry Leiber and Mike Stoller's songwriting empire, a giant in the world that Spector knew he needed to find his way into. In April 1959, Spector signed a publishing deal with Gregmark, the company Sill and Hazlewood named for their eldest sons. He then consummated the arrangement with a song he'd said he'd written with sister Shirley (under the pseudonym Cory Sands), 'Be My Girl', and which he had deliberately held back from The Teddy Bears' sessions. Spector was taking out insurance on his future.

The Teddy Bears' first Imperial single, in January 1959, was Spector's own 'Oh Why', the song he had tried so hard to foist upon Doré. In the marketplace, all of that label's reservations were proven. Imperial's own marketing push shoved the record to the edge of the *Billboard* Top 100, but no further. It inched a little higher on the *Cashbox* chart, finally peaking at No 75, but that was no consolation for either the group or the label. The album, *The Teddy Bears Sing*, was no more successful, and when Doré finally got around to releasing 'Wonderful Lovable You', having themselves been waiting hopefully for the group to strike gold again, that, too, died a death.

Even worse, however, was the news filtering back to the label from The Teddy Bears' camp itself. Although he had now followed his masterpiece with two consecutive flop singles, people who knew Spector like to say that he changed once 'To Know Him Is To Love Him' hit, that a polite and diffident young man became an aggressive and over-bearing bighead. There were signs of that in the studio, as the group worked to complete (or even commence) its album, and further tantrums once Jimmie Haskell moved in. Anybody, however, who had known him a year earlier, and now chanced upon him for the first time since the hit, would never have guessed it was the same person.

Those same people say that Bertha and Shirley changed with him; that they became louder and even more possessive, and aggressive towards anyone that they felt was threatening Phil. Donna Kass certainly felt that she was no longer wanted – as if the Spector women had ever led her to consider otherwise! – enduring endless bouts of rage with them both, while her boyfriend watched quietly, uncertainty daubed across his face. It was heartbreaking, but almost a relief regardless when Kass discovered that Spector was seeing another girl anyway. Though there never came a day when they formally broke up, their relationship was already sliding away.

Marshall Lieb and Annette Kleinbard were the next to find their security shaken when Shirley Spector announced that she was stepping in as The Teddy Bears' manager. It was a role that she would, initially, have to fight her way into – agent Ned Tanen had already booked the group onto their first run of gigs, spinning through New York and DC when they flew out to *American Bandstand*, and was in place to retain that position. New York publicist Bud Dollinger had already sewn up the group's promotion, and Imperial's own crew was on hand to make things ran like clockwork everywhere else.

Back in LA, however, Shirley pushed herself boldly into every situation she could, and quickly proving herself capable of transforming the most innocuous quest – such as picking up a cheque from the Doré/Era offices – into an excuse for a knock-down argument. And, when she did join the group on the road, early in the New Year as they travelled to New York to appear on the NBC network's *Kraft Music Hall With Perry Como*, it was clear to both of Spector's bandmates that he was already facing a crucial decision over where his deepest loyalties lay – to his bandmates, or to his family?

The journey was fraught from the outset, then, and it quickly got worse. Backstage at the television studios, as the group ran through a rehearsal of 'To Know Him Is To Love Him', Kleinbard told journalist 'Country' Paul Payton. 'My voice cracked in front of [bandleader] Ray Charles, and Phil came up to me and literally was going to pounce me on the head. Remember, we were kids – but he said, (very deliberately) "If you don't hit that note, you're going to destroy our lives, you're going to destroy me!" I was so horrified that when I went for that note – which I hit, thank you God – [but] the expression on my face was of such fright that I wouldn't hit it. It was right at the top of my range; what did I know? But I hit it. I hit it.'

Imperial had spent a lot of money on The Teddy Bears – that album alone was among the most expensive the label had ever recorded. To see the group falling apart before the company's eyes was the final straw. A second single was pulled from the album in April 1959, in the hope of remedying the group's collapse; and then a third in late summer. But 'If You Only Knew' scratched no higher than No 96 on the *Cashbox* chart, and 'Don't Go Away' vanished altogether. An attempt at salvaging anything whatsoever from the debacle, in the form of a solo Spector single, went no further.

Released under the pseudonym Phil Harvey (reversing, of course, Spector's two forenames) 'Bumbershoot' and 'Willy Boy' were a pair of chugging instrumentals built on the interest stirred up by 'Say You'll Be Mine', a twanging guitar number included on The Teddy Bears album. Recorded with guitarists Ernie Freeman and Howard Roberts, Spector imagined the latest releases might ride the recently ascendant Champs' coat-tails to glory; unfortunately, they did not. Neither did an attempt to launch a Phil Harvey Band, based around the ahead-of-its-time concept of fusing Spector's long-held love of jazz with rock 'n' roll, move beyond a few weeks of rehearsal and a solitary live show.

Lester Sill visited Spector at the studio on several occasions, and enthused, 'he amazed me with what he was doing with vocal harmonies. He looked like he was 12 years old.' As with The Teddy Bears album, it was apparent that Spector had plenty of fascinating ideas. He just hadn't yet figured out what he was going to do with them.

The final curtain was rung down on The Teddy Bears in September 1959. Shattered by Shirley Spector's continued interference in the band's career, and stunned by Spector's almost total diffidence to their own concerns, both Lieb and Kleinbard were already on the point of quitting the group when the unthinkable happened.

Taking one of the many winding turns and sharp bends that send Mulholland Drive snaking through the hills above Hollywood, Kleinbard suddenly lost control of her white MG convertible. The vehicle plunged off the road and down an almost sheer cliff, before coming to a shattered halt in a ditch. Kleinbard survived the smash, but her injuries were awful, leaving her with no immediate future beyond months of gruelling reconstructive surgery at the UCLA Medical Center.

Kleinbard recovered from the accident, and came bouncing straight back into music. Remaining with Imperial, she cut a single as Annette Bard, before reinventing herself as Carol Connors in 1961, and recording 'You Are My Answer', the first in a stream of 45s issued over the next five years. None were hits but you only had to hear them to recognise her voice, still as perfect as it ever was with The Teddy Bears. She began songwriting as well, first for sundry local bands (The Rip Chords and The California Suns among them), before shifting her attentions towards TV (*Star Search* and *Life Styles Of The Rich And Famous*) and the movies – she co-wrote the hit theme to Sylvester Stallone's *Rocky* movie and, more recently, supplied two songs for the soundtrack to Roman Polanski's Oscar-sweeping *The Pianist*.

At the time of her accident, however, one of the unkindest cuts of all was delivered by one of the friends who came to visit her during her recuperation. When Kleinbard asked if Spector had sent any messages, she was told that her former bandmate simply snarled, 'Too bad she didn't die.' The story was not true – Spector himself has vehemently, and consistently, denied ever saying any such thing. But, in years to come, as the legends began to accumulate around Crazy Phil, the tale would be constantly repeated regardless.

3 Brilliance And Brill

With The Teddy Bears now irrevocably shattered, Spector's first thought was to launch himself as a solo act, a one-man industry capable of writing, singing, performing and producing all his own work. Lester Sill, his own faith in Spector's abilities utterly untouched by the group's messy demise, was more than happy to let him get on with it. Spector, for his part, was studying the art of record production even harder than ever, often travelling as far afield as Phoenix, Arizona, to watch Lee Hazlewood working on Duane Eddy sessions.

'He absorbed everything we did like a sponge,' Sill reflected, both during the recording session itself and back in Los Angeles, when they took the tapes into Gold Star for overdubbing. And, after every session, Spector would be frantic to get back into the studio in his own right, to put the latest lessons he had learned into practice.

Shortly after Kleinbard's accident, Spector returned to Master Sound studios, to enact what he acknowledged was a virtual carbon-copy of The Teddy Bears sound. He was joined for the occasion by session singer Ricki Page (a minor star at Liberty Records, and wife of songwriter George Matola) and a young singer, Fairfax High student Russ Titelman, whom Spector had taken under his wing a year or so earlier, and frequently used on his own demo recordings – they were collectively known as Spector's Three.

The trio recorded four songs together, to be spread across a pair of singles issued on another of Sill and Hazlewood's operations, the Trey label ('I Really Do'/'I Know Why' and 'Mr Robin'/'My Heart Stood Still'). Each of the songs flirted with the co-ed vocal sound that The Teddy Bears had pioneered, and which was now breaking out all over (most notably in The Fleetwoods' recent hit 'Come Softly To Me'), but none especially stood out alongside the earlier group's greatest hit ('Mr Robin' was especially grating); and interest in the project was almost predictably minimal.

Even locally, the best the group could muster was an appearance on a local television show hosted by radio DJ (and future TV game show host) Wink Martindale, while Spector's own interest in the proceedings was evidenced by his refusal to actually appear on the show. Indeed, Titelman was the only member of the original group to actually perform; his girlfriend, Annette Merar and one of their Fairfax High classmates, Warren Entner, joined him. Fortunately, they were required to do nothing more strenuous than lip-synch.

Spector was now spending so much time at the Sill family house in Sherman Oaks that he virtually had his own room, shared with the Sills' youngest son, ten-year-old Joel. With Lester and his wife Harriet, and two other children, Mark and Chuck (Harriet's son from a previous marriage), he had entered into a 'complete' family for the first time since his own childhood and, apparently, he revelled in it.

Bertha and Shirley were still breathing down his neck, of course, but Spector had his own ways of dealing with them, instructing the Sills to say he was out if they called, and dodging their overtures elsewhere. He visited them on his own terms – though he was still a minor, he was no longer a baby and it was clear he was trying to establish at least a few 'normal' boundaries between himself and his family. He would never truly succeed. Years later, even after he married, Bertha was still turning up at the studio with cups of homemade soup and sandwiches for him and, if he was 'too busy' to see her, she'd simply wait until he wasn't. But whichever apron strings he could cut, he did, with the Sill's home a sanctuary from which she could never dislodge him.

Sister Shirley was another matter entirely. Though he never openly admitted it, it was clear that Spector attached at least some of the blame on the demise of The Teddy Bears to his sister's attempts at management; he was also less than happy with her handling of the group's finances, an emotion that both Marshall Lieb and Annette Kleinbard have since volubly testified to. But there were other issues for him to contend with. A temperament that Annette Kleinbard later described as 'very difficult, very unruly', had begun manifesting other problems, emotional and mental, and it was becoming clear that Shirley was going to need a certain amount of help and attention in the future. Psychiatrists were mentioned, and even hospital stays. Fearful for her future, but alert to his own self-preservation, Spector had a whole new set of reasons to keep Shirley out of his professional life.

However he enacted his escape, once he was free of their influence (some would say interference), Spector blossomed. He started dating again, and at 'home' in Sherman Oaks, he hung out with the kids, and let them in on his secrets – he even had Joel copying music charts for him. He was active in the studio: Trey singles by singers Greg Connors and the Clyde McPhatter-like Kell Osborne were both Spector productions. And, when Sill flew to New York for various business meetings, Spector would invariably tag along, following quietly along as Sill made the rounds of some of the biggest names in the recording industry.

The blossoming, however, brought its own restlessness. Los Angeles might well have been the entertainment capital of the world, but, so far as Spector was concerned, when it came to rock 'n' roll music, New York remained the centre of the universe. No disrespect to any of the companies that called the West Coast home, but New York was where the most important record companies, publishers and studios all lay, and his visits to the city with Sill only convinced him that it was where his own destiny, too, lay.

He knew precisely where he wanted to be, as well; at 40 West 57th Street, and the offices of Jerry Leiber and Mike Stoller. Both some seven years older than Spector, they – like him – first made their mark in Los Angeles, again through the auspices of Lester Sill. He was national sales manager for the Modern Records label at the time, when he happened to stop by the record store where Leiber was working. They struck up a conversation and Leiber mentioned that he and a friend were budding songwriters, then proceeded to regale Sill with a few highlights from their repertoire.

Sill was impressed, so much so that he began introducing the two boys – both were still at school (Fairfax, of course) – around some of the smaller labels he knew. In 1951, Leiber and Stoller saw their first song recorded, 'That's What The Good Book Says', by a local vocal group, The Robins. By the following year, they were supplying material to Johnny Otis who, in turn, introduced them to the blues belter Big Mama Thornton. It was she who brought the pair their first major hit, when her version of their 'Hound Dog' topped the Rhythm & Blues chart in 1953.

By 1955, Leiber, Stoller and Sill were partners in their own record label, Spark, with the duo not only writing, but also arranging and producing many of the label's releases. But, despite unleashing such future classics as 'Riot In Cell Block No 9', 'Smoky Joe's Café' and 'Framed', the label was never able to break any record outside of Los Angeles. It was time to go national. When Atlantic Records approached them with a production deal, Leiber and Stoller abandoned Spark and took the offer.

Atlantic's timing was, of course, spectacular. The following summer, Elvis Presley's version of 'Hound Dog' established the pair as the hippest young songwriters in the world, a status that they confirmed with the launch of The Coasters, a band formed from the wreckage of their old friends, The Robins. By late 1957, Leiber and Stoller had left LA and established themselves in New York; by the time Spector got to meet them, on one of his trips east with Lester Sill, they were so hot that even failures from their distant past were scoring major hits – Presley followed 'Hound Dog' with 'Love Me', a Leiber/Stoller song originally recorded for Spark in 1954 by the duo Willy and Ruth.

It was Sill who first broached the idea that Spector should be 'apprenticed' to Leiber and Stoller. In 1981, Leiber explained, 'Lester called us sometimes in the early 1960s [actually, spring 1960] and asked me if we would allow Phil to sort of apprentice himself to us. He was living in Los Angeles at the time and, at the time, Los Angeles wasn't that exciting. So we took [him] on.'

The arrangement was that Spector would work for Leiber and Stoller in New York, both as a producer and a songwriter for their Trio Music publishing house, but remain under contract to Sill and Hazlewood in Los Angeles, although the reasons behind the move were not wholly musical. At 20 years old, Spector was a prime candidate for the draft into the Army and, while his asthma might well have rendered him unsuitable, still it was a risk he was not prepared to take. Such full-time employment with Leiber and Stoller would provide him with a shelter should Uncle Sam come knocking.

The first shock for Spector came when he arrived at the duo's penthouse suite. They didn't remember him from their previous meetings – knew him, in fact, only from Sill's recommendations, and the inescapable 'To Know Him Is To Love Him'. Stoller wasn't especially taken with him, either. Describing him as 'very bright, a sharp young man, witty and sarcastic,' he also sensed 'a rather angry young man…a man on the make,' a suspicion that was confirmed when Spector announced that he had no place to stay, nor money to spare, so would it be okay for him to crash in the office? Wondering exactly what they had let themselves in for, his new employers agreed.

Once in New York, however, Spector swiftly made it apparent that he had no intention of allowing the grass to grow under his feet. He didn't want to sleep on the couch because he was broke, he wanted to sleep on it because it was there, and the less time he had to waste looking for a place to live meant he'd have more time to find his way around town – or, at least, those parts of town that interested him.

It would be several weeks before he finally took an apartment of his own, a first floor flat on East 82nd Street; in the meantime, Leiber and Stoller discovered that he would be out of their office the moment that the other offices opened, and making a beeline for the Brill Building, the bustling hive of publishers, songsmiths and entrepreneurs where hit singles were literally being churned out by the bucketload, by some of the most gifted names in American pop.

Eleven floors of offices sited over boxer Jack Dempsey's restaurant, the Brill Building was, essentially, a song factory. As English songwriter Graham Gouldman, who worked there during the late 1960s, put it, 'we were employed to write songs. Every morning we would clock in, go up to our offices, sit down at the piano and write. It was like any factory, only instead of little bits of cars, you'd make little bits of music.'

At the helm of this empire sat Don Kirshner, a native New Yorker who wrote his first song while working as a bellhop at a resort hotel in the Catskill Mountains. Finding himself carrying singer Frankie Laine's baggage one day, Kirshner tried to sell the song to him – Laine turned it down, but did explain how to get a demo made. Kirshner followed his advice and, six months later, the song was published. It was never recorded, but it gave him the taste for that side of the industry and, by 1957, he was writing for the then unknown Bobby Darin, whom Kirshner met outside a candy store one day.

Darin's career was slow getting off the ground, so Kirshner turned his attention instead to writing commercials for various shops and businesses. It was in the course of this enterprise that he encountered one Al Nevins, himself a successful composer and musician.

Despite his own lack of success so far, Kirshner was convinced that the secret to pop success lay in writing songs targeted exclusively at teens. Nevins agreed and, in May 1958, the pair pooled their resources (and their forenames) as Aldon Music, and rented office space directly opposite the Brill Building, at 1650 Broadway. They were still unpacking the furniture when they signed their first clients, as Neil Sedaka and Howard Greenfield walked in and proceeded to play them half a dozen of their own compositions. Days later, Kirshner had placed the first of them, 'Stupid Cupid', with Connie Francis. The ensuing single was a Top 20 hit and Aldon Music was off and running.

Aldon began actively searching for talent, always with the proviso, 'you're writing for teenagers, so write *about* teenagers'. Thus, their most inspired recruits usually were teenagers, or at least people young enough to remember what it was like to be one. Sedaka and Greenfield were followed by Barry

Mann and Cynthia Weil, Jack Keller and Harry Hunter, Carole King and Gerry Goffin, Jeff Barry and Ellie Greenwich, Doc Pomus and Mort Shuman, Neil Diamond, Bobby Darin and Gary Sherman.

By 1962, some 18 writers were on the Aldon books, all filing into their cubicles in the Brill Building at 10am every day, then sitting down at the piano and writing. Some had past track records, others came in on the recommendation of others – it was Sedaka, for example, who suggested Aldon recruit his ex-girlfriend Carole King; she brought along her husband, Gerry Goffin and within weeks of their arrival, in 1960, the first song they gave to Aldon, The Shirelles' version of 'Will You Still Love Me Tomorrow', was No 1.

As each new writer settled into his or her role, so styles and identities came to the fore, and partnerships – some of the best known in music history – were forged. The Brill Building would be responsible for close to 100 US hits over the next five years and, even after The Beatles came along to kill the entire concept of the contract songwriter dead (at least for a few years), most of its graduates would ride out the storm regardless, simply by beefing up their output and setting out to compete with the best of them.

Neither was songwriting the company's only attribute. Kirshner and Nevins also established themselves as independent producers, supplying finished masters to the various record labels with whom they worked, and utterly trashing the then two or less per cent royalty that most labels offered, by demanding a full ten per cent – half for the artist, half for Aldon. Again by 1962, they would be operating their own record label, Dimension, and running a West Coast office, overseen by former Doré A&R man Lou Adler.

That was still away in the future when Spector first visited the Brill Building. But still he could not help but find himself both impressed and inspired by Aldon's success, the manner in which two virtual outsiders had created one of the most powerful entities in modern music history. His first duty in New York, then, had to be the infiltration not only of Aldon, but of every major publisher that called the Brill Building home. And there were a lot of them. Kirshner, who first met Spector during one of Lester Sill's visits to the city, recalled 'Philly' as possessing 'that quality that was charming and warm and funny. He was such an oddball that you adopted him.'

Spector would call upon all those qualities as, methodically, he began on the first floor of the Brill Building and started working his way up, simply introducing himself to anybody who listened, reminding them why they might recognise his name, informing them that he was now in New York, working with Leiber and Stoller. A few people said hello, a few more said they might be in touch and one or two seemed genuinely interested. Weeks before Leiber and Stoller found time to do anything with their young protégé, Spector had already had his first taste of a New York studio, recording demo discs at Associated Sound, with songwriter Beverly Ross, a staff writer at the Hill & Range publishing house.

Paul Case, the same company's General Professional Manager, was another early convert to the Spector cause and, when it became apparent that there was little more than a basic songwriting chemistry between Spector and other people he was meeting, Case began introducing the newcomer to some of his own company's fellow writers.

Remembering Spector, Jerome 'Doc' Pomus (who died in 1991) laughed, 'Spector was Paul's special "case". He called me up one day and said there was this young fellow, hot as mustard, who Lester Sill had sent up from LA. Would I meet him, talk with him, see what he was made of? Well, I knew who he was …"To Know Him is To Love Him"…and then I met him. *This* was the guy who wrote *that?* He was absolutely a bundle of nerves, just hopping up and down, fixing his tie in the mirror and combing his hair, up and down, up and down. Then he'd open his briefcase and pull out a piece of bread.

'But we talked – *he* talked, and he was alright. I was staying at the Hotel Forrest at the time, then heading home to the wife at weekends, so Phil would come over, hang with the guys…we didn't get much writing done at first, but we had some laughs and that was what mattered, because it broke the ice.'

They began spending time together. Sometimes, the pair would jump in the car and simply drive around the city, Pomus filling Spector's head with all the experience of his 35 years, so many of them spent building the foundation stones of the still infant rock 'n' roll industry. Half-crippled by the degenerative bone disease that would eventually kill him, but more than compensating for his physical disabilities with a raw sense of humour and a magnetic memory for the most telling trivia, Pomus had an anecdote for every club they passed and every person they met, a repository of knowledge that Spector simply soaked up. Pomus described how, for years to come, people meeting Spector for the very first time would be stunned by his ability to rake some forgotten incident out of their past and retell it not merely as though it were yesterday, but also as if he himself had witnessed it. It would usually be much later, Pomus smiled, before they realised 'the story must have come from me'.

On other occasions, Spector would drive Pomus back to his home in Long Island, to spend a weekend with his family. 'I'd hire the car, Phil would drive and Willie [Pomus's wife] would fill him with all the Jewish cooking he could eat. And that's when the songs started coming.'

Another early ally with saxophonist Nino Tempo, a child prodigy who, by age nine, was already being touted as 'the next Mickey Rooney', but who had long since turned away from acting to concentrate on music instead. Now in his mid-20s, Tempo relocated to New York from his native Los Angeles to work in sessions, frequently for Leiber and Stoller, and when Leiber set off for a six week vacation abroad, he asked Tempo and Spector to housesit for him. Tempo would become one of Spector's closest friends, an occasional songwriting partner and, over the next 15 years, one of the first musicians he would call when he had a session looming. (The pervasive rumour that Spector produced one or more of the hit singles Tempo scored with sister April Stevens during 1963, however, is just that – a rumour. Tempo and Atlantic head Ahmet Ertegun were responsible for them all.)

Spector had been in New York for close to a month of frenzied activity before Leiber and Stoller themselves finally found a use for him, calling him into the studio to act as an occasional session guitarist. It was scarcely a job that Spector enjoyed. Although the duo were themselves renowned arrangers and producers, Spector found their actual recording methods stultifying, all the more so since he was more or less tied down to whatever guitar lines they'd already worked out in rehearsal. Occasionally he would rebel – engineer Tom Dowd recalled one or two occasions when Spector would deliberately miss a cue because 'what I wanted to play wouldn't fit', but for the most part, he simply played along.

The duo also paired him with a new songwriting partner, a streetwise Brooklyn boy named Phil Teitelbaum, who had enjoyed a fleeting flash of fame as a would-be teen idol a couple of years earlier under the name Terry Phillips. An appearance way down on the bill of *American Bandstand*, however, marked the peak of Phillips' accomplishments and he was about to go to law school when he met with Leiber and was taken on as a Trio Music staff writer.

Spector's immediate reaction was distrust – he'd been brought to New York to learn his trade, and now he was being asked to nursemaid a kid who was even greener than he was. As they talked, however, and as they settled down to see what they could come up with, Spector relaxed into the situation. Phillips was receptive to his ideas, willing to try things and not at all hung up on his own ideas. If he came up with something and Spector wanted to twist it slightly, there would be no screams of injured ego, no insistence that Spector concede something in return. So long as the song was improved, that was all that mattered. Although no more than a handful of Spector/Phillips compositions would ever make it onto vinyl – with Spector producing, country-soul singer Johnny Nash recorded 'A World Of Tears' and 'Some Of Your Lovin'' for a single in 1961 – still the partnership was a success. Soon, Phillips had even moved into the spare room at Spector's East 82nd Street apartment.

As Spector settled in, so Leiber and Stoller found other outlets for him. They had recently been approached to produce the latest single by Ray Peterson, a country singer who had recently hit the Top 10 with the death anthem 'Tell Laura I Love Her'. Flush from the success, Peterson and manager Stan Shulman were now launching their own label, Dunes (distributed by Hill & Range's Big Top label), and saw Leiber and Stoller as the ideal architects behind the label's flagship release. Unfortunately, their schedule was simply too packed to squeeze in another session, but when Spector pushed himself forward as a viable substitute, Peterson and Shulman gave him the nod. It wasn't, after all, as though they were placing their trust in the hands of some untried kid, and Spector would not disappoint them.

Insisting only that he be allowed to supply the single's B-side, Spector reached back to the first song he ever sold Lester Sill, the co-write with his sister, 'Be My Girl'. The A-side, meanwhile, was to be a reworking of the 1930s-era Red Nichols' jazz band standard, 'Corrine, Corrina' – a number that Spector knew from R&B singer Joe Turner's 1956 hit rendering, although Peterson's version would tone down Turner's gutsy tone somewhat, with Spector leaping aboard the chance to work with strings for the first time ever.

Calling in Leiber and Stoller's own regular arranger, Robert Mersey, to map out an orchestral score, and working closely with Bell Sound Studios engineer Eddie Smith, Spector pulled off a feat that Imperial boss Lew Chudd, for one, would never have believed possible. 'Corrine, Corrina' was completed in no more than half an hour. Just weeks later, in late November 1960, the single slipped into the chart, heading for a most commendable No 9.

A month later, it was joined on the listings by two more Spector numbers, as ex-Drifter Ben E King turned his tones towards 'First Taste Of Love', from the canon of Doc Pomus/Spector collaborations and, even more excitingly, 'Spanish Harlem', a song that bore the hitherto undreamed of writing credit of Phil Spector/Mike Leiber.

Leiber had written the lyric a few months earlier, intending the song for The Drifters themselves. Stoller was out of town at the time and Leiber simply wanted to get the number finished. He passed the lyrics over to Spector and asked him to see what he could come up with. The resultant melody slipped over the lyric like a glove – indeed, it was so perfect that, when Stoller returned to New York and heard it, the only contribution he could add was to replace Spector's haunting piano riff with an even more effective marimba. Recorded at the end of October (Leiber and Stoller produced, Spector played guitar), 'Spanish Harlem' became King's first ever solo hit, while enough DJs flipped the single to ensure that 'First Taste Of Love' made the chart as well.

The decision to relocate to New York could not have panned out better for Spector, but Lester Sill had not forgotten him. In early December, Sill called him home to LA to do some work for Trey Records. The label had recently signed the Paris Sisters, Priscilla, Sherrell and Albeth, a San Francisco troupe who had been recording since 1954 and still hadn't sniffed a hit. Normally, Sill explained, he would have been content to take his time with the act, and let them build up a natural head of steam – they had the talent, after all. All they needed were the right songs and the right guidance. However, Sill and Lee Hazlewood's own enterprise had recently run into a major crisis as a row with Duane Eddy, by far their greatest star, ended with the guitarist demanding to be released from his contract. His label, Jamie Records, and their distributors, Universal, backed him to the hilt and left Sill and Hazlewood with little choice but to agree. If ever they'd needed to establish a new hit act, it was now.

Spector agreed, of course. The opportunity to repay Sill for all his past kindness and help was not one that he would pass over in any case, but just as tempting was the possibility of setting himself up as a hit-maker on both sides of the country, a trick that precious few producers had ever managed in the past. They worked the East Coast or they worked the West. The idea that somebody could commute between the two, turning out effortless smashes every time he touched ground, was unheard of – and absolutely irresistible. Calling Gold Star studios, the Paris Sisters' own favourite haunt, Spector booked Stan Ross to engineer the session, and flew out to LA.

Turning down Bertha's offer to stay with her while he was in the city, Spector made the Players Motel his base, spending his first days in LA on the telephone, rounding up a virtual who's-who of past musical collaborators to appear on the session: Russ Titelman and Michael Spencer were joined by Johnny Clauder, one of the drummers who'd helped out with Spector's original trio, in his high school days. Next, he set about resculpting the Paris Sisters themselves, isolating Priscilla as the group's most distinctive vocalist and pushing her to the forefront. Then it was off to Gold Star to cut two songs, another go-round for 'Be My Girl' (retitled, of course, 'Be My Boy') and a new Phil Spector/ 'Cory Sands' composition, 'I'll Be Crying Tomorrow'.

Sister Shirley's (the 'real life' Cory Sands) condition was worsening; she was now spending a great deal of time under various doctor's supervision and, within a year, the first time Spector met singer Gene Pitney he openly admitted, 'my sister's in an asylum'. The songwriting revenue that Spector was now funnelling her way might not amount to a fortune, but every bit helped towards her medical expenses and, who knew? Maybe some success with such songs would help promote her recovery. (Over the next couple of years, Spector took to crediting Cory Sands as co-author of several other compositions, including The Ducanes' 'Little Did I Know' and The Paris Sisters' 'A Lonely Girl's Prayer'.)

Sill and Hazlewood's initial hope was to license the Paris Sisters' songs to another label. But, even with their own reputations, and Spector's again soaring name behind it, there was little interest. Only Herb Newman, now sole controller of Era and Doré Records (he bought out Lew Bedell in summer 1959) showed any excitement, and even he was cautious. Finally, in March 1961, 'Be My Boy' was released on Sill and Hazlewood's newly formed Gregmark label. Within a month, it too was inching up the chart.

With Spector's star in such vibrant ascendant, Stan Shulman immediately rebooked him to produce a second Dunes label single, 19-year-old Arizona nightclub singer Curtis Lee's 'Pretty Little Angel Eyes'. Written with the then-unknown Tommy Boyce, an LA-based songwriter who would go on to massive success writing for The Monkees, 'Pretty Little Angel Eyes' was little more than an average doo-wop song – but that did not hold back Spector.

Recruiting one of New York's top vocal bands, The Halos, a black harmonies-for-hire quartet, Spector transformed the number into a rambunctious slice of honking joy, dominated by The Halos' bassy 'bomps' and falsetto 'ooohs', and destined to become one of the quintessential doo-wop pop singles of the age. Then, suitably emboldened, he would wreak even more audacious magic on another Lee/Boyce composition, 'Under The Moon Of Love', at the same time as advancing his own science a few notches further.

Spector had long been fascinated by the potential of percussion – a potential that few other producers or musicians had ever dreamed of trying to tap. The norm was simply to mike up the drum kit, and let it rip. Spector, however, had heard that an engineer over at Mira Sound Studios on West 47th Street, Bill MacMeekin, had perfected a new technique, by placing the microphone *inside* the bass drum. The result was a virtual thunderclap. Allying this to the massive echo that the old studio walls naturally produced, and with a little help from another mike set up outside in a stairwell, Spector created a record that rumbled like an LA earthquake, but sounded crisp as a New York winter.

Barely had 'Pretty Little Angel Eyes' completed its Top 10 run in summer 1961, than 'Under The Moon Of Love' was charging into the chart itself, and when, some 15–20 years later, British rock 'n' roll revivalists Showaddywaddy turned their own chart-topping attention to the same two songs, it was no shock to hear them follow Spector's arrangements all the way down the line. The original performances simply could not have been improved upon.

Spector did not always get his own way. Early in 1961, Paul Case apparently approached Spector and Terry Phillips about contributing some songs to the next Elvis Presley movie, *Blue Hawaii*. Presley had recently turned his attention to the Doc Pomus/Mort Shuman catalogue, and Hill & Range were keen to push some of their other talent in the same direction.

Details of precisely what Spector offered 'the King' are sketchy, although Doc Pomus did recall submitting a Spector-produced demo of 'Night Rider' (a Pomus/Shuman rocker) for Presley's consideration, during the summer of 1961. Somewhat amusingly, the demo itself was so powerfully arranged that Presley himself despaired of ever translating the song to his own style, and gave up on it after struggling for about an hour. (It would finally be recorded the following year.)

According to Terry Phillips, however, he and Spector actually wrote a number of songs for the project, immersing themselves so deeply in the experience that they scarcely gave a thought to the fact that they were under contract to Leiber and Stoller, and had no business freelancing out for any other concerns – at least not without first clearing it through their own paymasters. For two weeks straight, the pair cranked out songs – before, inevitably, Leiber and Stoller got wind of what was going on.

It was no big deal, they said. But their own Trio Music would require a full 50 per cent of the publishing on all the songs that *their* employees had written for the project. Hill & Range turned them down and, when Trio's lawyer, Lee Eastman (Paul McCartney's future father-in-law) threatened legal action, the company simply abandoned the entire project. Phil Spector and Terry Phillips were left high and dry.

Spector was not going to go down without a fight. He had been just 20 when he signed his contract with Trio Music – a minor. The laws that had governed his past contractual agreements, which had seemed such a silly inconvenience at the time, could now be turned around to fight on his behalf. Days after Spector learned that he'd wasted two weeks of writing and work, Trio received a letter from Spector's attorney, informing them that his contract was void. They promptly wrote back agreeing with him.

4 Atlantic Crossing

It was early spring 1961, and Phil Spector had arrived in precisely the place he wanted to be. He'd placed four singles on the American chart in the past six months – Peterson, King, Lee and the Paris Sisters. Leiber and Stoller, despite the manner in which his employment had ended, were still numbered among his closest allies. Hill & Range were still firmly on his side and, every time his telephone rang, it was with another offer of work. He could afford to pick and choose, and he did.

Of all Spector's most persistent suitors, Atlantic Records was by far the most alluring. The label was formed in October 1947 by Ahmet Ertegun, the son of Turkey's US ambassador, and Herb Abramson, a jazz promoter and a part-time record producer with National Records (he was also a co-founder of Jubilee Records, in 1946.) They were joined at the label's helm by Abramson's wife Miriam and, in 1953, *Billboard* journalist Jerry Wexler (the man who created the term 'Rhythm and Blues' to replace the earlier 'race records' on the magazine's chart). Ertegun became Atlantic's President in 1958.

Atlantic prospered from the outset, swiftly establishing a reputation for fair dealings both artistically and commercially. Early signings included the vocal groups Delta Rhythm Boys, The Clovers and The Cardinals; bluesmen Leadbelly and Sonny Terry and jazz musicians ranging from Art Pepper and Erroll Garner to Dizzy Gillespie and Sarah Vaughan. The Drifters established the company as a commercial power as early as 1953; Clyde McPhatter, LaVern Baker and Ray Charles joined them as chart regulars, while Joe Turner's 'Shake, Rattle and Roll' not only topped the R&B chart in 1954, it also provided the springboard for country band Bill Haley And The Comets' leap to stardom.

Spector himself had had dealings with the Atlantic family in the past, of course. Not only had the company distributed both Trey and Ben E King's label, Atco, it also supplied Leiber and Stoller with the lion's share of their own workload. The label knew how to score hit singles. Just as impressively, however, Atlantic was also a frontrunner in the world of LPs. Where other companies (Imperial immediately came angrily to mind) viewed long-players as little more than a way of making fans buy the same singles twice, Atlantic were renowned for some of the best quality, best value LPs on the market, spending money not simply on the songs and sessions, but on the album's sleeve as well.

Spector could not wait to leap into the high-pressure cooker of creativity that was Atlantic. But he learned very quickly that the grass was not always quite as green as it seemed. Many of the label's biggest artists were in decline now, and Atlantic had little idea, it seemed, of how to reverse the trend. Spector also found himself to be little more than a medium-sized fish in a very big pond – not only was he competing for work with Leiber and Stoller and Ahmet Ertegun, but also with Tom Dowd and Jerry Wexler, and the occasions when he was given a session to oversee frequently found him working alongside one or other of these far more experienced peers.

He was also unhappy with the equipment on offer at the various studios Atlantic used. Industry lore insists that the only difference between a four-track and an eight-track recorder is, one is twice as 'big' as the other; instead of having only four musical tracks to record on, there are eight. Spector, however, wasn't merely accustomed to having no more than four tracks, he actively preferred it. To his ear, overdubbing was not simply a matter of layering different instruments over one another. Other factors came into play – the sound of other instruments as they bled through onto different tracks, the ambience of the room, the very echo of the music ricocheting off the walls. Especially the echo – as one percussionist discovered when he pointed out that the echo was turned up way too high. Spector stopped whatever he was doing, and glanced around almost innocently. 'Too much echo? What does that mean?' he asked. There could *never* be too much echo.

To many producers of the day (and of many subsequent days as well), the recording studio is an almost sterile environment, wherein the greatest achievement is to place each instrument pristinely into the mix. Eight-track recorders were ideal for that – and, in later years, of course, eight would expand to 16, 32, 64 and so on. Spector disagreed. For him, the challenge was to crowd the instruments together, to make a vast sound…a Wall of Sound.

Greg Shaw, author of an excellent 1982 essay on Spector for *The History Of Rock* magazine, explained, 'in today's studios, each musician can have a track of his own, and the whole thing can be mixed at leisure later on. But with three-or four-track equipment, it is necessary to keep "bouncing down" several tracks onto one as the session proceeds, and to combine many instruments on each individual track.

'Spector's approach was to perfect his rhythm track (drums, piano, bass, sax, guitars), dub it all down to one track, then add strings and vocals. Ordinarily, this muddies the original "bed track" out of all recognition, but through experimenting, he devised ways to apply different forms of echo to each track as it went into the mix; and by using several different tape machines, he constructed a sound that was both well defined and "big" at the same time.' Atlantic, however, was not the place to be doing that.

Neither was Spector over-enamoured with Atlantic's love of stereophonic recording. At a time when other companies viewed the new technology as little more than a high-end inconvenience, Atlantic had embraced it as far back as 1958. Larry Levine, the Gold Star sound engineer who would later become one of Spector's most trusted sidemen, detailed how '[Spector]'s big motivation for mono was that what he heard in the studio and captured on tape, would always be that way. The down side was, it was hard work to get that all mixed. The up side was, it was thrilling to work that way.'

Spector's first commission at Atlantic was a meeting with singer Bobby Darin. Inducting Darin into the Rock 'n' Roll Hall of Fame, Ahmet Ertegun detailed one of his own first encounters with Spector's perfectionism. 'We went to Bobby Darin's house... I introduced him to Phil Spector and he barely said hello to him...and then he started playing a few songs. He started playing me a song called "Jailer, Bring Me Water". I said "Well, that's great. What else have you got?"...he sung two or three [other] songs, and I said "That's great, that's great, but what else have you got?" because eventually, he would come up with a big hit. [But] after the third song, Phil...looked at me and said "Are you crazy or am I? These songs stink!"'

Darin was furious, ejected Spector from the house and, for the next year or so, Ertegun alone worked with him. And then, one day, 'Bobby said to me, "We've been doing very well, but there are some of these young kid producers who are really terrific. Do you think you could work with one of them?" I said, "who do you mean?" He said "well, I heard this guy Phil Spector's very hot," and I said, "that's the guy you threw out!"'

In the event, at least eight, and maybe more, singles released by Atlantic over the next year or so featured Spector's production techniques in some way or another, including releases by Billy Storm, Ruth Brown, The Top Notes,

The Castle Kings and LaVern Baker. None, however, were hits, and increasingly it seemed that Spector's greatest successes with Atlantic were the records where he played a mere supporting role, as session guitarist or pianist on Leiber and Stoller hits by The Coasters and Drifters – his guitar solo helps highlight Garry Sherman's arrangement of 'On Broadway'. Quickly it became apparent that, brilliant though Spector was, his brilliance needed to fly solo. He was not a team player, he was not a collaborator. Either a record was made his way or, so far as he was concerned, it was not made at all.

Back in LA, Bernard Alfred 'Jack' Nitzsche, a dazzling young arranger who had recently been brought on board by Lester Sill, explained, 'Phil was different than the A&R men and the record company people I had been working with' – a role-call that included Specialty Records A&R man Sonny Bono, who brought the 20-year-old Michigan farm boy on board in 1957 as a writer and saxophonist. 'In those days, A&R men would hire me to do an arrangement or arrange for a three hour session, and no matter what, we had to get it done before the three hours were over. Phil Spector was the first one to go into the studio with one song, and if it needed two sessions to do the rhythm section, that's the way it happened.'

Ertegun and Wexler were willing to persevere with Spector. There would, after all, come a time when, like them, he would be working alone in the studio and, though he could be difficult, he was also profoundly talented and it was that, his restless quest to push his own ideas forward, and the pursuit for perfection that followed, which lay at the heart of most of his blow-ups. Already Ertegun had granted Spector permission to begin auditioning hopeful new bands, but it was a sign of Spector's own increasing disenchantment that, many times, he failed to even turn up at the auditions. He did spend time at the offices, of course, often working at his desk until late into the night. It was only after Spector had moved on, however, that Wexler claims he found out what the mercurial misfit had been doing – making long distance phone calls back to California and elsewhere, on the company's dime.

In the midst of this torment, Spector received another call from Lester Sill. With the Paris Sisters' 'Be My Boy' having proven a hit, Sill returned to New York for a few days in early April, touring the publishing houses with Spector in tow, in search of a sure-fire winner. Almost predictably, they found it at the Brill Building, dropping by Aldon Publishing to have Don Kirshner pull out a number that Barry Mann and Larry Kolber had only recently finished, the soft, lilting teen ballad 'I Love How You Love Me'.

Spector was back in LA in early May to begin work, with Michael Spencer welcoming him home with a party for every old friend and associate he could find. Spector bathed in the congratulations of them all, but one in particular now caught his eye. The last time he saw blonde-haired, green-eyed, Annette Merar was back in the Spector's Three days; she was Russ Titelman's girlfriend, who stepped in for Ricki Page on the Wink Martindale show. He remembered she was pretty, but that was about it. Tonight, however, she was beautiful. Walking over to where she was standing, Spector's first words were along the lines of, 'would you like to model for the sleeve of an LP I'm recording?'

Neither was that a simple off-the-cuff pick up line. Spector was indeed preparing to record an entire LP...a veritable concept album if you will... arranged around the whims of the teenaged heart.

Working side by side with Hank Levine, the arrangement Spector grafted onto 'I Love How You Love Me' was the inspiration behind the long-player; that, and the memory of the abortive Teddy Bears album. There, too, the notion of a teenage opera had been at the heart of his endeavours, but he'd been too young, and too easily dissuaded, to follow the dream through to its conclusion. Now, however, all the pieces were in place.

'I Love How You Love Me' itself was nothing short of a symphony, with Priscilla Paris' honey-smooth lead vocal almost dripping off the strings. Eight violins led the melody; behind them, the guitar, bass and drums that Spector worked so furiously into shape contributed little more than a gentle wash. Other songs slipped sweetly into the same mould and mood. By the time the album was complete, some $10,000 in recording costs later, Spector had spent close to six weeks at Gold Star, driving the session musicians to distraction with his relentless search for the perfect 'sound'. And he achieved it. With 'I Love How You Love Me', Spector touched sonic heaven for the first time – and, with Annette Merar, he seemed to have found it on Earth as well. Aside from the time he spent in the studio (which, admittedly, was rather a lot), he and Merar were almost inseparable throughout his time in LA.

And what a time that was turning out to be. He'd cut the perfect record, he'd met the perfect girl and now, just days before he was due to fly back to New York, he found the perfect business partner.

For some months now, Lester Sill's partnership with Lee Hazlewood had been growing increasingly strained, as the two men's musical interests began to diverge. Sill, for his part, had found much of what he was looking for in Spector. Hazlewood, however, had never really recovered from the loss of

Duane Eddy from his stable, all the more so since he knew that, if he were to cut himself loose from Gregmark *et al*, he could probably engineer a reunion with the guitarist.

The Paris Sisters' sessions were still dragging on when Hazlewood finally delivered his ultimatum. So much of Sill's time was being spent at Gold Star with Spector – whose methods had never especially interested Hazlewood – that simply pinning him down to discuss company business was becoming an unutterable chore. Finally Hazlewood marched into the studio and told Sill outright. Either he remembered everything else that the pair were meant to be working on – or Hazlewood would walk. Sill suggested that he walk, and then offered Spector the chance to make all his dreams come true. A 50–50 recording and publishing partnership, with the record company end christened for its two founders, Phil and Les...Philles; and the publishing wing named in part for Spector's mum, and in part because it almost sounded like another word entirely. Mother Bertha...as in 'you low-down muthabertha'...

It would take time to get the enterprise off the ground, of course – indeed, it would be close to Christmas, a full six months distant, before Philles Records would make its public bow, a period during which Spector returned to New York and brought his time with Atlantic to a close. Restoring his 'independent producer' swagger, he swore never again to involve himself in somebody else's empire. From hereon in, he was his own boss.

Spector would remain in New York to scout talent for the label, while continuing to ply his trade as a freelance producer. He cut, say acquaintances, a distinctive figure – although no period photographs even hint at such flamboyance, still he is said to have aroused considerable concern among the clean cut all-Americans among whom he circulated, cultivating shoulder length hair and a cloak that swiftly saw him nicknamed D'Artagnan. And it really doesn't matter whether or not these tales are true. Something certainly forced people to notice Spector and, having noticed him, they queued to get in touch.

Among the first calls he answered was one from Aaron Schroeder, the manager of singer Gene Pitney. Schroeder had been trying to persuade Spector to record Pitney for some months now, and Spector's interest was only fuelled by the fact that he knew, and liked, Pitney himself – they first met at the Brill Building earlier in the year.

Though his songwriting career was taking off, Pitney's singing ambitions were less well realised. Pseudonyms such as Jamie and Jane (for a duet with Ginny Arnell) and Billy Bryan had gone nowhere, while his first release under his own name, 'Please Come Back', was not especially blinding, either. At the beginning of the year, however, Pitney finally scored a hit as '(I Wanna) Love My Life Away' scraped the Top 40.

What was remarkable about the single, however, was the fact that Pitney himself produced it – almost as if he was telling Spector, if you won't produce me, then no one will. And, whether that was the intention or not, Spector took the bait, demanding only that he be allowed to choose the A-side – which would, in turn, permit him to reach an arm into the Brill Building, a connection he was desperate to consolidate. He selected 'Every Breath I Take', a song composed by Carole King and Gerry Goffin, and published by Aldon. Pitney himself then added one of Spector's Terry Phillips collaborations, 'Dream For Sale', to his repertoire.

The recording session took place at Bell Sound, where Spector lined up alongside a glittering array of talent. Pitney was also recording another Aldon track with Leiber and Stoller the same day, co-written by 'I Love How You Love Me' author Barry Mann and his new writing partner, Cynthia Weil. They were already in attendance when Spector's session began; so were Carole King, Gerry Goffin and Don Kirshner himself – and that was before one began to count the session musicians Spector recruited. All told, some of the most powerful talent in New York City were crammed into the room for a session that overran its three hour allotment by almost twice as long. And, with that army of session players commanding double time for every minute of that overrun, Schroeder later claimed the entire session cost over $13,000 – at a time when most singles cost no more than $500.

Despite such expense, 'Every Breath I Take' was not to be the massive hit that Pitney and Schroeder hoped – in climbing to No 42, it actually stalled three places lower than its predecessor. Part of the problem, sad to say, was the song's arrangement, and The Halos' backing vocals. Though they certainly doo-wopped with exquisite charm, they did so at a time when the doo-wop style itself was seriously starting to lose its commercial appeal, and 'Every Breath I Take' suffered accordingly.

If you stepped beyond the actual song, however, Spector achieved everything that he was recruited to do, a strident orchestral backdrop punctuated by flirtatiously squalling strings, and a drum beat (from Gary Chester) that echoed like a mid-town jackhammer.

But Schroeder did save some money. When he went to hand Spector his fee for the session, the producer turned it down. Though Philles was still under wraps, Spector had no intention whatsoever of being drawn into even a loosely defined financial arrangement with anybody else. Telling Schroeder to regard the session as a favour, he strode happily out of the studio and into the early morning light.

Most of Spector's days were spent, still, at the Hill & Range offices, where Paul Case was constantly throwing suggestions and ideas in his direction. Out of friendship as much as professional courtesy, Spector pulled off a handful of low-key productions from the Big Top label, recording sides by Sammy Turner and Karen Lake. It was at Hill & Range, too, that he found the groups that might serve to debut Philles records, a black Brooklyn girl group called The Crystals, and a couple of white vocal acts, The Creations and The Ducanes.

It was The Crystals – Barbara Alston, Delores Kennibrew, Mary Thomas, Mema Girard and Pattie Wright – that interested him the most. Although Spector recorded all three of the groups, by year's end he had passed both The Ducanes and The Creations off to other labels: Goldner, the eponymous company launched by The Chantels' old mentor, George Goldner, and Jamie, home to Lee Hazlewood's guitar protégé Duane Eddy.

The Crystals auditioned for Spector personally at Hill & Range. They were performing a song composed by their friend, Leroy Bates, 'There's No Other (Like My Baby)', and were more than slightly taken aback when Spector began throwing suggestions at them – 'let's hear you sing it like this…like that… like this'. He turned out the lights, and had them sing in the dark; apparently he wanted to see how romantic it could sound. Then, when the first audition was over, he asked them to come back the next day…and the next and the next and the next.

For two weeks, Spector had the five girls standing in the dark, singing the song again and again and, if that was not exhausting enough for them, there were other ears in the office who also fancied their chances with the group. Big Top label staffers Bill Giant and Bernie Baum came extraordinarily close to signing The Crystals to their own company – so close that, when Spector got wind of their intentions, on 28 June 1961, he paged the five Crystals at their high school graduation ceremony, and called them into the city to become Philles Records' first act.

The group's first recording session followed just days later. Returning to the Mira Sound Studios where he cut the Curtis Lee hits, Spector was conscious enough of Philles' own limited budget (Lester Sill was still juggling the various shareholders and partners that the venture required) to pull in a remarkably restrained battery of musicians. Drummer Gary Chester, who so impressed Spector at the Gene Pitney session, bassist Richard Zeigler, guitarists Wallace Richardson and Bob Bushnell, and a small string section, were joined by Spector's old LA comrade, pianist Michael Spencer, himself now based in New York, while studying at the Mannes College of Music.

Two days were deemed sufficient in which to record – in fact, that was all Spector could afford, and the song that sounded so heavenly in the dark at Hill & Range emerged less than perfect, slow enough to drag in places, with the vocals often sounding quite at odds not only with the smooth instrumentation that drifted behind them, but with the melody itself. Occasional flourishes, however, worked phenomenally well – a flash of Spencer's piano in the opening moments; the occasional chime of guitar; and the moment, around the midway point, where the strings really kicked in, all had their charm. Spector himself was happy enough to send the finished masters to Sill; he in turn was delighted to finally know how Philles Records would debut.

Hill & Range, however, were less than overjoyed. Though they knew full well that Spector was rehearsing The Crystals; knew, too, that he had taken them into the studio at the end of June, the assumption always was that he was moulding them for Big Top Records. That deal had not been signed, of course, but it was certainly in someone's in-tray and, so far as the Hill & Range hierarchy was concerned, Spector hadn't simply hijacked The Crystals. He had stolen them outright. The friendships and relations he had so carefully built up since his arrival in New York 18 months before were simply flushed away, but Spector didn't even seem to care.

'That was one of the things I loved about Phil,' Doc Pomus reflected later. 'He knew what the game was, and he played it. Every businessman is your best friend until they've sucked you dry of whatever they want. Phil just got to them before they got to him, and they didn't like it one little bit. And I must admit, not a lot of people felt especially sorry for them when it happened.' The boot, the feeling seemed to be, had finally found its way onto another foot.

Spector had good reason to be feeling so confident, of course. Even as one door closed, another flew open when Liberty Records offered him the post of Head of East Coast A&R, a virtual free hand in the label's New York operation, at the same time as acknowledging his independence to work the Philles Records catalogue. The salary alone was stupendous – $25,000 a year was a small fortune, especially when Spector was then able to convince his immediate boss, 'Snuff' Garrett, to pay the entire amount upfront. In one deft move, Spector had dispelled all doubts over Philles' ability to fund its first few releases, negating a handful of the deals that he and Sill had already been forced into making, and ensuring that he would never need to skimp on any of his recording costs again.

He moved house, settling into a one bedroom apartment on West 58th Street – soothingly for his new paymasters, it was just a block away from the Liberty offices, although the hours that Spector put in at his desk (commandeered, stylishly, from the company's conference room!) were scarcely commensurate to the salary he was drawing. Indeed, few people could ever claim that Liberty ever got their money's worth. Spector remixed and dubbed Timi Yuro's forthcoming single, a delicious duet with Clyde McPhatter, 'What's A Matter Baby'; and, early in 1962, he cut further sides with Troy Shondell, Obrey Wilson and a young Lester Sill-discovery named Bobby Sheen. But the label itself scrapped a session he cut with The Ducanes, a country-ish number called 'Tennessee', and when he saw his freedom fly out of the window, Spector felt little compunction about following it. He resigned from the label in May 1962 – $25,000 better off, of course.

In his defence, Spector scarcely had time to catch a breath in those last months of 1961, let alone try and reason with ears that could not possibly hear things the way he did. After close to a month of virtual inactivity on the record shelves, the Paris Sisters' 'I Love How You Love Me' finally entered the chart in September 1961 – the dawn of a four month run up the chart that would see it peaking at No 5. Neither was the magic, this time, to be contained in just one song. Curtis Lee aside, Spector had never yet proven himself of sustaining more than one hit per artist, no matter who he worked with. But 'I Love How You Love Me' looked set to be followed up by 'He Knows I Love Him Too Much', a song custom written for the Paris Sisters by Goffin/King, and Spector knew that there were further hits just biding their time on the album.

Unfortunately, the album was not to be. One day, Sill asked his assistant to throw out a few shelves of the unwanted dubs and demos that were cluttering up his office. What he didn't realise until the job was done, and the tapes had been destroyed, was that the master tapes for the entire Paris Sisters LP had been accidentally misfiled among the out-takes. Everything was lost, everything bar the handful of songs that had already been selected as the sisters' singles. They alone survived the disaster; they alone testify to how magnificent the album could have been.

Spector and Sill's relations with the Paris Sisters (and, as it transpired, with one another) never survived the loss of the album, all the more so when it became apparent that the actual cost of recording it was still to be deducted from the group's earnings. A series of furious meetings ensued, with the Sisters' rage rightfully stoked further by Spector's own apparently lackadaisical response to the situation...a kind of 'shit happens' shrug, followed by an abrupt departure from the room. He, too, was devastated by the loss of the album, but he knew there was nothing that could be done about it. Plus, someone had to pay for it.

The Paris Sisters fled the Gregmark label for a new deal with MGM, but Spector was not about to allow them to have the last word. George Goldner, still thrilled with the Top 100 success of The Ducanes single, had recently approached Spector about producing a new single by Arlene Smith, the former lead vocalist with The Chantels. Spector agreed, and promptly offered up the same song he'd earmarked as the Paris Sisters' next single, 'He Knows I Love Him Too Much'. (Spector and Priscilla would be reconciled and, in 1967, the producer contributed liner notes to her LP *Priscilla Sings Herself*.)

Goldner himself was in the midst of a considerable tug of war over Smith's recording contract with Big Top, a battle that the label was desperate to win, but looked increasingly likely to lose – as Goldner proved with his recruitment of Spector. The label's own misgivings over Spector (sparked, of course, by The Crystals incident) were simply brushed aside. Goldner wasn't simply one of the most powerful men on the New York scene, he also had the contacts to back up that power. Probably in a very unpleasant manner.

In the event, Spector did not truly rise to the occasion, but perhaps he wasn't meant to. Goldner called him in to put one over on Big Top, and Spector agreed, to put one over on the Paris Sisters. Although a few weeks would divide the two releases, the idea of spiking their next single with a rival cover version really was a rather delightful one.

But, with less time in which to record it, and no real enthusiasm for trying to outdo what he had already done to the best of his ability, Smith's single was never going to hit the same heights. Neither did Big Top feel disposed to promote it heavily – continued negotiations with Goldner meant that they were going to lose Smith regardless of how far back they bent. While the Paris Sisters' version made the Top 40 in early 1962, Smith's version flopped. (Nevertheless, by way of a thank you to Spector, Goldner released Arlene Smith's next single, produced by Richard Barrett, on the specially formed one-off Spectorius label.)

By this time, of course, Philles had already debuted, and proven itself as excitingly successful as Spector and Sill always dreamed it would be. Released at the end of October, 'There's No Other (Like My Baby)' entered the chart on 20 November and, by the New Year, was Top 20-bound. Now his mind was working towards their follow-up.

Spector had already tried recording Barry Mann and Cynthia Weil's 'Uptown' with 'Little' Eva Boyd, Carole King and Gerry Goffin's 19-year-old live-in babysitter. The end result was less than satisfactory – apparently, Spector was not at all keen on the girl's voice, and scrapped the recording (Eva recorded the song again for her debut album with Carole King). Nevertheless, Spector had determined that the smartest move he could make would be to firmly ally Philles Records with Don Kirshner's Aldon Publishing, home to precisely the kind of writers whose songs most fitted his own visions of great pop music. No matter that the arrangement might occasionally necessitate running with B-sides that were of a lesser quality than Spector might have preferred, still it guaranteed him what amounted to the first choice on any suitable new songs in the catalogue.

Recorded at Mira Sound in January, 'Uptown' emerged a dramatic soundscape of smouldering Latino soul and brittle New York City vibrancy. Drawing more than a passing breath from 'Spanish Harlem', layered beneath The Crystals' shrill vocals, Spector threw cellos, mandolins and even a rattlesnake castanet into the brew, accentuating each with almost operatic bravado. Certainly the resultant mélange had little in common with its own writers' original vision of the song but that, of course, was one of the reasons why so many people wanted to work with Spector. Other producers and arrangers could transform a song. But Spector was able to transcend it.

Anybody doubting the truth behind that statement needed only wait for the release of the next Crystals' single. 'He Hit Me (And It Felt Like A Kiss)' was written by Gerry Goffin and Carole King, after Little Eva returned from a weekend away with her boyfriend, covered in bruises. The boyfriend seemed to have spent the entire weekend hitting the girl but, when Goffin and King questioned her about it, Eva didn't bat an eyelid. He hit her because he loved her. And, in the song, because she believed she deserved it.

It was a brutal number, as any attempt to document such violence must be, and Spector's arrangement only amplified its savagery, framing Barbara Alston's lone vocal in a sea of caustic strings and funereal drums, while the backing vocals almost trilled their own belief that the boy had done nothing wrong.

That the lyric was itself a violent reaction against the kind of attitude that it seemed to be excusing; that, in a more understanding age, 'He Hit Me' would have been recognised for the ironic riposte that it was, is unavoidable. But it was not an understanding age, and its sentiments were accepted at base face value. Lester Sill, in particular, loathed the song and, while radio play was initially encouraging, listeners' complaints quickly began pouring in, not only to the DJs and programme directors, but also to shops that carried the record.

So far, Spector had defended 'He Hit Me' against every one of his industry colleagues who objected to it. But, with the general public itself apparently preparing to rise up in protest against the record, igniting one of those periodic feeding frenzies to which popular culture is so oddly prone, Spector backed down. All too often in the past, he had witnessed the damage that one mistimed comment or deed could wreak on a seemingly unstoppable career, the ease with which the gods could be humbled by their subjects. He had no intention of joining any of them on the sacrificial altar. In June 1962, just days before 'He Hit Me' was confidently expected to breach the Top 100 (for controversy can encourage sales, as well as cripple them), Philles pulled it off the shelves.

Although Spector and The Crystals were already established as Philles' number one selling point, they were not its only artists. Lester Sill had already produced two singles for the label, by Joel Scott and Spector's most favoured saxophonist, Steve Douglas, while Ali Hassan (aka Al Hazan, the star of B Bumble And The Stingers' 'Nut Rocker') self-produced one of the most distinctive singles the label would ever release, the instrumental 'Malagüeña'.

Neither was Spector's own work confined to Philles alone – just weeks before the release of 'He Hit Me', MGM released a new single by Connie Francis, written and produced by Spector as a favour to Don Kirshner – 'Second Hand Love' went to No 7 that summer.

Nevertheless, the withdrawal of 'He Hit Me' left Philles facing a long summer without any scheduled releases whatsoever. With time on his hands, Spector set about seeking out new talent for the label, at the same time making certain that nobody would distract him from his task by announcing that he was burned out on studio work and was off to Spain for a vacation. And, just to make sure that everyone believed him, he littered both his office and his apartment with holiday brochures and Berlitz guide books.

Later, it became apparent that such careful carelessness was simply his way of confirming that outrageous alibi. Spector had no more intention of going to Spain than he did of taking a break from the studio – indeed, just weeks later, Spector was back in LA, preparing to start cut The Crystals' next single. Except he would not actually be employing The Crystals on it.

Fanita James, Gloria Jones and the sisters Annette and Nannette Barrett had been playing around Los Angeles as The Blossoms since the mid-1950s; a new member, Darlene Wright – soon to become infinitely better known as Darlene Love – was recruited to their line-up in 1956, after Annette became pregnant. It was their vocal coach, Eddie Bill, who landed the group their first recording date, singing back-up on actor James Darren's recorded debut but, from there, they did indeed blossom. A session with Sam Cooke followed and, though Love had to excuse herself from the group for the birth of her first children, The Blossoms stuck together to become regular session singers around LA – Shelley Fabares, Jan and Dean, the list went on.

By summer 1962, The Blossoms – now a three piece of Love, Jones and Barrett – had just finished work on Bobby Darin's *Sings Ray Charles* album, when Love received a call from Lester Sill. They'd worked with him in the past and she expected it to be another, similar job. Instead, Sill asked if she would come down to the studio on her own, to meet with his partner. A few days later, Love was ushered into the presence of 'a little man in a toupee, sitting at a piano'. She had just met Phil Spector.

Still uncertain why she had been called to the studio without the rest of The Blossoms, Love was even further baffled when Spector began quizzing her about The Crystals – a group, she had to admit, she had never even heard of. He was working on their new single, a Gene Pitney song called 'He's A Rebel', but he didn't have time to fly the group out from New York to record it, nor the patience to return to the city himself.

He was tiring of the New York studio scene, with the closed circle of musicians who simply couldn't understand what Spector was trying to accomplish in the studio, and didn't think twice about telling him so. LA was more open, more willing to try something new. Henceforth, Spector would record almost exclusively in the City of Angels.

It was some time later before Love, or anyone else for that matter, discovered the 'real' reason why Spector was in such a hurry. He'd just got off the phone with Pitney's manager, Aaron Schroeder, and learned that songstress Vicki Carr had already recorded a version of the song, for release in September. Spector was determined to beat it to the punch – or, at least, smother it at birth. And, as for why he'd called Love herself in to sing, he'd heard that she had exactly the kind of vocal timbre that would convey the lyric's street-smart sashay.

Love agreed, then watched in amazement as, once they got to the studio on 13 July 1962, the room began filling in with the kind of stellar talents she had only glimpsed at past sessions. Arranger Nitzsche, engineer Larry Levine, saxophonist Steve Douglas, drummer Hal Blaine, pianist Al Delory, guitarists Howard Roberts and Tommy Tedesco, bassists Ray Pohlman and Jimmy Bond and many more. (Nitzsche rounded the musicians up – they comprised, he told *Goldmine* magazine, 'a lot of the same guys I had been working with for years. Phil didn't know a lot of these people; he had been in New York in 1960–1962. Leon Russell, Harold Battiste, Earl Palmer, Don Randi Glen Campbell...a lot of the players came out of my phone book.')

In the midst of what could have been chaos, 'He's A Rebel' took shape. Love's Blossoms bandmates, Fanita James and Gloria Jones, were invited along to handle backing vocals, together with Bobby Sheen, the young vocalist whom Spector had signed so unsuccessfully to Liberty during his time there. And, so frenetic was the pace, so dramatic was the sound that, when Love came to sing, she was so overwhelmed that she lost all sense of the rhythm, and travelled through the song's hind-quarters completely out of time. Horrified, she begged Spector to give her another chance. He simply smiled at her. 'I like the mistake.' It would become one of the most distinctive moments in the entire performance.

'The moment you heard "He's A Rebel", you knew it would be a smash,' Larry Levine told *The History Of Rock* magazine. But, as summer 1962 turned to autumn, Love herself barely gave the recording another thought. Exciting (and lucrative – Spector paid her $3,000) though the session itself had been, she did not especially care for the song and genuinely was not expecting to ever hear it again.

From the moment it was released in September 1962, however, 'He's A Rebel' was everywhere, indeed trampling Vicki Carr's version into the dust as it stormed to No 1. And no surprise. The record itself spent just a fortnight at the top, in late November, before being bumped down again by the Four Seasons' 'Big Girls Don't Cry'. But still, in the face of all he had done in the past, in defiance of all that he would accomplish in the future, 'He's A Rebel' remains many people's idea of the ultimate Phil Spector record, the peak not only of his achievement, but of the entire Brill Building/girl group epoch that modern writers and historians now wax so rhapsodic over.

'He's A Rebel' itself was the latest in that extraordinarily long line of teenage love songs in which a girl attempts to justify her lover's rough-shod charms by pointing out, beneath the gruff exterior, that there beats a heart of gold. Spector, however, might well have had other thoughts in mind when he rushed the song into production.

Sonny Bono, Jack Nitzsche's mentor at Specialty Records, had recently come on board as Philles' promo man, and mused, 'though he always knew what he wanted in the studio, and wasn't shy of telling you, Phil didn't really say much on a personal basis – either you knew what he was thinking, in which case words didn't matter, or he didn't. One of his big things, though, was signalling with song titles. The whole time he and Ronnie Ronette were together (later in the Philles saga), all the songs she sang were messages from him to her. But even before that, he was sending out these little musical telegraphs… you never got them at the time, of course, but afterwards, it was "uh *yeah*!"'

At the risk of reading way too much into things, 'He's A Rebel' might well have been intended as one of those telegraphs. For Phil Spector himself was about to rebel.

He was tiring of making other people money. It wasn't even big-headed for Spector to sit around the house and ask himself where would the likes of Lester Sill be without him? Looking for the next hit, of course, rather than simply lying back and knowing precisely where it was coming from. It was time, Spector decided, to begin cutting people loose.

Neither did he care what damage such ruthlessness might inflict upon his own reputation. '95 per cent of the music business is heavily infiltrated by morons,' Spector told *Time* in 1965. 'If [people] hadn't been so greedy and vicious, I wouldn't have tried to control them.' Fortunately, he continued, 'I function well in a world of hostility.'

To his foes, of course, it was the same old story. When Spector needed someone beside him for moral or financial support, to grease wheels or oil palms, he did everything in his power to accommodate whoever was necessary. But, once he'd achieved the ends towards which he was working, it was time to raise the bar even higher and cut off the dead wood that clung on from past entanglements. And, by late 1962, Lester Sill was dead wood.

Spector made no secret of his intentions, and Sill received the message very early on. Looking back on his own contributions to the Philles catalogue, Sill admitted outright that he knew the records had few musical merits, confessed that he made them simply to aggravate the increasingly autocratic Spector, and remind him that there were two syllables in Phil-les. Without such oddities as 'You're My Only Love' and 'Lieutenant Colonel Bogey's Parade', the label would have had a 100 per cent ratio of hits-to-releases, a level of perfection that no other record company on earth could boast. And, knowing how much that perfection meant to his partner, it amused Sill to ensure that it never happened.

He knew what the upshot of such sabotage would be, of course; pointed song titles notwithstanding, Sill had been in the music business long enough to recognise all the signs that Spector was now flashing at him – the failure to turn up for meetings or return telephone calls, the grunted replies to the most innocuous questions, the gradual distancing of other people within the partnership's orbit. Even before Sill flew to New York that September, for a meeting that he strongly suspected would turn into the final showdown, he was well aware that Spector had been moving forward behind his back, conspiring with likeminded souls at distributors Universal, and so it proved. In a meeting that was fraught with anger, emotion, resentment and regret, Sill agreed to sell out his entire stake in both Philles Records and Mother Bertha Publishing for just $60,000.

It was a laughable sum, but Spector had only just started joking. When, weeks later, Sill contacted him to demand the actual cheque, Spector's lawyer, Universal's Harold Lipsius, informed him that they were holding back while they worked out some final calculations – how much money had Spector already lost in royalties on the long-ago Paris Sisters album debacle. Then, when Sill, out of patience at last, brought his own lawyer in to launch legal proceedings, Spector retaliated with a gift that was almost breathtaking in its pettiness.

Gathering together The Crystals, Michael Spencer and a handful of other musicians, he booked Mira Sound for a day and cut a one-off, not-for-public-consumption, single especially for Sill, a two-parter called 'Let's Dance The Screw'. With the girls in full Andrews Sisters mould, Spencer's piano plunking a jaunty boogie and Spector himself interrupting every 30 seconds or so with a spoken 'dance the screw', here was one musical message that nobody could ignore. The fact that it was such a mindlessly catchy little number only infuriated Sill even further. Even Spector's foulest insults sounded like No 1 singles.

The split did little to affect the innermost workings of Philles. Chuck, Sill's stepson, continued working at the label with his father's full blessing – no matter how much bad blood now flowed between Sill and Spector, Sill himself was smart enough to realise that the boy's own career could only benefit from remaining in the producer's orbit. Jack Nitzsche and Steve Douglas, both of whom also owed their salaries to Sill, remained on board too, again at their employer's behest.

Interviewed in the early 1990s, Nitzsche explained, 'Lester knew that Phil was only going to get bigger, and…I dunno, maybe he got some satisfaction about seeing "his" people still tied to Phil's star, knowing that when they did break away from him, some of that stardust would always accompany them.' He happily admitted, 'my fee was $50 a song, [but] I don't feel any bitterness about the money or payment whatsoever. The credits helped secure employment for years. Phil knew what he wanted. He put my name on many of the singles as arranger. I loved it. What an education!'

He elaborated in a later interview, 'I was getting jobs simply because of the Spector association.' By late 1963, he had scored a couple of hit singles in his own right, the instrumentals 'The Lonely Surfer' and 'The Rumble', while his writing partnership with Sonny Bono would soon hit the jackpot when their 'Needles And Pins' topped the chart with The Searchers. He also became a vital component in the success of The Rolling Stones' mid-'60s recordings, 'But it was the stuff with Phil that people remembered. Neil Young [whom Nitzsche worked with during the early 1970s] once told me to my face that he'd brought me on board for the Spector connection, and all I had to do was make sure I didn't disappoint him.'

Alone now at the top of Philles Records, and about to embark upon the most dazzlingly productive year of his life, Spector opened this new era with a surprisingly constrained release. Back in his Atlantic days, Spector produced a single by soul singer Billy Storm – who was now the brother-in-law of 'He's A Rebel' backing singer Bobby Sheen.

Storm's latest venture was The Alley Cats, a six-piece vocal harmony combo formed with Sheridan Spencer, James Barker, Brice Coefield and the brothers Chester and Gary Pippin, and working with Lou Adler, The Teddy Bears' A&R man at Doré – now heading up Don Kirshner's West Coast office. Essentially enacting a favour to everyone, Spector agreed to split the next Philles single, by The Alley Cats, between himself and Adler. They would even produce one side apiece, with Spector handling the A-side, 'Puddin 'n' Tain'.

The song was a children's favourite. Pre-empting the bubblegum blast of five years hence, when the Brill Building songsmiths Jeff Kasenatz and Jerry Katz held the nation in thrall with their musical adaptations of singalong ditties 'Simon Says' and 'Yummy Yummy Yummy', Gary Pippin had taken the playground chant of 'ask me again and I'll tell you the same…puddin 'n' tain…,' and transformed it into a stirring teenage love song. On release it marched straight into the Top 40.

From the outside, the single – and, indeed, the entire gesture surrounding the single – seemed only to strengthen the ties between Spector and Aldon Music. Spector, however, knew that quite the opposite was true. His next release, The Crystals' rendition of Mann and Weil's 'He's Sure The Boy I Love', in December 1962, was to prove Spector's final visit to the Brill Building for another two years. With Lester Sill out of the picture, it was time to bring Mother Bertha into play.

Of course Spector had already proven his compositional talents many times in the past, not only in the writing of his own songs, but also in the breathtaking manner in which he reshaped others'. Throughout his dealings with Aldon Music, however, he never attempted to take a piece of the songwriting credit for himself, no matter how much he poured into a performance. That was to change. Henceforth, any outside song that he recorded in his inimitable fashion would have his name appended to the writing credits. And, with every such appendage, Mother Bertha's coffers would swell a little further.

Don Kirshner, whose own dealings with Spector would inevitably lessen under this new regime, was not worried by the loss of income, of course; rather, he could not help but take pride in just how readily, and ruthlessly, Spector established himself as a major player in his own right. 'Philly was becoming a bit impetuous, he was super cocky. [But] he wanted to rule the roost. He wanted to be the king pin.'

In fact, impetuosity was one of the last charges that could be levelled at Spector. Rather, he timed his move perfectly, his decision coinciding precisely with his discovery (or, rather, rediscovery) of an exciting young New York songwriter named Ellie Greenwich. Born in Brooklyn but raised in Leavittown, Long Island, Greenwich had been writing and performing since she hit her teens; her first group, The Jivettes, was formed with a couple of high school friends, and became a familiar sight around local hospitals, schools and charity benefits, primarily performing Greenwich's own original songs.

She was still at school when her mother arranged a meeting with Cadence Records president Archie Bleyer, hoping he might advance her career. In fact, though Bleyer certainly encouraged her efforts, he was concerned that she finish school before entering the precarious world of songwriting. Greenwich apparently agreed. In 1962, shortly after graduating with top honours from Hostra University, she was recruited to Trio Music at Terry Phillips' suggestion (he was dating her best friend at the time). Shortly after she was introduced to Spector, and attempted to interest him in some of the latest songs she'd written.

She failed. Spector had already grown to dread his periodic visits to the Brill Building, taught himself to completely tune out the aspirant buffoons who would corner him in corridors or trap him in the lift, so they could serenade him with the latest fluffy jingle they'd created. And because he didn't tell them outright that he hated it, then they'd get his number and call him, to ask when they'd be getting together again. But they weren't only wasting his time, they were wasting theirs as well. When Spector visited a publisher, he always knew precisely what he was looking for, and he usually knew within the first four bars of a song whether or not he'd found it.

Greenwich, however, wasn't aware of any of this. All she saw was a little man who seemed more interested in combing his thinning hair than paying attention to anything she had to offer, and who simply walked out of the room when she objected.

By February 1963, however, she was experiencing her first chart success, with The Exciters' take on her 'He's Got The Power'. Her own new band, The Raindrops, too, were poised for action (their debut single, 'What A Guy', was on the eve of release) and, when Spector heard a clutch of demos that she'd co-written with Tony Powers, he arranged a meeting at his own home.

Setting a pattern that would become familiar to so many future artists, Spector arrived late for the appointment...very late. But, when he saw Greenwich and Powers still sitting patiently in the lobby, he smiled – as if they'd passed a test, as so many other of his guests have said. Ultimately, Greenwich and Powers would write only a couple of songs for Spector. But, in tandem with her husband Jeff Barry, Greenwich herself co-wrote every Philles label release of the next 12 months, and remained among Spector's favourite songwriters for several years beyond that.

Spector himself was constantly involved in the writing process. Greenwich laughed, 'it was a hotchpotch...the three of us were spewing out piano, Jeff would be playing a tambourine and Phil would be strumming his guitar, and the three of us singing away like maniacs at the top of our lungs... We'd find something that hit all of us at once more or less, because our minds were sort of on the same wavelength...and before you knew it, a song emerged.' Another aspiring writer, Harry Nilsson, had his own recollections of writing with Spector, when he told *Goldmine* how their collaboration, 'Paradise', began life as a Spector original called 'Stand By Him'. 'We started working on it [and] he kept changing it, trying to make it better: "I want something more Hawaiian, rainbows, paradise!"'

Such alchemy was still to come, of course, when Spector summoned Darlene Love back to the studio, this time with fellow Blossoms James and Jones on board, to try out a new song. 'Da Doo Ron Ron' was one of the first songs Greenwich and Barry handed him; and one, the writers merrily confessed, that meant absolutely whatever you wanted it to. Indeed, although countless interpretations of the title have been delivered up over the years, Greenwich and Barry's own recollection is that they'd simply run out of words to fit, so they ad-libbed in the hope that something better would present itself. When it didn't, they relied on the listener's imagination to fill in the blanks. Which, of course, it did.

Spector intended the song as the follow-up to 'He's A Rebel', but he did not reckon with Darlene Love's demand that, this time, she receive some sort of credit on the record – either her own name, or The Blossoms. Spector initially seemed amenable to her request. He assured her it would be done; insisted that, even as they worked on the song, his lawyer was drawing up the contracts. But not until Love walked out of the studio with just a few more vocal lines remaining, furious that Spector had forgotten the document once again, was the contract finally delivered.

Love and James signed (Jones had already announced she was leaving the group)...and Spector promptly cancelled the release of 'Da Doo Ron Ron'. Instead, he had another song he wanted The Blossoms to work on, a reworking of 'Zip-A-Dee-Doo-Dah', from the 1947 Disney flick *Song Of The South*, which he intended releasing under the pseudonym Bob B Soxx And (after a brief flirtation with The Holidays) The Blue Jeans. That, Love later smiled, was when she *knew* Phil Spector was crazy.

5 Philles Comes First

Joining Darlene Love and Fanita James on 'Zip-A-Dee-Doo-Dah', once again, was Bobby Sheen, his falsetto vocal the key note on a ruthless deconstruction of the once-innocuous children's song, now revised as a dramatic gospel number and cut through by a wicked fuzzed guitar solo from Billy Strange.

At a time when oddball novelty records were showing up on the US chart with ever-increasing frequency, 'Zip-A-Dee-Doo-Dah' was more oddball than most – even 'Puddin 'n' Tain' sounded conventional alongside it. But the sheer vastness of the production insisted that this was no mere novelty. Rather, it was Spector proving to the world that anything was now possible, including the conversion of the basest nursery singalong into a flawless sonic concerto. Or, as Love put it, 'if I had any doubts that Phil had his finger on the pulse of American teenagers, they were erased when 'Zip-A-Dee-Doo-Dah' hit the Top 10 [in November 1962]. If he could make that song a hit, I thought, then he could make anything a hit.'

In fact, so far as Spector was concerned, 'Zip-A-Dee-Doo-Dah' was little more than an experiment – or, rather, the results of an experiment. Although he nonchalantly insisted 'He's A Rebel' emerged sounding precisely as he'd intended it to, in fact the sheer enormity of the record shocked him.

He had, after all, done little more to that song than he did to any other. Doubling up on instruments was already a time-honoured habit, while his relentless pursuit of a single sound, the repetition of one bar, one note, one chord, over and over until it filled the entire room, was already notorious among the musicians he chose to work with. Indeed, for many of those players, their most potent memory of sessioning for Spector was the mind-numbing tedium and wrist-breaking agony of going over the same simple sequence again and again, while Spector sat impassively in the control room, ordering them to do it once more.

For Howard Roberts, 'He's A Rebel' proved the final straw – an accomplished jazzman who despised rock 'n' roll to begin with, no amount of money was worth the physical pain that the constant repetition caused him. By the time the song was complete, his fingers were literally raw and bleeding.

Spector himself did his best to relieve the tedium, alternating moments of dictatorial concentration with bursts of almost childlike mischief. He delighted in darting around the studio, sticking silly notes on the musicians' backs... 'Hi! I'm Betty Boop' or 'I'm WC Fields' mother-in-law'. Other times, Spector would stage solemn gift-giving ceremonies, handing individual musicians the most lavishly wrapped packages, then whooping gleefully as they opened them to discover a box of condoms, a pair of garters or, for Hal Blaine himself, 'a perfectly sculptured, red and white striped peppermint candy penis.' Jack Nitzsche once laughed, 'Phil was a kid. He would call me up at 4:00am and want to go out for ice cream.'

At the same time, however, he made certain that the players never forgot precisely who they were working with, redecorating the studio with signs and posters proclaiming 'Phil the King' and similar homilies. And there were times when it was impossible to argue with that, as he strove to conjure a sound that was unlike any other record on earth, that was as vast as the most accomplished classical performance but as immediate as the tinniest transistor radio. He achieved it on 'He's A Rebel'; now he had to prove to himself that he could repeat it. Recorded at Gold Star on 24 August, with two guitarists, two pianists, two saxophonists and three bassists, plus drums and a battery of percussionists, 'Zip-A-Dee-Doo-Dah' delivered that proof.

By now, Spector had more or less established a core of musicians with whom he was happiest working, the so-called Wrecking Crew of Tommy Tedesco, Howard Roberts, Glen Campbell and Bill Pitman on guitar, Carol Kaye and Ray Pohlman on Fender bass, Lyle Ritz and Jimmy Bond on upright bass, saxophonists Steve Douglas and Nino Tempo, horn players Jay Migliori, Ollie Mitchell, Roy Caton, Virgil Evans, Lou Blackburn and Tony Terran, keyboard players Al Delory, Larry Knechtel, Don Randi and Leon Russell and drummers Hal Blaine and Earl Palmer.

Countless other musicians passed through, however. Blaine remembered Spector habitually hanging a 'closed session' sign on the studio door, knowing that it would attract an army of other musicians and producers, all of whom could then be press-ganged into playing some minor part in the recording. Soon, many of the musicians who were booked upfront for each date were bringing boxes full of additional instruments along with them, to hand out as the studio filled with extras.

Bob B Soxx And The Blue Jeans toured in the wake of 'Zip-A-Dee-Doo-Dah', heading east to headline some of the most legendary venues in the country – the Brooklyn Fox, the Harlem Apollo and so forth. It was a short outing, cut even shorter when the group – Love, James and Sheen – finally tired of the lousy fees, bitter weather and, occasionally, hostile crowds with which they were faced. The Fox Theater show was especially hard; although it was common knowledge among industry insiders that The Crystals did not sing on 'He's A Rebel', the people who actually bought the record never suspected a thing. When emcee Murray The K introduced Love and James as the voices on that hit, 'we could hear the crowd bristling.' Love explained, 'The Crystals were local heroes, [and] this was a big slap to them.'

Back in California, Spector finally seemed ready to follow through on his promise of launching Darlene Love as a solo performer – it was, in fact, now that he rechristened her with the name she still bears today. His inspiration was the gospel singer Dorothy Love, a passion that Darlene herself shared; and, when they went into the studio in November, it was to cut what Spector assured her would be her first solo single, Barry Mann and Cynthia Weil's 'He's Sure The Boy I Love'.

One again, however, he released it under The Crystals' name, insisting that radio would be far more receptive to the latest record by a known group, than the debut by an unknown. And so it transpired. 'He's Sure The Boy I Love' reached No 11 in early 1963, while Love was forced to console herself with a second Bob B Soxx single, the distinctly under-performing (No 38) 'Why Do Lovers Break Each Other's Hearts?'

Perhaps only Spector, well aware of how disappointed Love was by his prevarications, saw the true irony of that title. However, nobody who knew him could miss the significance of Bob B Soxx's next release, 'Not Too Young To Get Married'. For he was indeed about to be wed, and his in-laws to be were not at all certain that the 19-year-old bride, Annette Merar of course, wasn't herself too young.

No matter that much of Spector's time was being spent in New York. Since that trip to LA back in May 1961, their courtship continued long distance, and reignited wholly whenever he returned to California, before she herself moved to New York, to study English Literature at Hunter College. Merar herself had long become resigned to the fact that, so far as Spector was concerned, the recording studio would always take precedence over anything and anyone else in his life; still she knew that she came a close second.

She was party to his episodes of intolerance, of course – her place by his side made her an instant witness to the dismissal of Lester Sill, the swerve away from Don Kirshner and a breakdown with Lou Adler. The jealousy that scarred his years with Donna Kass, always needing to know where she was and why she was there, ensured that her own wishes were always subservient to his, while his regular visits to a Park Avenue psychiatrist, Dr Kaplan, often filled her with a nagging fear, as she wondered what new demons might be conjured up out of the latest session.

But she was also privy to his magnanimity and concern for the people he loved – his continued generosity to Shirley, in the form of fresh co-written compositions; his habit of rewarding, or at least immortalising, other friends and associates with B-sides of their own. His psychiatrist was the titular star of the instrumental 'Dr Kaplan's Office', while the famed Brother Julius hamburger stand, conveniently sited in the Gold Star parking lot, was the eponymous subject of a Crystals' B-side. Annette herself would become a songwriter, sole author of such future Philles flips as 'Big Red', 'Beatle Blues' and 'Pete Meets Vinnie'.

Perhaps the greatest gift he gave her, though, was the B-side of the latest Bob B Soxx single. Another Spector/Sands effort, it was one of Spector's loveliest instrumental numbers, and it was titled, simply, 'Annette'. In addition, the words 'Phil and Annette' would be scratched into the run-off groove of every Philles single released that year.

The couple wed on 18 February 1963 in a ceremony of extraordinary privacy. Held in the Central Park West study of a rabbi, the marriage was witnessed by just three guests, photographer Pete Bitlisian, Liberty Records staff producer Ed Silver and arranger Arnie Goland. The reception, on the other hand, overflowed with glitterati, as Johnny Mathis' manager, Helen Noga, threw open her Central Park South apartment for the occasion. And, while there was no time for a honeymoon, the couple's new home, an already furnished penthouse on New York's 62nd and York, was itself quite as luxurious as any hotel bridal suite.

Business, of course, continued around the festivities. Just days after the wedding, Spector flew to LA alone, for a few days at Gold Star and, as soon as he returned to New York in March, he became instantly preoccupied by his latest discovery – a group that he would soon describe as his greatest ever signing.

Like The Crystals, The Ronettes were New York through and through. Two sisters, Veronica, or Ronnie, and Estelle Bennett, had been singing with their cousin Nedra Talley, since childhood. Originally they called themselves the Darling Sisters; they became The Ronettes when they graduated from local hops to the more exacting stage of New York's Peppermint Lounge, and DJ Murray The K's holiday dance shows at the Brooklyn Paramount.

Such exposure quickly brought the group recognition. In 1961, they linked up with Stu Phillips, a staff producer at Columbia's Colpix label, and a couple of singles for that label were followed by three more on the R&B specialist May subsidiary. Nothing hit, however, and by early 1963 the group were doing little more than session work for whoever would hire them. It was while they gnawed at this loosest of loose ends that they hatched the idea of simply telephoning the most famous producer they could think of, and asking if they could audition for him.

No less than any other music-hungry teens of the time, the three Ronettes had devoured Spector's most recent hits, and were convinced that whatever he'd done for The Crystals, he ought to be doing for them. They tracked him down through directory enquiries; they knew Philles had recently moved to a new office on 62nd and York, and had heard that Spector himself lived in the same building. They had no idea, however, that when they rang the number, the secretary would patch the caller – Estelle – straight through to the great man, nor that he would actually deign to talk to them. By the time Estelle got off the phone, she could barely speak for excitement. They were to meet Spector the following evening at Mira Sound Studios.

The audition was like a dream. Instinctively recalling all that they had learned from their singing tutor years before, they began with 'When The Red Red Robin Comes Bob Bob Bobbing Along'. Spector listened, laughed and then asked them if there was anything else they could do – something, perhaps, that came from the heart. The trio responded with a breathtaking trawl through the Frankie Lymon catalogue; followed up with the Little Anthony songbook... by the time Spector suggested they break for a bite to eat, The Ronettes were already convinced that they'd passed the audition.

Now he had to pass theirs – that is, meet the girls' mothers and persuade them that he was honourable, then extract them from their Colpix contract. Moribund though it appeared to be – they'd not heard from the label in months – they were still legally bound to it. But it was not Spector's businessman guile that enabled them to break away. Rather, it was Veronica and Estelle's mother, who simply called the company and explained that it was time for the girls to get on with their rest of their lives. The singing had been fun, but Ronnie was off to become a nurse, Estelle and Nedra were planning to attend secretarial school…by the time Mrs Bennett put the phone down, she had achieved what it might otherwise have required a battery of lawyers to accomplish.

Larry Levine was not a Ronettes fan. 'When I met [them], I didn't think they were going to be a very good group,' he wrote in the liner notes to their first album. 'Phil had said to me, "I found this group, they're good looking, but they don't sing too well." So I said, "Well, why bother?" He said, "I kind of promised their mother".'

No matter. Besides, if they weren't particularly good when he met them, they soon would be. From the moment The Ronettes signed with Spector, at the end of March, he rehearsed them constantly, every night of the week, according to Ronnie. He already had a song in mind for them, Ellie Greenwich and Jeff Barry's 'Why Don't They Let Us Fall In Love', and later, Spector's friends would wonder whether this was not another of his coded musical messages, as The Ronettes' rehearsal space at Arnold Goland's apartment increasingly became the scene of a gentle, but ever more sincere, romance between Spector and Ronnie Bennett.

Ronnie found herself being favoured in other ways, as well. Rather than record the group in New York, Spector insisted they cross the country to Gold Star and, when it came time to travel out to California, Ronnie and her mother travelled by air; her sister and cousin followed behind in Bobby Sheen's new station wagon. In LA itself, when Spector took them out to show off the city, it was Ronnie who had the front seat view. The others were simply passengers.

Into Gold Star for a few days, the group recorded a tremendous version of 'Why Don't They Let Us Fall In Love', but Spector had already decided not to release it. Rather, he was already working feverishly on another Greenwich/Barry number, 'Be My Baby', confident that, by the time he was ready to present the finished backing track to The Ronettes, its title, too, would have come true. As Darlene Love later pointed out, he was not simply making a record. He was declaring his love for Ronnie.

April 1963, meanwhile, finally saw the release of Darlene Love's first single, '(Today I Met) The Boy I'm Gonna Marry.' It was, she told in her autobiography, 'a sort of doo-wop meets gospel ballad that really lets me blow off some steam – and by then, I was a pressure cooker.' However, much as she enjoyed performing the song, she could not help but feel betrayed once again. Spector, after all, had led her to expect to debut with 'Da Doo Ron Ron' – only for him to suddenly turn around and restore The Crystals to favour.

The group had recently brought a new member on board, as 15-year-old Dolores 'La La' Brooks replaced the pregnant Mema Girard, an event that completely rejuvenated the group, both as an act in their own right, and as a power in Spector's eyes.

Understandably over the course of two hits that they did not even sing on, the group had begun feeling sorely overlooked – Gene Pitney met the group at a gig in Washington DC, just as 'He's A Rebel' broke through, and found himself teaching them the words to the song before they went onstage. Royalty payments were slow in arriving, if they even came at all, and the rumours about Spector's burgeoning fling with Ronnie Bennett were distracting as well. It certainly explained why he wasn't even rehearsing them anymore.

The first time he heard Brooks, however, it was as though the past months of neglect had never happened. Her treatment of 'Da Doo Ron Ron', so vastly different to Darlene Love's knock-out assault, enchanted him from the moment he even imagined it – by the time he had it down on tape, it was mesmerising. The follow-up, 'Then He Kissed Me', was even more impressive and, had Spector not discovered and fallen so heavily for The Ronettes, The Crystals could easily have counted on any number of further, equally impressive releases. But he had, he did and, though there would be two subsequent Crystals 45s released during 1964, his interest in them was at an end.

Darlene Love, too, would ultimately suffer as The Ronettes' career took off, although not until she'd at least run up a clutch of memorable hits, and certainly not until Spector had completed work on what he was convinced would prove his *Mona Lisa*, his Sistine Chapel, his 'Lady of Shallot'. He was going to record a Christmas album.

Since his disastrous experiences with both The Teddy Bears and the Paris Sisters' long-players, Spector had generally steered clear of albums. Both The Crystals and Bob B Soxx saw LPs released in their names during 1962–63, and both had moments of sublime magic far beyond the expected peaks of the hit singles (and the makeweight lows of sundry instrumentals). There was a collection of Philles' singles-so-far, *Philles Records Presents Today's Hits*; while Spector also threw together a Crystals *Sing The Greatest Hits* album, filling in around their own singles with Wall of Sound-ified versions of other people's recent smashes...Dee Dee Sharp's 'Mashed Potato Time', Chubby Checker's 'The Twist' and, though The Crystals' *Twist Uptown* debut album featured the original recording of Mann/Weil's 'On Broadway', still most people were more familiar with The Drifters' later hit version. (Spector also played guitar on the latter.)

None were pieced together with anything like the attention that hallmarked Philles singles, and none sold especially well; The Crystals' *He's A Rebel* was the biggest, and it climbed no higher than No 131. Early in the summer of 1963, however, Spector finally shrugged off his antipathy towards the format and announced that December would see the release of his most grandiose gesture yet, an album of rock 'n' rolling Christmas tunes that would pull out every sonic stop in his arsenal. It was, he said, his most brilliant brainwave yet – although Darlene Love remembers that the musicians he roped in were more prone to calling it an earthquake.

The idea itself was not wholly original. Elvis Presley cut his first Christmas album as far back as 1957, since when artists as far apart as Frankie Avalon and the Four Seasons had dropped their own festive offerings into the record racks. Presley notwithstanding, none of these records had actually charted, suggesting that the general public preferred to maintain their seasonal merry-making on a more traditional footing. But Spector had his own reasons to believe that this year, things might be different. *Billboard* magazine, whose weekly pop charts were generally regarded as the bible of such statistics, had just announced that 1963 would see the inauguration of a special chart for Christmas-themed records only. Regardless of how his Christmas album fared on the 'regular' pop charts, there would be little to keep Spector from dominating this new specialist listing.

Sessions for the album kicked off in mid-summer, and everybody agreed that it felt awfully peculiar to spend all day and half the night sequestered away within Gold Star studios, picking painfully away at 'Frosty The Snowman' and 'Rudolph The Red-nosed Reindeer', then stepping out into the heat of an August night in LA.

Spector and Darlene Love were in charge of picking the songs – Love adored Christmas music and, in any case, was thrilled that Spector was finally permitting her to have some say in one of his records. Of the 13 songs on the final record, Love sang all three of the songs she chose, 'Winter Wonderland', 'White Christmas' and 'Marshmallow World', while she also wound up with a fourth that Spector had originally commissioned (from songwriters Ellie Greenwich and Jeff Barry) for The Ronettes, but which the latter group had proven strangely unable to handle.

Of course their failure did the rest of the world a favour, as Darlene Love's version of the positively shimmering 'Christmas (Baby Please Come Home)' became one of *the* quintessential festive pop hits, an evergreen that still dominates the radio for a few weeks every year. (Pianist Leon Russell, too, excelled at that session – he threw one lick into the mix that so thrilled Spector that he leaped out of the control room and handed Russell a cheque for $100 on the spot.)

It was September before the album was complete, and every promise Spector had made during the recording was absolutely borne out by the end result. Even the closing rendition of 'Silent Night', with Spector himself quietly thanking everyone who had bought his records over the year, had a sentimental charm that outweighed its mawkish qualities – 'a lot of people thought the song was corny,' Ronnie later agreed. 'But, if you knew Phil like I did, it was very touching.'

A Christmas Gift For You was released in America on 22 November 1963 – later than Spector had hoped, but still in plenty of time for the holiday buying spree. A single, Love's gorgeous rendering of 'Christmas (Baby Please Come Home)', was imminent and, if any man was ever justified in believing that he was on the top of the world, and was still soaring higher, it was Phil Spector. Instead, the news that broke out of Dallas, Texas, the following afternoon pulled the entire edifice out from beneath him. President Kennedy had been assassinated – and Christmas was cancelled.

It seems so melodramatic, looking back across 40 years, to pinpoint the death of a distant political figure as the moment when another, wholly unconnected, man's life completely changed; and even more so, the cancellation of a simple record release.

In the context of the time, however, Kennedy was more than simply a President. The youngest ever incumbent of the Oval Office, he in turn was portrayed as an icon of youth, a man who may not, in the manner of Bill Clinton 30 years later, have deliberately courted the country's pop-loving teenagers (there would have been no point – the voting age was still 21), but who certainly appeared to understand the concerns and desires of Young America, and was working to represent them as fervently as he upheld the country's more traditional values. He was even photographed doing the Twist with his wife.

In life, he represented hope; in death, therefore, he became a symbol of hopelessness. And that hopelessness, like the hope before it, spread far beyond the avenues that might normally have suffered the shockwaves, and far deeper into the American psyche as well. The death of a leader was always horrifying. The death of such a beloved one, however, went beyond that. It was necrotising, and America slipped into a state of grief from which time alone could rouse it. Television programming was cancelled, movie houses were closed and pop music all but shut down. By the beginning of December, and for the remainder of the year, the top-selling single and LP in America were recordings by the 30-year-old Belgian Sister Luc Gabrielle, the Singing Nun. Behind her, other records were listed, but they were scarcely selling.

The Christmas chart was no less pious. While The Chipmunks' *Christmas With... Volume Two* at least gave the smallest children something to smile about, older ears were wrapped around festive offerings from Johnny Mathis, Robert Giulet, Bert Kaempfert and his orchestra, Mantovani and *his*, the Mormon Tabernacle Choir, the New Christy Minstrels and Andy Williams. Nat 'King' Cole sat at No 1 with *The Christmas Song*. And, all the while, unsold copies of *A Christmas Gift For You* sat piled up in warehouses around the US, awaiting destruction.

Although it was released on schedule in Britain, Spector could not bear to bring the album out into the sea of mourning that had consumed America; could not, perhaps, stand the idea that the album might fail in the lachrymose climate of the day. So, rather than risk anything, he chose to scrap everything. 'A President died and the public changed,' he explained. 'How would you like to put out a $55,000 album the same week as something like the President being assassinated took place?'

It would be another nine years before America finally received Spector's Christmas Gift, until the album was hauled out of legend for reissue by The Beatles' Apple label. In the meantime...Darlene Love summed up the legend that history loves best. 'As Phil withdrew *A Christmas Gift For You*, so he also started to withdraw himself.'

Yet withdrawal is very much in the eye of the beholder and, if Spector dropped out of some arenas, he certainly remained busy in others. A new Ronettes single, 'Baby I Love You', was released on schedule in December and, though the loss of the Christmas album *did* upset Spector's commercial applecart, there is little to say it would not have been upset anyway. Six weeks after Kennedy's death, just as America was beginning to find its feet once again, four long-haired lovers from Liverpool flew in, and draped the new phenomenon of Beatlemania across the entire United States.

The difference was, while other artists complained that they could not compete with the Fab Four, Spector made another decision entirely. He chose positively *not* to compete.

But the popular belief that he recorded less music in 1964 than he had in '63 is exploded simply by counting up the number of releases; and, if the likes of The Crystals and Darlene Love felt sidelined, that was only because he preferred to spend time with The Ronettes and, later in the year, his next discovery, the Righteous Brothers. His wife, Annette, saw less of him, but Ronnie Bennett saw much, much more. And, when he seemed to suddenly disappear from view in America, early in the New Year, that was only because he'd just crossed the ocean, and was visiting Britain instead. Two could play at the Invasion game after all, and no matter how deliriously America's pop aristocracy flocked towards The Beatles, in Britain Spector was to be feted just as furiously.

6 With The Beatles

Britain originally responded slowly to Phil Spector's music. 'To Know Him Is To Love Him' was a massive hit in 1958, while 'Pretty Little Angel Eyes', 'Corrine, Corrina' and Ben E King's 'First Taste Of Love' ('Spanish Harlem', intriguingly, was relegated to the B-side) fared reasonably well during 1961. But neither Gene Pitney nor the Paris Sisters meant a thing across the ocean, with insult poured upon indignity when the UK release of 'I Love How You Love Me' was beaten out of sight by a starkly inferior spoiler cut by local singer Jimmie Crawford.

From the moment 'He's A Rebel' arrived in October 1962, however, Spectormania was always just around the corner. 'Da Doo Ron Ron' was Top 5, 'Then He Kissed Me' spent a fortnight at No 2, 'Be My Baby' rose to No 4 and, in every place where artists came together to talk, Spector's name…Spector's brilliance…was never far from the surface.

Back home, Spector was almost blasé about the fulsome praise of the rich and powerful. Beach Boy Brian Wilson was still talking about the first time he ever heard 'Be My Baby' on the radio, and had to pull over to the side of the road until the song had finished, and he was not alone in his admiration.

British bands, too, flocked to venerate him. The Beatles adored his work; The Rolling Stones raved about it and their manager, Andrew Loog Oldham, was so enamoured that he came close to actually emulating him, enacting a stream of productions (for the Stones and otherwise) that so joyfully revelled in the Master's magic that, occasionally, they even outdid them.

Spector, on the other hand, knew little more about Britain than he heard on the radio. British bands rarely broke through in America, and the handful that did seldom caught his ear. Of course he'd won that Fairfax High talent contest with his own rendering of Lonnie Donegan's 'Rock Island Line', but since that time, the only British record that really interested him, and made him seek out more music by its maker, was The Tornados' instrumental 'Telstar', the freakish tempest of electronics and science fiction sound effects that topped the US chart for three weeks at the end of 1962.

The Tornados themselves were simply a group of session musicians – Spector, of course, was more curious about their producer, an apparently reclusive paranoid named Joe Meek. Like Spector, the grapevine buzzed with rumour and legend about his methods; like Spector, he expected nothing less than absolute loyalty and obedience from the artists with whom he worked. And, like Spector, he was so unhappy with the industry standards and restrictions of the day that he simply tore them up and refused to acknowledge them.

An independent producer who launched his own record label, Triumph, back in 1959, Meek had now turned his back upon even the most open-minded recording studios in the land, and literally built his own, in the modest flat he rented above a leather goods store in north London. It was there, surrounded by boxes, wires and other assorted electronic gismos whose functions, it seemed, were known only to him, that Meek worked his alchemy, turning base beat groups into solid gold.

Yet, while Spector brimmed with curiosity over this trans-Atlantic twin, Meek only bubbled with resentment. Like everybody else in the country, he, too, talked incessantly about Spector. But only to impress upon people what a thieving scoundrel the American was, as he painstakingly picked apart the latest Wall of Sound extravaganza, and seized triumphantly upon even the tiniest nuance that he could claim he had utilised beforehand...the fuzz, the echo, the perfectionist overdubbing, the sound of chains being dragged across a piano's keys. Spector was no more a stranger to sonic gimmickry than Meek. But, in every instance, the Londoner insisted, it had been his gimmick first.

Meek's friends – his songwriting partner, the late Geoff Goddard among them – remember Meek angrily switching the radio off every time the DJ announced a Phil Spector tune. But worse was to come. On 24 January 1964, Spector himself was coming to England, accompanying The Ronettes on their first British tour. The enemy wasn't simply at the door, he was about to walk straight through it.

It is quite possible that many of these tales are apocryphal. Biographies of Meek published in the years since the murder-suicide that ended his life in 1967 have concentrated so heavily on the weirdness that swirled around him, that it is frequently difficult to determine precisely what is and isn't true within the Greek tragedy that was his life.

What does not seem to be in doubt, however, is Meek's response the afternoon, some time during that final week of January, when he picked up his telephone to hear an unfamiliar American voice announce, 'hello, this is Phil Spector'. Leaping back as though he'd been scalded, Meek slammed the telephone back into its cradle with such strength that he literally shattered the instrument. Spector never tried calling him again.

Others were far more welcoming, of course. Accompanied by Ronnie and Estelle's mother, The Ronettes flew into London two weeks ahead of Spector, to launch a three week tour with The Rolling Stones, then riding the success of their second single, 'I Wanna Be Your Man'. The Ronettes themselves were originally intended to top the bill, but the Stones were pushed ahead of them just a few days before the tour opened, as the sheer enormity of their following began to establish itself.

The Stones themselves were not convinced that they deserved the promotion. 'Those Ronettes stopped us dead in our tracks,' Mick Jagger admitted. 'We were just knocked out by their looks, sense of humour and everything.' Keith Richard followed through, 'they do such a tremendous act. It's not just the singing. They twist around and shake like mad. I think all the American groups have a similar styling, but The Ronettes have that something extra that puts them above the rest of the crowd.'

Nevertheless, an audience drawn almost exclusively from the burgeoning army of Stones-loving teenyboppers would never have appreciated such qualities, and The Ronettes knew it. Besides, if they were disappointed by their demotion, Decca Records – whose London subsidiary was Philles' UK representative – did their utmost to ensure the group's comfort elsewhere. They were introduced to The Beatles on their first night in the country, and the only major shock they received was when The Rolling Stones themselves seemed studiously to ignore them. Finally, Ronnie cornered Andrew Loog Oldham to demand at least some sign of civility. His response astonished her. 'Darling, the boys are your biggest fans. We'd all *love* to talk to you. But we got a telegram just before the tour started that forbids us from fraternising with you.' He did not need to tell her who the telegram was from.

Spector arrived as the tour wound down, to be met at the airport by Loog Oldham. With the American installed in a flat at the Mirabelle Hotel, with a Rolls-Royce at his permanent disposal, the pair of them readily became a formidable double act – much, apparently, to the despair of most of Oldham's own associates.

Oldham himself described Spector as looking 'more like an act than most acts. His appearance and attitude would just upset people. Little men in red corduroy jackets with black suede patches on the sleeves simply didn't alight from large Rolls-Royces in Mayfair.' He did not seem to realise that, for many observers, Spector was only half the problem. '[They] were a nightmare together,' Decca's Tony King smiled 30 years later. 'Andrew got hooked on Phil's not behaving well. They were terrible, like two irresponsible schoolboys.'

Oldham and Spector were all but inseparable that week, dining and clubbing together, but also hatching an audacious scheme. Through their UK record deal with Decca, The Rolling Stones' records had so far appeared on the London label in America (just as Spector's appeared on London in Britain). So far, however, London had done little to prove that they could break the Stones in that country; displayed, in fact, no more interest in the band than they did in any other import that their UK counterpart sent over.

Spector, on the other hand, absolutely loved the Stones, and had a label that could translate that love into lucre. If only Philles could take over the Stones' Stateside distribution...

On 4 February, Oldham and Spector paid a visit to Sir Edward Lewis, the venerable old head of Decca Records, to outline their scheme. Lewis listened, then turned them down flat. The Stones' future lay with London Records – and, of course, the band would prosper accordingly. As the two entrepreneurs departed the meeting, however, their mood was foul. They vowed revenge – and exacted it that same evening.

The Stones were booked into their customary Regent Sound studios that evening, to record the B-side for their next single, their third. The A-side, a startlingly distinctive revamp of Buddy Holly's 'Not Fade Away', was already in the can – this session, therefore, promised to be relaxing, if nothing else. As the evening approached, however, it appeared that nothing could have been further from the truth. For some long-forgotten reason, the Stones themselves were in an evil temper, and recording was the last thing on their mind.

How convenient, then, that Gene Pitney, flying in from Paris at the outset of his own promotional visit, should join Oldham and Spector in the studio, to announce that it was his 23rd birthday, and induct the band into an old family tradition, of draining a full glass of cognac, which he'd thoughtfully picked up at the duty free store. Only he and Oldham, of course, knew that the visit was by no means a coincidence; that Oldham had called Pitney just a few hours earlier, to ask him to come down and brighten up the day. It wasn't even his birthday for another 13 days. But the subterfuge did the trick. 'The Stones now had a friendly audience,' Oldham laughed. 'They had to perform – it's in the blood.'

With Pitney seated at the piano, and Spector joining two further new arrivals, The Hollies' Graham Nash and Allan Clarke, on assorted percussion (Spector himself tapped an empty cognac bottle with a half dollar coin he had in his pocket), the Stones recorded five songs, the B-side 'Little By Little'; two cuts destined for the band's debut album – 'Can I Get A Witness' and the aptly titled 'Now I've Got A Witness (Like Uncle Phil and Uncle Gene)'; and two numbers that Bill Wyman admits 'were very rude', 'Spector And Pitney Came Too' and 'Andrew's Blues', an astonishingly ribald 'tribute' to Decca head Sir Edward Lewis. That would teach him for shooting down people's dreams.

Spector would not go unrewarded for his appearance at the session. The writing credits for 'Little By Little' (plus the two unreleased numbers) would bear his name alongside the Stones' Nanker Phelge alter-ego, while he also knew that, in Oldham, he had found a friend who didn't simply understand his own dreams and motivations, he shared them. As Oldham's then-wife, Sheila, put it, 'they shared a passion about what they were into – little tweed hats, music, you name it... It was almost like [they'd] met [their] other half.'

Contrary to Joe Meek's fears, meanwhile, Spector maintained a relatively low media profile during his time in London. In those innocent years before paparazzi-style photographers began dogging even semi-celebrities' footsteps, most of Spector's activities during his fortnight in town were conducted for the benefit of his immediate companions alone.

He was extraordinarily gracious in an interview with the *Evening Standard*'s Maureen Cleave, happily raving about The Beatles and even confessing, the first time he heard them, he 'thought they were a great Canadian outfit'. The day after arriving in London, he made an appearance on BBC television's Saturday evening *Juke Box Jury* show, offering his opinions on the week's potential hits and misses; the following Friday, he popped up on *Ready Steady Go*. And then he was off, flying back to New York on 7 February, the same flight as The Beatles took to make their own triumphant debut in America. The flight, he said later, 'was a lot of fun. It was probably the only time I flew that I wasn't afraid, because I knew that they weren't going to get killed in a plane [crash].' In fact, according to Paul McCartney, 'he "walked to America". He was so nervous of flying, he couldn't sit down, so we watched him walk up and down the length of the plane all the way.'

The Ronettes' latest single (and, of course, latest hit) was 'Baby I Love You', released in January 1964 and, though no-one would ever have guessed from listening to it, it was the first of the group's singles to be recorded by Ronnie alone, cut during the autumn, while her bandmates (and another cousin, Elaine) were touring the US aboard impresario Dick Clark's Caravan of Stars tour.

Just as significantly, 'Baby I Love You' was also the last in that unbroken sequence of Philles singles to be penned by Ellie Greenwich and Jeff Barry. The couple had recently launched their own Red Bird label, in partnership with Leiber, Stoller and George Goldner, with the best of their songwriting output, inevitably, now destined for their own concern. Indeed, Red Bird's very first release, The Dixie Cups' 'Chapel Of Love', was a song that Spector had already cut with both The Ronettes and Darlene Love. However, when it became apparent that he had no intention of releasing either version any time soon, Greenwich and Barry lost no time in recording their own with The Dixie Cups – and it rocketed straight to No 1.

Spector was furious. Slicing Greenwich and Barry out of all future calculations, when he linked up with The Ronettes in London he was carrying with him a new song for them to record, 'The Best Part Of Breaking Up', composed by a new set of writers. Many of The Ronettes' final days in London were then spent holed up in their hotel room, rehearsing the song.

It was Paul Case who introduced Spector to Vinnie Poncia and Peter Andreoli, a Rhode Island duo who moved to Manhattan at the behest of Peer-Southern Music, and were now resident at the Hotel Forrest. There, perhaps inevitably, they met with fellow guest Doc Pomus, who in turn alerted Hill & Range to their abilities. Introduced now to Spector, the pair was nervously running through the songs they'd already written when Poncia happened to mention that they were working on a new one, 'The Best Part Of Breaking Up Is Making Up'.

Spector was sold on the spot. The title alone was solid gold; if the song was even half as good, he'd take it. Subject, of course, to a one-third songwriting credit, to take into account all that he would be bringing to the performance. The duo agreed and, soon after he returned from England, Spector was in the studio, recording '(The Best Part Of) Breaking Up' with The Ronettes. He also bought out half of Poncia and Andreoli's contract with Hill & Range, and installed the pair as Mother Bertha staff writers, while Poncia remembered the duo served another purpose as well – as *de facto* bodyguards whenever Spector was in New York.

Spector's need for personal protection has long been regarded as one of his most pointed quirks – as Poncia was quick to point out, Spector himself did not actually need any kind of protection. There was nobody gunning for him, nobody approaching him in the streets with violent intent. Rather, it was Spector himself who would instigate any problems, wheeling around on total strangers in restaurants, clubs or bars, and demanding to know why they were bothering him. Of course, most of them responded with precisely the same hostility; it was the admittedly meaty-looking Poncia and Andreoli's task to calm the situation and remove Spector from harm's way. And, of course, humour him as he rebuked them for not allowing him to kill his tormenter, 'because I could have, you know'.

But it wasn't mischief, madness or even ego that saw Spector become, as so many people have put it, 'obsessed' with muscular protection. Rather, Paul Case, his old friend at Hill & Range, told biographer Richard Williams, it was personal experience; the night on The Teddy Bears' first tour when Spector was confronted in the men's room by four concert-goers, who locked the door behind them, and proceeded to piss over him. It was an incident, Case averred, 'that Phil never forgot, and he said to himself "this will never happen again".'

In fact, if Spector had any tormenters as 1964 unfolded, it was the boys he'd flown across the Atlantic with. The Beatles dominated America that year, flooding the media, swamping the chart. By year's end, the group had placed no less than 30 different songs on the *Billboard* chart, as B-sides, EP and album tracks all wrestled for supremacy with the hit singles themselves.

Behind them, too, the Anglo-floodgates broke. British bands topped the US charts for no less than 26 weeks that year, as Peter And Gordon, Manfred Mann and The Animals joined The Beatles at the top, and Gerry And The Pacemakers, The Swinging Blue Jeans, Cilla Black and, of course, The Rolling Stones welled up behind them. Suddenly, America's own music industry was in absolute chaos and Spector, though he could certainly claim to have seen it coming, and was certainly present at its birth (he was first off the plane behind The Beatles, when they landed at Kennedy Airport back in February), was as powerless to resist as anybody – perhaps even more so.

Once the most futuristic noise imaginable, the 'Phil Spector Sound' was now out-of-date, last year's news. Spector himself was confidently expected to bounce back – great producers never die. But the lavish walls of music upon which his reputation was founded had been crushed and demolished by the simple twanging and happy-go-lucky instrumentation of the British Invaders.

It was a new world and, if Spector wanted any part in it, the nay-sayers insisted, he would have to renew himself, too.

Of course, Spector's own supporters dismissed such accusations with a shrug. When British journalist Keith Matthews suggested that Spector was old hat to The Ronettes, before their London Palladium show in January, Estelle Bennett retorted, 'it's not old-fashioned and it's still around. The same sound is still there, but its being widely imitated. When we use it, it sounds more natural…and so it goes on and on.'

Yet there was some truth to the accusations. Although both The Crystals and Darlene Love had more or less faded from his attentions by now, Spector's continued devotion to The Ronettes ensured that he remained wholly in league with the 'girl group' of what suddenly seemed such a long-ago era, with no sign, either, of even attempting to update his approach. The emergence of Greenwich, Barry and co's Red Bird label certainly proved that there was still mileage in the great teen anthem – The Dixie Cups' version of 'Chapel Of Love' went to No 1, even as The Ronettes' '(Best Part Of) Breaking Up' stalled at No 39; while Detroit-based Tamla-Motown had already launched The Supremes.

The Shangri-Las, another Red Bird outfit, were on the verge of breaking through, too, with a producer, Shadow Morton, who was just as revolutionary in his way as Spector had been in his. The difference was, they *had* changed with the times. Every new Supremes single sounded like it had been cut just the day before. A new Spector production, however, could have been recorded any time in the past three years.

Spector tried to break out of the straitjacket. Released that summer, The Ronettes' 'Do I Love You' grafted horns to the Wall of Sound, and allowed, for the first time, for silence to play its own part in the construction, as one of Jack Nitzsche's most tantalising arrangements allowed for momentous slabs of emptiness to simply hang in the air. But 'Do I Love You' barely fared better than its predecessor and, that autumn, Spector found himself playing a game that he might once have deemed several fathoms beneath him, attempting to cadge a ride aboard The Beatles' bandwagon by recording a song about them.

It was not a bad idea in itself. Shortly before Christmas, television actor Lorne Green would top the American chart with 'Ringo', while the release racks all around creaked beneath similarly grisly (and, occasionally, enjoyable) odes to the moptopped horde.

Vinnie Poncia and Peter Andreoli's 'I Love You Ringo' was to fall firmly into the former court. Indeed, Spector himself indicated his own disdain by bypassing Philles altogether, and issuing the record on a newly formed subsidiary named Annette – a gesture, of course, to his wife. It was to prove a short-lived label…much like the Spectors' marriage, in fact…and would see just two further releases, a duet between Spector and Doc Pomus, Harvey & Doc's 'Oh Baby', and a cover of The Beatles' 'Hold Me Tight', by Vinnie [Poncia] and Pete [Andreoli] themselves.

'I Love You Ringo', meantime, was recorded with a girl who'd been hovering around Spector's inner sanctum for a couple of years, a tall, striking teenager named Cherilyn LaPierre, or 'Cher'. She was dating Sonny Bono at the time, the Philles promo man who reflected, years later, 'that was my official title. My unofficial duties included buying burgers from Brother Julius', singing back-up in the studio, banging tambourines, chauffeuring everyone around…' his voice trailed away a little wistfully, a little resentfully. 'But my ambition was to have Phil record Cher.'

The first attempt at making that dream come true arrived in early 1963, at Gold Star. Cher told TV interviewer Melvyn Bragg, 'I was just hanging out with Son [Bono], and one night Darlene didn't show up, and Philip looked at me and he was getting really cranky, y'know. Philip was not one to be kept waiting. And he said, "Sonny said you can sing?" And so, as I was trying to qualify what I felt my…"expertise" was, he said, "Look, I just need noise – get out there!" I started as noise, and that was "Be My Baby".'

Documenting the session in his autobiography, *And The Beat Goes On*, Bono himself had less pleasant memories of the occasion. 'There was absolutely no chemistry. The two of them stood opposite each other in the antechamber of the studio and eyed one another like a cat and a dog.'

Spector broke the silence. 'Sonny tells me you want to sing.'

'I like to sing,' Cher replied, and Bono broke in, 'she's incredible. Man, Phil, you should hear her.'

Spector sighed. 'I suppose I will.'

Slowly, over a period of months, the mood between the pair lightened. Cher joined Bono among the backing vocalists on a number of subsequent recordings, but still Spector showed no interest in pulling her out of the chorus and giving her her own break. 'And then he came up with The Beatles thing,' Bono said, 'and that's when he called her.' It would not be released under her own name, however; instead, Spector came up with the pseudonym Bonnie Jo Mason and, doubtless, Cher was grateful that the record sank without trace. 'Philip thought that all girl acts should have very American names,' Cher shrugged.

"[It] was not one of Phil's better projects,' Sonny Bono continued. 'In fact, it was a total flop. There were numerous reasons. First, the song wasn't that good. Second, Beatle fans loved Paul more than Ringo.' And third, as Cher admitted to British television's *The South Bank Show*, 'the radios wouldn't play it, 'cos they said it sounded like a guy singing "Ringo I love you"...and so, that wasn't happening.'

Neither Cher nor Bono would remain at Philles for much longer. Indeed, Bono later acknowledged that he'd been skating on thin ice for several months, ever since a phone call he made to Spector in October 1964, after he visited LA radio station KFWB with a hotly pressed copy of the new Ronettes single, 'Walking In The Rain'.

The record itself was an instant classic, a return to the proven pastures of Mann and Weil that returned, too, to the outer limits of Spector's imagination, as he drenched the performance in the sounds of a genuine thunderstorm.

But the meeting did not go well. 'When the deejay played [it] he gave me a less-than-enthusiastic look – actually, a grimace. "You know, the thunder and the tricks and the Wall of Sound...it kinda sounds tired".' The jock agreed to add the record to his playlist, but could not promise when that might be and, when Bono relayed the news to Spector himself, he made what he described as 'my fatal mistake'. He didn't quite repeat back all the deejay had told him. But he did suggest that maybe it was time to change the sound.

'In retrospect,' Bono wrote, 'I can tell myself, "okay, who were you to tell Phil Spector to change his sound?" But I was his trusty confidant, his right-hand man, his connection to radio stations that were the bread and butter of his operation. He often requested my opinion and, even when he didn't, I usually gave it anyway.'

This time, however, he had given too much. The silence on the other end of the phone stretched on so long that Bono thought...hoped...for a moment that the line had been interrupted. Finally Spector did say something, non-committal but pregnant all the same. 'I limped out of the phone booth, doomed.'

Of course Bono would be alright in the long run. Making a clean break from Spector, he and Cher launched their own career as Sonny and Cher and, by summer 1965, they were top of the American chart with the proto-hippy anthem 'I Got You Babe'. And Spector survived the break-up as well – in February 1965, he achieved what many industry insiders had truly believed he would never do again, and scored another US No 1. And he did it with a Wall of Sound that no band on Earth could have vaulted over.

7 The Loving Feeling

On 3 January 1965, the prestigious *New York Herald Tribune*'s magazine section, *New York*, published one of the longest interviews Spector had ever granted, a profile by the much-respected author Tom Wolfe, titled 'The First Tycoon Of Teen'. It was an apt heading. Just turned 24, Spector was already a millionaire and he had, indeed, built his wealth upon the fortunes and misfortunes of teenaged America.

The article focused on Spector in all his guises, from the nervous traveller who kicked up so much fuss on a flight out of Los Angeles that they turned the plane around for *him* (and then checked his luggage for bombs, just in case), to the bold entrepreneur seated in his New York office who suddenly announced that he was relocating the entire company to LA, so he wouldn't have to fly anymore. From the hard-nosed businessman who bucked the entire American music industry by refusing to pay any*one* any*thing* for the privilege of playing his records ('we need this guy, Phil, he's the biggest distributor out there'; 'I don't care') to the karate king who could literally 'kill a guy like *that*'.

It discussed his hatred of the music industry establishment, how Universal Distributors' influence over the label's finances was severely cut back as Spector chose to launch his own distribution network, under the supervision of Chuck, Lester Sill's long-suffering stepson and now, Philles' general manager. 'They're a bunch of cigar-smoking sharpies in record distribution,' Spector snarled. 'They've all been in the business for years, and they resent you if you're young. That's one reason so many kids go broke in this business.' He hadn't gone broke, because he played them at their own game – no, not their own game. He played *his* game, and let them believe it was theirs. It was only when they turned around to chuckle about how smart they were, that they discovered there really wasn't much for them to laugh about.

But finally, Wolfe settled on Spector's most important role of all, the man who, from 'To Know Him Is To Love Him' to 'Walking In The Rain', had developed, orchestrated and accomplished a canon of music that encapsulated every emotion, every dream and, of course, every heartache that the teenage soul was capable of sustaining – and, who could fight for rock 'n' roll's dignity until the cows came home. 'People are always saying…"why doesn't anybody write lyrics like Cole Porter anymore?"' he told Wolfe. 'But we don't have Presidents like Abraham Lincoln anymore, either.' Rock 'n' roll, the music that he made, and The Beatles made and so many other artists made, had 'a spontaneity that doesn't exist in any other kind of music. It's very today. It's what people respond to *today*.' And to Phil Spector it was that response, that immediacy, that mattered.

His last few records, though he would not admit it outright, had not had that immediacy. Though he let Bono believe he was fired for calling the Wall of Sound out-of-date, in truth the little gofer had told him nothing he didn't already know. Indeed, if Bono had only paused to think back a few months for a moment, he would have known that Spector had already taken the future into consideration with a record he'd cut at Gold Star that autumn, with both Sonny and Cher in attendance. It was called 'You've Lost That Lovin' Feelin'' and, after all the apparent mis-steps of the past 12 months, it was everything a Phil Spector record needed to be.

The Righteous Brothers – the unrelated Bill Medley and Bobby Hatfield – had been performing around southern California for some three years before Spector encountered them, honing an energetic act that trailed from doo-wop to R&B without a pause, but one whose local live popularity never transformed itself into record sales. A string of releases on the local Moonglow label included a couple of lower-rung hits – 'Little Latin Lupe Lu' went to No 49 in mid-1963, 'My Babe' peaked at No 75 later that same year – but nothing more.

Spector was well aware of them, of course. Another of their singles was one of Sonny Bono's own compositions, 'Koko Joe', while the duo were also regular guests on television's *Shindig*. More recently still, they'd been booked to open for The Beatles on their first US tour in August and September 1964. But even at their best, they lacked one thing – a song to match their voices, and a sound to match the song. Spector knew he could provide both.

Armed with a Barry Mann/Cynthia Weil song that he could not imagine recording with anybody else, Spector contacted Moonglow to arrange a deal that would allow him to 'lease' the Brothers to Philles. The label agreed and, in October 1964, Hatfield and Medley joined Spector at Gold Star studio A to record their next single.

'You've Lost That Lovin' Feelin'' represented new pastures for Spector. A towering edifice before he even sang a word, Medley's lead vocal itself would be the sonic selling point, with the band – boosted for the occasion by Spector's old-time idol Barney Kessel – merely adding flourishes around the masterstrokes. It was within those flourishes, however, that Spector worked his greatest magic, coaxing a performance that could not help but draw Medley's voice into ever greater heights of passion and which, as Spector and arranger Gene Page worked on, quickly tore through all the previously recognised boundaries of a hit single.

Larry Levine insisted, 'Spector was never hung up with the idea of [the] sound that he had until…he got into the Righteous Brothers. Up until then, it was always what the song said, what the song needed.' This time around, things were different. Predicting the gauntlet he would throw down a decade later, when he would literally challenge the world's top producers to try and outdo him, Spector cast his eye around at the 'competition' – George Martin with The Beatles, Andrew Oldham with the Stones, Brian Wilson with the Beach Boys – and set out to prove that, no matter how grand they might sound, he could sound grander. And he succeeded.

Spector knew 'You've Lost That Lovin' Feelin'' was a hit from the outset; indeed, when Bobby Hatfield, sidelined by his partner's lead role in the song, asked the producer if there was anything at all for him to do, Spector is said to have simply replied, 'start counting the money'.

There was only one drawback to the recording – and, if Sonny Bono was looking for other reasons why he (and, because she was already regarded as inseparable from him, Cher) were so peremptorily dismissed from the Philles set-up, another clue may have lain there. As the session progressed, Spector found himself in need of some additional backing vocals, specifically a solo part that only one person in the room, he decided, could handle. But when he turned to Cher and asked her to step in, Bono shuddered, 'she refused'. He was already aware that nerves frequently got the better of her when asked to simply perform – 'the indomitable strength disappeared, her voice went into vapour lock'. That is what happened there. 'With tears in her eyes, she ran into the hallway'. Spector may have understood her fears, he may not. But he never invited her to sing a solo part for him again and, just weeks later, he ensured that she would never even be in a position to.

The session lasted, as usual, for an eternity – at least 39 takes were required to complete it and, when they played the song back on the tiny car radio speakers through which Spector tested all his takes, it went on forever as well. At a time when few hit singles exceeded three minutes in length, 'You've Lost That Lovin' Feelin'' emerged an epic that nudged the four minute mark, territory that precious few other acts had ever tapped before. Even The Animals' similarly protracted 'House Of The Rising Sun' had been crudely hacked for radio play and it was only late into its chart life that enterprising DJs began digging out the longer album version, and giving that a spin.

Spector would not edit 'You've Lost That Lovin' Feelin''. What he was willing to do was reverse the last two digits of the song's actual timing, and give radio DJs the longest 3.05 of their lives. It was, apparently, some weeks before many programme directors figured out why their tightly programmed shows were suddenly over-running, but by then, 'You've Lost That Lovin' Feelin'' was already ground into the Planet Pop consciousness. It was not cut, it could not be cut and, on 6 February 1965, 'You've Lost That Lovin' Feelin'' officially became the longest record ever to top the *Billboard* chart.

It was just as successful in the UK; indeed, there its achievement was even greater, as it battled not only against the usual crop of post-moptop chart-toppers, but also against a powerful cover version, cut by George Martin and singer Cilla Black.

Spector purists objected furiously to the blasphemy of Black's rendition – Andrew Oldham and his business partner Tony Calder, in fact, were so aghast that they took the absolutely unheard of step of buying an advert in the *Melody Maker*, to help promote a record they could not hope to profit by: 'this advert is not for commercial gain. It is taken as something that must be said about the great new Phil Spector record… Already in the American Top 10, this is Spector's greatest production, the last word in Tomorrow's Sound Today, exposing the overall mediocrity of the Music Industry.' Oldham himself had considerable advance warning of the power of the record. Back in October in New York, at the outset of the Stones' latest American tour, he spent a couple of nights crashing on Spector's sofa. He expected the office to be empty when he let himself in following the band's appearance on the *Ed Sullivan Show,* and was surprised to find Spector and Danny Davis, the former Big Top promo man who'd replaced Chuck Kaye at the head of the Philles family, still on the premises, listening loudly to a white label test pressing that had obviously just been delivered.

'The room was filled with this amazing sound,' Oldham remembered. 'I had no idea what it was, but it was the most incredible thing I'd ever heard.' For a moment, he wasn't even certain that it was a Spector production – 'it was certainly nothing like his usual up-tempo avalanches of fulfilled and celebrated love, heavy with percussion, pianos, guitars, keyboards, stabbing horns and wailing black nubiles…yet it *had* to be Phil.' And, of course it was.

Against such a backdrop – 'I'd never heard a recorded track so emotionally giving or empowering' – of course, Cilla Black's version of the song stood no chance of being accepted. The charts, however, told another story entirely. Both Black and the Righteous Brothers entered the UK listings on 14 January, both were in the Top 3 by the end of the month, but it was Black who had her nose in front, touching No 2. The following week, however, while Cilla dropped a place, the Righteous Brothers leaped up two. Spector had his first British No 1.

'You've Lost That Lovin' Feelin'' was not Spector's only appearance on the chart that month. On 17 January 1965, The Rolling Stones checked into the RCA Studios in LA to record their own next single, 'The Last Time'. It was a dynamic session, and Oldham was convinced he'd just produced what would prove to be the Stones' breakthrough American hit; so convinced that he called Spector to ask him to cast an ear over the tape, and predict how high it might go. Spector arrived at the studio just 45 minutes later, turned the tape up as loud as it would go, and then chuckled. 'Number 10, guys, number 10.'

In fact it went to No 9, but before he left, Spector had a second gift for the group. Knowing that the only other song to cut, the scheduled B-side, was the delicate ballad 'Play With Fire', guitarist Brian Jones and the rhythm section of Charlie Watts and Bill Wyman returned to their hotel, leaving Mick Jagger, Keith Richards and arranger Nitzsche to get on with it. Picking up a bass, Spector joined in for his first recorded musical performance in some five years. 'Play With Fire' itself would mosey up to No 96 on the American chart.

Throughout the early months of their courtship, Ronnie Bennett had no idea that Spector was married. On one of her rare visits to his apartment, to meet with Ellie Greenwich and Jeff Barry, he explained away the odd feminine article that lay around the room as belonging to his sister. Neither did Spector encourage anybody to speculate on the true nature of his relationship with the 19-year-old. Their circumspection could lead them into trouble on occasion, however – such as the time the Delmonico hotel in New York City busted Ronnie for prostitution, after seeing Spector creep surreptitiously away from the room they'd booked, five minutes before she came down the stairs.

Cornering her while they spilled out their accusations, the house detectives allowed Ronnie to make one call; of course, she rang Spector at the studio. He asked her to pass the phone to one of the detectives, and Ronnie admitted that even she felt sorry for the man, as he put the receiver to his ear. 'You could hear Phil shouting all the way across the room, "That's my wife you've got in there! And, if you lay one more grubby hand on her, I'll sue you, the hotel, the New York City Hotel Commission. And then I'll personally arrange to have you killed." '

They let her leave.

Despite the pains that the couple took to conceal their relationship, however, rumour began to circulate anyway, until finally Darlene Love confronted Ronnie during one of The Ronettes' increasingly frequent visits to Los Angeles, sometime in spring 1964. They were in the bathroom at the Purple Onion discothèque when Love detonated her bombshell and, years later, she could still hear herself saying 'this man is already married' – and wondering how Ronnie had managed to block her mind to the knowledge. 'To this day,' Love averred, 'I don't believe she didn't know. How couldn't she have known? She wasn't stupid.'

Neither was Annette Spector, although she, too, was among the last to discover what had become an open secret both within and without Spector's immediate circle of acquaintances. Even then, she learned only that he was having a relationship with *one* of The Ronettes, and she later admitted that her first guess would have been Nedra. Still, it was clear to Annette that the marriage was over. Alert, as ever, to the secret messages that Spector filed through the songs he recorded, she knew the truth the moment she heard 'You've Lost That Lovin' Feelin''. The first line of the first song he recorded after they re-met at that party back in 1961 had said so much to her: 'I love how your eyes close whenever you kiss me.' And now he was speaking directly to her again – 'you never close your eyes anymore...'

Nevertheless, another 18 months would elapse before she and Spector finally separated for good. Their divorce, granted in late 1965 under the loose laws of a Mexican court, saw Annette receive a $100,000 alimony spread across five years of weekly payments. Just days later, Spector bought a new home for himself and Ronnie, a 21-room, 5-bedroom, castle-like mansion owned by veteran English actor Reginald Owen (whose films included *National Velvet* and *Mrs Miniver*), and his wife Barbara.

1200 La Collina Drive lies deep in the heart of Beverly Hills – turn off Sunset Boulevard when it changes to Doheny Road, and it's the third major turning on your right, a secluded street that simply dribbles to a dead end. Eartha Kitt was Spector's closest neighbour, at No 1230 (that building is now occupied by Vanguard Films); otherwise, the house wasn't simply off the beaten track, it was practically invisible.

Spector himself would not take up residence in his new home for close to a year; New York still occupied much of his time, with the success of 'You've Lost That Lovin' Feelin'' – coupled with the highbrow circulation of the Tom Wolfe article – having suddenly reminded America that he was still around.

Spector reacted cautiously. The previous August, he joined Leslie Gore, Bobby Vinton, Goldie Goldmark and Jack Keller among the guests on David Susskind's *Open End* show, and any hopes he entertained that such a bastion of establishment entertainment might treat him with a little more respect than the average rock 'n' roller were swiftly disavowed.

Pop stars, after all, were little more than performing freaks to the old guard entertainers, something to be tolerated for the sake of the ratings alone, and Susskind quickly made it apparent that he viewed Spector with no less disdain. Spector responded with matching venom. 'I didn't have to come here tonight,' he told his startled host. 'I could have stayed at home, making money.'

This time around, he was booked onto Johnny Carson's *Tonight Show*. Ella Fitzgerald was also guesting and, as was the show's format, the pair sat down with Carson for a cosy chat – which collapsed when Fitzgerald asked Spector who his biggest act was. Bearing in mind that 'You've Lost That Lovin' Feelin'' was currently No 1, on its way to selling a previously unheard of seven million copies, a surprised Spector answered 'the Righteous Brothers'.

'I've never heard of them,' Fitzgerald sniffed – to which Spector flashed back, 'that's alright. They've never heard of you.'

In the wake of 'You've Lost That Lovin' Feelin'', the Righteous Brothers' popularity exploded. Moonglow promptly unleashed *three* of their earlier recordings, 'Bring Your Love To Me', 'You Can Have Her' and 'Justine' and, though none was more than a nominal hit, it was difficult not to cast one's mind back a mere 12 months, to a time when every label that had an old Beatles song on board was suddenly raking in the cash from their undying popularity. The Brothers' own intended follow-up, Gerry Goffin and Carole King's 'Just Once In My Life' itself arrived in April and, borne once again on a magnificent wave of Spectorsound, it cracked the Top 10.

Goffin and King had not been Spector's original first choice as writers. Among the promises he made Barry Mann and Cynthia Weil, when they handed over 'You've Lost That Lovin' Feelin'', was the pledge that they would supply the follow-up single as well, a stately ballad titled 'Love Her'. Since then, however, he had changed his mind. If the Righteous Brothers were to succeed, they needed to diversify, emotionally if not musically, and 'Love Her' was just a little too close to its predecessor for comfort. Precipitating what would become a major bone of contention between producer and songwriters, Spector turned away from them, and the success of the new song bore out his decision. (So did the failure of 'Love Her' – quickly recorded by the decidedly similarly themed Walker Brothers, it failed to make either the US or UK chart.)

Midway through the year, and the Righteous Brothers alone represented one of Spector's most successful spells ever, so much so that, a pair of barely noted Ronettes singles notwithstanding, Philles' entire output was turned to the new duo's success. It was a bubble, Spector was convinced, that could never burst; and it was certainly one that he did not intend endangering by allowing other acts to distract his attention.

Indeed, a label that had never overflowed with 'stars' was suddenly looking dreadfully threadbare. The Crystals were now ensconced at United Artists, and celebrating with the sharply titled 'You Can't Tie A Good Girl Down'. Vinnie Poncia and Pete Andreoli would soon be moving on, shifting over to Red Bird and immediately hitting with The Tradewinds' 'New York's A Lonely Town'.

Darlene Love was still around, but she and The Blossoms had more or less faded into session work; away from Spector's empire, the group was still in demand as session singers, swelling the line-up with Jack Nitzsche's wife Grazia, and the mercurial voice of Merry Clayton and guesting for friends as far afield as country singer Johnny Rivers, and LA's own Beach Boys.

Demos regularly poured into the Philles offices, not only from songwriters but also, increasingly, from fully formed bands who wrote and performed their own music, and needed only a visionary producer to bring their brilliance to light. Rock was growing more serious, and both Danny Davis and Vinnie Poncia were constantly trying to impress upon Spector that he needed to turn his attention to that mood. He was already familiar with The Beatles and the Stones, the Beach Boys and The Byrds...would it hurt him to find an act in a similar mould, that he could nurture into the future?

Spector listened to their speeches and occasionally listened to the demos that they played him. Few, however, caught his ear. He was not sick of music, he was not sick of work. He was, however, sick of never hearing anything that excited him enough to do something about it. In 1969, he would tell *Rolling*

Stone, 'I'm…tired of hearing about…everybody's emotional problems.' Modern notions of music, borne in on the psychedelia that, in 1965–66, was just beginning to swirl beneath the mainstream surface, were 'too wavy…like watching a three- or four-hour movie. No concept of melody, [it] just goes on and on with the lyric.' Musicians, he complained, were no longer writing songs. 'They are only writing ideas. They don't really care about repetition, they don't care about a hook or melody.' So he no longer cared about them.

Even those groups that did interest him were unlikely to actually hear from him. For a few days in spring 1965, for example, Spector seemed utterly obsessed with a New York group called The Lovin' Spoonful, whose 'Do You Believe In Magic' demo was seldom off the Philles office turntable. But, though he liked their sound – a jugband bluegrass variant; and though he loved the song, even playing his own guitar along with it, he hated the group's name and never got in touch. Weeks later, John Sebastian and co signed with the Kama Sutra label and spent the next three years among America's best-loved bands.

Outsiders accuse Spector of similar short-sightedness that same summer, when Danny Davis approached him about The Rascals, a Long Island blues-rock band fronted by the effervescent Felix Cavaliere. The Rascals' manager, concert promoter Sid Bernstein, put him onto the band, and it turned out that Vinnie Poncia knew of them too – his wife Joanna's own band often gigged alongside The Rascals at the Barge, a club in Westhampton, Long Island. It took days of cajoling to persuade Spector to finally agree to drive out to see the band one evening in August, only for him to be left sorely disappointed when he got there.

Thrilled when they heard Spector was coming, The Rascals put aside their own songs and rehearsed some of his old numbers instead, to be performed as a tribute when he arrived. All Spector heard, however, was a covers band and, though Poncia persuaded him to stay for the full show, he would not be deterred from his first impression. If Poncia loved the group so much, he should produce them, and Spector would release it on a new label he was launching with Davis, Phi-Dan. Otherwise, they should be left for labels that really wanted them. Jerry Leiber and Ahmet Ertegun were both numbered among The Rascals' circle of acquaintances, and Spector simply did not care enough for the group's sound that he was willing to launch another feud with either man. And that is how it turned out. Weeks after Spector caught the band, Atlantic despatched producer Tom Dowd to check them out and, before the end of the year, The Rascals were chartbound with the sparkling 'I Ain't Gonna Eat Out My Heart Anymore'.

Phi-Dan, on the other hand, would never take off. Formed when Danny Davis complained that Spector wasn't releasing enough records for him to actually promote, the label released no less than eight singles during 1965, although not one of them was actually a Spector production. He instead turned the reins over to Poncia and Andreoli, session man Leon Russell and various others, all potential members of a production stable he was intending to forge.

In the event, Spector never built that stable, the dream a casualty of the ultimate failure of Phi-Dan. Just one single on the label broke through, and that did so only via a slice of industry-wide controversy that at least kept readers of the trade papers enthralled for a few weeks. Produced by another of Spector's hopeful young protégés, Jerry Riopell, Bonnie And The Treasures' 'Home of The Brave' was released in mid-August, just days before Capitol released a version of the same Barry Mann/Cynthia Weil song by Jody Miller.

Anxious to get a jump on Capitol, Spector placed an ad in *Billboard* asserting that, though he'd heard that 'it was gonna be covered by a major label,' his record was the original. Capitol promptly issued a statement insisting that their 'Home Of The Brave' was recorded at their own Capitol Tower Studios in Hollywood on 8 July, and was previewed at their sales meeting at the Sheraton San Juan Hotel, Puerto Rico, a week later. According to the Los Angeles Musicians Union, meanwhile, the Phi-Dan version was not cut until 24 July.

Spector struck back immediately, arguing that though The Treasures' own version was cut on that date; the actual arrangement dated back to 1964, when it was intended for a Ronettes single. This formed the basis for Riopell's new recording, recorded with a young singer named Charlotte Ann Matheny, herself a friend of one-time Philles recording artist Al Hazan. In a wire to *Billboard*, Spector maintained 'that the idea behind the song, of doing the song, and of its hit potential and the fact that it would now be apropos is what constitutes in my opinion the word "cover". All these things were first thought of and originated by the Philles organization.'

In the public arena, however, his protests were to little avail. While Bonnie And The Treasures climbed no higher than No 77, pop-country vocalist Miller's version reached No 25. (Miller would return to taunt Spector six years later, after George Harrison's 'My Sweet Lord', a Spector co-production, was accused of being 'borrowed' from The Chiffons' 'He's So Fine' – Miller covered the latter in the style of the former, and scored a Top 60 hit for his trouble.)

One band that Spector did express an interest in was the Beach Boys. Three years had passed since the Wilson siblings-and-friends first burst onto the chart scene with their songs of endless summers filled with cars, girls and surfboards, a period that had seen frontman Brian Wilson's genius swell with the band's success and, as it did so, offer up further indications of how the tide was turning against the Wall of Sound. The most devoted pupil of all, the man once had to stop his car so he could marvel at the Spectorsound, was himself now being feted as the new King of sonic perfection and, as 1965 rolled along, hits like 'Help Me Rhonda', 'California Girls' and 'Barbara Ann' evidenced how firmly Wilson was grasping that mantel.

Even at his peak, however – and he was certainly approaching that point, that summer – Wilson remained in absolute awe of Spector. 35 years later, he told *Mojo* magazine, '…Phil Spector…was probably the biggest influence of all. That's where I learned how to produce records. Anybody with a good ear can hear that I was influenced by Spector. I would listen to his records and pick up ideas. I'd try to work out how much echo he was using on particular instruments, and how he achieved that particular sound.'

Wilson and Spector had met on several occasions ('I found him very easy to talk to,' the Beach Boy affirmed); had even discussed the possibility of Wilson producing The Blossoms. Now they were planning to collaborate. Wilson had recently written a song for The Ronettes, 'Don't Hurt My Little Sister', and he told *Mojo*, 'he cut a track for it and he asked me to come down to Gold Star studio and watch him produce it. So I got my ass down there…' With Jack Nitzsche handling the arrangement, and Wilson playing piano, 'he *did* produce it, but he never finished it. So that never appeared.'

Not in its intended form, anyway. But when Spector was approached to contribute a song to a public service campaign, informing minority groups that new employment opportunities were opening up for them, he promptly retrieved 'Don't Hurt My Little Sister', and entrusted Jerry Riopell with adapting it to the Equal Opportunities Commission's needs. He came up with 'Things Are Changing', recording it at Gold Star with Darlene Love and The Blossoms; subsequently, the same backing track was utilised by The Supremes and Jay And The Americans, for their own contributions to the campaign.

Another version was recorded by Puerto Rican singer Lucecita, as part of a settlement arranged between Spector and Lucecita's manager Alfred D Herger, after he cut Spanish-language versions of 'Be My Baby' and 'Then He Kissed Me', without having first cleared the recordings through their American publishers. Generously, Spector permitted the use of his (or, rather, Riopell's) backing track for the performance.

Spector's high hopes for the Righteous Brothers came tumbling down in September, as the act that he intended would sustain him for the foreseeable future began growing rebellious beneath his hand. Philles' original deal with Moonglow had leased him the band's contract for four years. However, when Spector came to deal with the duo themselves, he found them somewhat less pliable than label head RJ Van Hoogten.

Barely had 'You've Lost That Lovin' Feelin'' hit the streets than the Brothers began agitating to record a full album. Spector, who now regarded the format with almost superstitious dread, refused, and it took all of Larry Levine's powers of persuasion to change his mind, convincing him to grant the go-ahead for Bill Medley, himself an aspiring producer, to handle the LP itself, for release on Philles. Spector agreed (Medley had, in any case, produced the single's B-side) and, though he found himself lumbered with an extraordinarily unpalatable potpourri of warmed-up MOR ballads, highlighted by just one shimmering moment (the title track, 'You've Lost That Lovin' Feelin'', of course), still the album was a massive hit.

Emboldened by the experience, Medley quickly began demanding a follow-up. Again Spector demurred; again he found himself convinced to step aside. *Just Once In My Life*, released in May 1965, was a marginal improvement on its predecessor – this time, two Spector productions made it onboard, both recent singles. And again it was a hit, but Spector could not help but notice that Medley's newfound power was undermining the strength of the duo itself, as Bobby Hatfield began chafing beneath his partner's apparent supremacy.

Looking to reunite the pair, Spector himself hatched the idea of a third album for release in time for Christmas. *Back To Back* would emphasise the two Brothers' differences, yet maintain a united front to the world, by having Medley produce his own material, while Spector oversaw the majority of Hatfield's contributions to the album. One of those, Hatfield's stirring version of 'Unchained Melody' (one of the songs that Lew Chudd had drafted into The Teddy Bears album!) was already climbing the singles chart as work began on the album in September, and Spector had already bookmarked its follow-up, a fabulous re-enactment of the old Frank Chacksfield hit 'Ebb Tide'.

Behind the scenes, however, problems were brewing. A clause of Spector's contract with Moonglow granted him the Righteous Brothers only for the US, Canada and the UK – Moonglow were to handle their releases elsewhere around the world. But where were the masters that Spector was contractually obligated to deliver? In mid-September, Van Hoogten notified Spector that he was in breach of contract and that their arrangement had now been terminated. At the same time, he instructed Medley and Hatfield to down tools on the then in-progress album, seemingly unaware that they had just received back the results of an independent audit of Moonglow's accounts, and found themselves owed almost $30,000 in unpaid royalties.

A major stand-off resulted, with the Righteous Brothers now arguing that, because Moonglow had breached *their* contract, then the label's own arrangements with Spector were of no concern to them. They also pointed out that Philles, too, had been remarkably lax about paying them their due. And, finally, they were sick of the fact that, every time they released a new single, the papers simply described it as the latest Phil Spector release.

Neither was any party willing to even try and thrash out a compromise. Although Spector and Van Hoogten put their own differences aside, and separately begged the Righteous Brothers to complete the album to catch the Christmas market, Medley and Hatfield stood firm – apparently, the difficulties that Spector had perceived brewing between the pair were less injurious than he had estimated.

Finally, Spector gathered up the handful of songs that had been completed, padded them out with a handful of Medley-produced out-takes and demos and released the resultant hodgepodge as it stood. The Righteous Brothers promptly added that to their list of grievances, as well.

Unfortunately, the duo was too swift to celebrate what they believed to be their emancipation. The first *Billboard* of the New Year featured the news that the Righteous Brothers were newly signed to MGM's Verve subsidiary, despite MGM themselves having already been warned off by Philles' solicitor, Jay Cooper. Worse was to follow, as the pair marched into the studio to record a new Barry Mann/Cynthia Weil composition, the soaring '(You're My) Soul and Inspiration.' For the writers, it was just retribution for Spector not allowing them to handle the follow-up to 'You've Lost That Lovin' Feelin''; for the Brothers, another chart-topper proved that they didn't need Spector after all. For Phil himself, it was treason. He would never deal with Mann and Weil anymore; he washed his hands of the Righteous Brothers and he pursued MGM so vigorously that they quickly settled his lawsuit for over half a million dollars.

Four years on, the entire incident still left a foul taste in Spector's mouth. Although he conceded, in his 1969 *Rolling Stone* interview, that the Righteous Brothers *should* have been able to make it without any help from him, he continued that they themselves probably weren't equipped for the job.

'[They] were a strange group in that they really were non-intellectual and unable to comprehend success. They couldn't understand it and couldn't live with it and accept it for what it really was. They thought it was something that could be obtained very easily and once it was attained, it could be consistently obtained. Really, they were not sophisticated enough to present themselves honestly.

'I just think it was a great loss, because the two of them weren't exceptional talents, but they did have a musical contribution to make. I loved them; I thought they were a tremendous expression for myself. I think they resented being an expression. I think now if they had it to do again, they never would have left.'

But what would they have had if they'd stayed? A record label that now lay like a western ghost town, through which a breath of sonic tumbleweed might occasionally pass through as its landlord saw fit...and a landlord who himself spent more time at home playing pinball than he did in the studio or on the town. Or so says the legend.

Unfortunately for the legend, and this is true throughout Phil Spector's career, the people who offer the most precise pinpointing of the moment when he dropped out of orbit, are in fact usually pinpointing the moment when he first dropped out of *their* orbit.

Whether through circumstance or design, 1965 found Spector again sloughing away many of the associations he'd built up over recent years and, for so many of them, 'that's the moment when I realised he had changed'. Not the moment when he realised he was bored of their company, not the moment when he decided they had nothing more to offer him, not even the moment when he lost their phone number and just never got around to finding it again. *That* was when he changed. In fact, it's just as likely that that's when he realised that he *could* change.

8 The Last Dance

As 1965 moved towards its close, Phil Spector showed no sign whatsoever of either slowing down or sliding away. He continued his wrangling with the Righteous Brothers. He allowed ABC television cameras into his world, to prepare a one-hour documentary on his life and times, for broadcast on 28 January 1966. And he discovered a new band, the Modern Folk Quartet, who represented all the frontiers that the likes of Danny Davis and Vinnie Poncia had been talking of, but who did so on terms that he himself understood.

He found them playing just down the road. Lining up as photographer Henry Diltz, future Monkees producer Chip Douglas, latter-day Lovin' Spoonful member Jerry Yester and Cyrus Faryar, the Modern Folk Quartet were regulars at the Whisky and the Troubadour, and turned out to be as pure and alluring as their name suggested. 'I played the banjo and harmonica and sang,' Diltz recalled. 'We were actually a vocal group. I mean, we all played instruments, but we did four-part harmonies, so the vocals were a big part of it.'

Spector was entranced – one night, according to LA scenester Kim Fowley, he even joined the Quartet onstage at the Trip club for an impromptu set of '50s-era oldies. The knowledge that half the people in the audience probably didn't even know who he was only added to the thrill.

With a crop of singles and two warmly received Warner Brothers albums to their name, the Quartet were no starry-eyed ingénues. Spector, however, made them feel like kings, inviting them back to the house to hang out and scarcely able to contain his excitement at the thought of working together.

In October, Spector booked the band into Gold Star. He already had a song for them – visiting publisher Perry Botkin the previous year, Spector was introduced to a young singer-songwriter named Harry Nilsson. It was one his songs, 'This Could Be The Night', that Spector deemed suitable for the Modern Folk Quartet (two others, 'Here I Sit' and 'Paradise', were subsequently recorded by The Ronettes), and the group pounced upon it, turning in such a bravado performance that when, the following month, Spector was invited to helm a concert movie being shot at the Moulin Rouge Theater, he reserved 'This Could Be The Night' for the theme music.

Staged over two nights, 29 and 30 November, *The Big TNT Show* was the brainchild of producer Henry Sapperstein, who saw the film as a successor to the smash hit of the previous year, the *TAMI Show* (Teen Age Music International) – itself a live rock 'n' roll spectacular for which Jack Nitzsche had himself compiled a band from the best of Spector's regular session musicians: Leon Russell, Nino Tempo, Glen Campbell and Sonny Bono.

This time around, Spector himself was hired as both associate producer and musical director (he oversaw the live orchestra), and he took to the task with relish. The acts he booked for the two nights of filming ranged from The Lovin' Spoonful to Bo Diddley, from Roger Miller to Ray Charles, from Petula Clark to The Byrds. Joan Baez was spellbinding, teaming up with a piano-playing Spector for a plaintive 'You've Lost That Lovin' Feelin'', while The Ronettes turned in a tremendous 'Be My Baby', and actor David McCallum at least had fun with the Stones' 'Satisfaction'. And even that feast was simply the foreplay, as the show built up to its closing salvo.

At *TAMI* the previous year, the final battle between James Brown and The Rolling Stones was absolutely mesmerising. This year, although nobody would even bother placing a wager on a head-on collision between Donovan and Ike and Tina Turner, still the two performances round out the movie with delicious poise; on the one hand, Donovan at his most sweetly sincere; on the other, the Turners at their raunchiest. *The Big TNT Show* emerged one of the last great rock 'n' roll films of the genre's protracted infancy, before the music itself divided into so many cells, and such a gathering of so many different facets and faces would have been rendered impossible by the laws of demography.

Although Spector played a large part in selecting the acts who would appear at *Big TNT*, there was one he would have selected, another of the discoveries he made as he traversed the clubs and dives of the Strip, who he was reluctantly forced to omit: Lenny Bruce.

Much, sadly, had changed for the outrageous comic in the near-decade since Spector and Marshall Lieb were so thrilled to follow in his footsteps on *Rocket To Stardom*. The son of vaudeville and burlesque comedian Sally Marr, Bruce made his name on the LA stripjoint circuit of the mid–late 1950s, with a routine that frequently left the audience utterly torn in their responses. *Variety*, the leading trade paper of the age, condemned Bruce for 'only trying to make the band laugh' – he appeared, in the style of the day, with an accompanying jazz combo. Others were alternately horrified or excited by the willingness with which Bruce assaulted each of entertainment's most sacred taboos – religion, race, sex – with a vocabulary splattered by obscenities. *Time* magazine described him, simply, as a 'sick comic'.

Bruce's greatest talent, however, was the ease with which he moved beyond simple shock value to address issues that themselves were of vital importance – societal flaws and failings, hypocrisy in law and language, government incompetence and so on. It was the kind of material that, by the 1980s, was the preserve of some of the best-loved young comics around; indeed, as writer Grover Sales pointed out, when Bruce used the word 'cocksucker' on stage in the early 1960s, he was busted. When Meryl Streep used it in a movie (*Sophie's Choice*) two decades later, she won an Oscar.

Bruce's popularity grew. Had such a term not been rendered meaningless by years of subsequent misuse, he was the first rock 'n' roll comedian, most comfortable in a field framed by be-bop jazz and beat poetics, and directed toward the same ears that held the words of Bob Dylan and John Lennon in such high esteem. But he was never able to enjoy his success. His first bust, in San Francisco in 1961, accused him of violating the California Obscenity Code. He was acquitted, but remained a marked man. He was deported from Britain, and busted for either obscenity or drugs from coast to coast.

He continued gigging, mainly thanks to a near-residency at Basin Street West in San Francisco. By late 1965, however, he had been declared a legally bankrupt pauper, and was spending most of his time in a narcotic haze, alone in his home at 8825 West Hollywood Boulevard. Bookings dried up as the best venues, painfully aware of his dilapidating lifestyle, refused to engage him for fear of him cancelling out at the last minute, while Bruce himself was scarcely in a fit state to perform even if he'd been asked to. No longer a comedian, or even a social commentator, he was a martyr, a victim, a scapegoat and he wore those roles like an old overcoat. An old *unwashed* overcoat.

Spector had followed Bruce's career for years, idolising the man, lionising his work. He even hung a massive blow-up portrait of the comedian over his bed. But he only got to know him towards the end, when Bruce returned to playing poorly advertised stand-ups at the seedier end of the Strip. To many people, their friendship appeared terribly one-way – Spector genuinely wanted to get to know Bruce, Bruce cared only that he'd found someone else to lend him money. Soon, both Bruce and his nine-year-old daughter Kittie were living almost entirely off Spector's largesse, while Spector – horrified at the treatment meted out to a man whom he considered America's only truly worthwhile comic and commentator – busied himself in planning a major relaunch of Bruce's career.

An album, *Lenny Bruce Is Out Again*, was the first step towards Bruce's rehabilitation. Released in October 1965, it comprised a collection of material dating back to 1962, while its liner notes included a long list of the lawyers Bruce had hired over the past four years – whose fees were the main reason he was now broke. Spector's own involvement in readying the tapes for public consumption was minor – the recordings went out very much warts and all. But the album was only the first step in Spector's plan. The second was to finance a 15-day residency at the Music Box Theater, on Hollywood Boulevard, impressively billed as *Phil Spector Presents Lenny Bruce*.

The show opened on 11 February 1966 – and it was a disaster. A minute crowd turned out to watch as a barely coherent Bruce wobbled before them, to do little more than read aloud from the sheaf of legal documents he had with him. Occasionally, he would break off from his recitation to rail against the powers that brought so many charges against him, but even Spector was horrified by the lifelessness of the performance. For once, however, he had his met his match. When Spector demanded that they cancel the rest of the run, Bruce demanded that they complete it. It was Spector's money but it was Bruce's reputation, and this was his last chance to reclaim it.

Meekly, Spector acquiesced, but the shows failed to improve, either in terms of performance or audience. Finally, after ten days of diminishing returns, even Bruce had had enough. Shows booked through to 25 February were scrapped and, though Spector never dropped him from his social circle, he never tried working with him again. Rather, he merely sat and watched while Bruce threw 'parties' for whoever he could gather around himself, sometimes at his own home, other times at Spector's.

One evening, Allen Ginsberg was among the revellers, and Spector apparently talked enthusiastically of recording an album with him. In his mind, however, he was formulating another notion that would take him far from that direction; far, even, from the promises that he had given the Modern Folk Quartet while they waited for his attention to snap back in their direction. He was going to retire from the music industry – and he was going to go out with the biggest bang he had ever made.

Why not? He was 25 and rich beyond his wildest dreams. Any insecurities he had ever nursed towards his talent had long since been assuaged – of course they resurfaced occasionally, but only, he noticed, when he started to wonder what form his next musical masterstroke might take. When he stopped worrying about that, he was amazed at just how simple everything seemed – how easy it was to allow one day to simply drift into another, with nothing more pressing on the agenda than reading a book or watching TV.

It was a life, he knew, that few people from his background, first generation Brooklyn Russian Jews, would ever experience. For them, work was everything, for there was always something else that they needed to work for. But Spector had everything he wanted already: a magnificent home, a powerful reputation, a famous name, a beautiful soon-to-be-wife. He could continue making records for the sake of it, but how much better to live life for the sake of life itself?

Of course, inactivity was as dangerous a bedfellow as insecurity, but Spector had already thought of that. Actor Dennis Hopper had recently moved into Spector's orbit, and the pair immediately hit it off. Like Spector (and, indeed, Lenny Bruce), Hopper saw himself as a rebel at best, a pariah at times. Unlike Spector, however, his chosen industry offered few of the opportunities for maverick freelancing that music presented and, just as Bruce had swathed himself in the finery of an outlaw maverick, and been drummed out of conventional comedy circles, so Hopper was himself widely regarded as the actor whom Hollywood forgot.

Four years Spector's senior, Hopper had been making movies since his teens. He was barely 17 when he debuted in Nicholas Ray's western *Johnny Guitar*, and in 1955 he appeared alongside James Dean in another Ray classic, *Rebel Without A Cause*. The following year, Hopper rejoined Dean for *Giant* and, in the wake of his co-star's death, he was widely tipped to become the next James Dean – not least of all by himself. By the early 1960s, however, his reputation for causing problems on set had all but exiled him from the Hollywood mainstream (filming Henry Hathaway's *From Hell To Texas*, Hopper apparently insisted on up to 100 reshoots for certain scenes), condemning him to spend the first half of the '60s ploughing the b-movie circuit.

His luck began to change in the mid-1960s, as the counter-culture began swirling around America's midriff. In those circles, Hopper's image was recast as the epitome of cool and he was already toying with a major comeback when he hooked up with Spector. All he needed was a financial backer who shared his vision – an independent movie that would blow away the establishment.

Spector would become that backer. He just had one final gesture to expel from his system, a new record that would overshadow everything he had ever accomplished before…that anybody had ever achieved before. He didn't care if it was a hit, he didn't even care if anybody liked it. When he went over the entire process in his mind, he explained, quite simply, 'I just wanted to go crazy for a few minutes, for four minutes. That's all it was. I just wanted to go crazy…I didn't really think there was anything for the public.'

He knew who he wanted to go crazy with, as well. As he was scheduling *The Big TNT Show*, the inclusion of Ike and Tina Turner was no accident. Spector first sighted the duo at the Galaxy on Sunset Boulevard – 'somebody told me to see them and their in-person act just killed me. They were just sensational.' Their performance at the Moulin Rouge, Tina Turner resplendent in white go-go boots and a micro-skirt, only deepened his enthusiasm for the Turners and soon his daydreams were filled with nothing more than the possibility of having Tina to himself, of unleashing the powerhouse battle cry that she called a voice onto something more potent than the succession of simple R&B belters that husband Ike seemed so content grafting her onto.

Of course, he knew that was just a dream – the Turners were more or less inseparable; hire one, and you got them both. He knew, too, that Ike could be as stubborn as he himself could – indeed, with a career that reached back to the very dawn of rock 'n' roll, the notoriously irascible Turner could easily turn on him altogether, and laugh the young whippersnapper out of the room. Yet the very first meeting between the two men, shortly before Christmas, completely disavowed him of all such notions.

Turner remembered the day when '[Spector] had his secretary call me to say he wanted to produce an album of Tina himself. He came over to my house and said he wanted to do it all on his own. He didn't want me to participate in the studio, in producing it. I said "great".'

All Turner wanted, he explained to Spector, was a hit. It mattered not that, since they hooked up in 1958, he and Tina had won the esteem of every R&B fan in the world, artists coming out of the woodwork to celebrate their performance. They had released close to 30 singles together, of which just 7 even made the Top 100, and it was 2 years since that had happened. They did fine on the R&B charts, but on the pop listings – the ones that promoters, record stores and everybody paid attention to – they weren't even a flash in the pan. 'I got no attitude,' Turner continued. 'All I care about is success. It ain't how you win, it's "did you win?" So I told him, "okay" and he had Tina come to his house to sing.'

Echoing the deal that he made with Moonglow for the Righteous Brothers, Spector arranged to 'lease' the Turners from their usual label, the Warners subsidiary Loma, for one album, at a rumoured cost of $25,000. And then the work began.

While Ike Turner busied himself in the studio cutting a single with the Turner act's backing singers, The Ikettes, for release on Phi-Dan, Tina made the daily drive to West Collina to plan for her studio date. She and Spector would be recording five songs together, and the sessions for the Motown standard 'A Love Like Yours (Don't Come Knockin' Every Day)', 'Everyday I Have To Cry', 'Hold On Baby' and Doc Pomus and Mort Shuman's 'Save The Last Dance For Me' passed by relatively quickly. It was the fifth and final number that would stretch everybody to the limit.

'River Deep – Mountain High' was written by Spector, Ellie Greenwich and Jeff Barry – he flew the pair to LA to join him for a week of writing, putting them up at the Chateau Marmont Hotel while they pieced together a song that was worthy of his ambitions. The end result would be born of no less than three separate tunes, superimposed atop one another to create an almost discordant whole, which Turner would – and she alone could – bind together through the sheer force of her vocal.

Darlene Love heard the song very early on and, unaware that it was already taken, made her own play for it. Who else in the Philles stable, after all, could have made a go of it? She documented the conversation in her book. '"What's that?" I asked. "Oh, it's just a song," Phil said. "Who's it for?" "Oh, I'm not sure yet".' But, of course, he was.

Turner herself spent two hours a day with Spector, every day for a fortnight, simply working on the melody for the verses – an experience she later equated to 'carving furniture'. Occasionally, she would be tempted to launch into one of her own vocal routines, the crowd-pleasing screams that trademarked so many of her other records. Politely, Spector would bring her back on track, tell her to concentrate on the melody and leave the melodramatics to him. For he had more than enough to spare.

If the song's structure was monolithic, the band that Spector assembled was even vaster. Close to two dozen musicians were required at three separate sessions, in February and early March, to lay down the backing – four drummers, four bassists, three keyboards, two percussion a brass section. The first time Tina heard the song, Spector stopped by and played it on an acoustic guitar. The next time she heard it...'Wow!' And he still hadn't added the strings!

'It was amazing to watch "River Deep" grow,' Jack Nitzsche told *Goldmine*. 'Even during the cutting of the track, Tina was singing along as we cut it and [she] was so into it she was holding her crotch on the high notes. Oh man, she was great, doing a rough, scratch vocal as the musicians really kicked the rhythm section in the ass. Once in a while, a vocalist would run through a song, but…Tina made everybody play better.'

'Tina told me [Spector] had 78 broads singing "de-do de-do de-do…"' Ike Turner marvelled. '78 voices. You don't even hear them on the record' – but they were there all the same, amid a cacophony so vast that even the echo had an answering echo. Tina Turner herself reckoned she must have sung the opening line, 'when I was a little girl,' 500,000 times, and she never did figure out if she ever got it exactly the way Spector wanted to hear it.

Still she slammed so much energy into the performance that Larry Levine, engineer at the session, admitted, 'the one thing that stands out in my memory is Tina. When she came in, she was electric. And she couldn't swing the song with all her clothes on, so she took her blouse off and sang it just wearing a bra. It was unbelievable, the way she moved around.' The Loma label's Bob Krasnow agreed. '[She] grabbed that microphone and she gave a performance that…I mean, your hair was standing on end. It was like the whole room exploded.' Even Ike Turner, who'd seen Turner give such performances so many times in the past, was spellbound. 'Ike was blown away,' Tina said. 'He sat there and went "God, that's amazing".'

If onlookers were stunned, listeners were astonished. Spector had no less than 16 different mixes of the song prepared, and played each one in turn to his most trusted advisors, to ascertain which one they preferred. Few could tell little or any difference between them, but all were agreed that this record – not 'He's A Rebel', not 'Be My Baby', not 'You've Lost That Lovin' Feelin'' – was Spector's ultimate masterpiece.

Just a handful of people demurred. Ellie Greenwich was horrified when she first heard the finished record, confessing that she listened to the acetate once, before hurling it against a wall. Co-writer Jeff Barry, too, was shocked, telling Spector biographer Richard Williams, 'to me what he's saying is, "It is not the song I wrote with Jeff and Ellie…it's me."' Even Darlene Love, making what would become her final appearance at a Phil Spector session amid the multitude of backing vocalists, felt Spector had completely swamped the song. If there was a wall of anything in the production, she wrote, 'it was a wall of water and everyone was drowning'.

Larry Levine put a technical spin on her thoughts. '[Spector] was always trying to create more and more, and I think it finally ate him up at the end, because the technology was not able to keep up with him. I think probably "River Deep – Mountain High" should have been greater than "You've Lost That Lovin' Feelin'", but it wasn't. [And] I think the reason it wasn't was because he tried to go beyond the scope of what we could do [technically].'

Still it would have been a brave soul indeed who predicted that 'River Deep – Mountain High' was anything less than a surefire No 1. Throughout the industry, where Spector's retirement plans remained his secret alone, 'River Deep – Mountain High' was widely tipped as the record that would surpass any of the apparently omnipotent peaks that he had scaled in the past. But the moment the first advance pressings went out to American radio, in mid-May 1966, it was clear that those presentiments were utterly misplaced. Few stations played the record, even fewer placed it into rotation.

The trade papers, those then most highly influential organs whose opinions guided the record shop buyers the nation over, were similarly disdainful – stuck for a B-side for the follow-up single, 'I'll Never Need More Than This', Spector recalled the most venomous of his assailants with the pointedly titled '*Cashbox* Blues (Whoops, We Published The Wrong Story Again)'.

In Britain, where Phil Spector remained a god, 'River Deep – Mountain High' soared to No 3, the Turners' first hit in that country, and their biggest until 'Nutbush City Limits' came along seven years later. In America, however, it merely drifted to No 88 and then began falling. 'Benedict Arnold,' Spector murmured as he studied the sales figures, 'was quite a guy'.

'That record just never found a home,' Tina Turner mused. 'It was too black for the pop stations and too pop for the black stations.' Other observers found their own reasons for its failure. Bob Krasnow blamed rivalry between radio stations, singling out one chain of station owners in particular, Drake-Chenault, for all but blackballing the record simply because a rival LA station, KRLA, was granted the first exclusive preview. Jack Nitzsche rounded on an industry prejudice against Spector in general – 'when anybody's had that much success without a break, like Phil had, they've won too many times, and people like to see them fall because they prefer to support the underdog'.

Ike Turner, however, disagreed with all of those scenarios and, without ever saying as much, suggests that he and Spector spoke of far more than production credits and hit records the first time they met up to cement their arrangement. 'Some people say that "River Deep" is the reason Phil Spector quit the record business,' Turner averred. 'But I don't agree with that.' Spector had already made up his mind that he wanted a complete change of scenery and had no more time for pop music. America's rejection of 'River Deep – Mountain High' just gave him an excuse that everybody would understand.

'There's a difference between being an egomaniac and being egotistical,' Spector explained to the *New Musical Express* a decade later. Had he been egotistical, the failure of 'River Deep – Mountain High' might have knocked him back. 'But I'm not egotistical. I am an egomaniac. My ego is so high you just can't beat me down.' Talking with journalist Richard Williams, too, he denied that the record's failure in any way affected his plans for the future. 'Making something good was always more important than success. The fact that [something] was successful was just the icing on the cake. It wasn't the main purpose at all. It was always to try and make something that was good and moving and important. Because if I didn't make anything that was better, I might as well have left it to Fats Domino.'

In fact, if 'River Deep – Mountain High' caused Spector to adjust his schedule in the slightest, it was its British success, rather than its American failure, that caused the delays. On the back of this massive hit, the duo were booked to tour with The Rolling Stones; work on completing their scheduled album, the songs that Ike Turner himself was producing, could only begin once they returned, and Philles issued *River Deep – Mountain High* that summer, wrapped in sleeve photographs taken by actor Hopper.

Neither is it true, as so many subsequent histories insist, that, with the album ready to ship, a demoralised Spector then cancelled the release. In America, for sure, it saw a tiny release, but only because the same DJs and journalists who rejected the single showed no more interest in the entire LP. But in Britain, *River Deep – Mountain High* climbed to No 27, Philles' first ever hit album in that country. And, while the Turners celebrated that coup, Spector got on with his new career, as independent movie mogul.

9 The Boy I'm Gonna Marry

By mid-May 1966, Phil Spector and Dennis Hopper had finally isolated the project they had spent so long scheming, Steven Stern's *The Last American*. Over the next six months, Stern himself would pull together a screenplay, while Spector and Hopper scouted locations in Mexico, and booked the Cherabusco Studios in Mazatlán. A crew was hired, Hopper's friend Peter Fonda was brought in to co-star and, by the time Spector returned to Los Angeles in July, *The Last American* was in excellent shape.

So was Spector, throwing himself into his own vision of Hollywood with the same gusto as he had assaulted the music industry – for it was an assault, he believed, an attempt to muscle in on the major studios and established stars with a film that would reject all the time-honoured clichés and practices, and target precisely the same kind of audience as his records, the teens.

There was a story, he'd explain, but that wasn't the point of the film. Rather, *The Last American* was a series of inter-connected vignettes that traced two friends, Hopper and Fonda, as they journeyed through the American counter-culture, investigating both the lives and lifestyles that bound it together. There would even be a role in it for Spector himself.

Barely had he returned to LA, however, when tragedy struck once more. In the months since the closure of Lenny Bruce's Music Box showcase, with Bruce himself stunned by the ferocity of his failure, the comic had worked hard to clean himself up. He had beaten his last outstanding court case, he'd written and rehearsed a mass of new material and, over two nights in June 1966, he returned to live performance, headlining the Fillmore West in San Francisco and receiving some of the best reviews of his life.

He was still in debt, and still battling against his heroin addiction; he might still have despaired over his future. From the outside looking in, however, Bruce was on his way up once again – which is why the news out of Hollywood on 2 August 1966 was so hard for anybody to comprehend. Bruce was dead, felled by a massive overdose of morphine.

Spector both paid for Bruce's funeral and delivered the eulogy. He also took out an advertisement in *Billboard* magazine, headlined simply 'Lenny Bruce Is Dead', outlining the plans the pair had hatched ('His last album… was to be the first of many we had planned'), but unequivocally pointing the finger of blame precisely in the direction he believed it deserved. 'America's foremost, and certainly most truthful philosopher…died from an overdose of police.'

Spector's grief was as public as it was genuine. But Ronnie Bennett – who later described August 1966 as 'probably the darkest month of my life' – claims that she was not even aware Bruce was dead until days after the fact. Spector never actually told her what had happened, and his longstanding refusal to allow magazines into the house meant that she was more or less isolated from any show business news whatsoever. When she saw how depressed he was, how much time he spent alone in his study up on the second floor, she assumed he was simply still seething over 'River Deep Mountain High'. One evening, however, after Spector retired to the bedroom, she found herself in his study, staring at a pile of photographs, black-and-white shots of a naked Bruce lying beside the toilet.

At first, she thought they were faked, some sick, bizarre joke that Spector and Bruce had come up with to help promote some new venture. But then she saw the needle on the floor beside the body, and the truth dawned on her. These weren't publicity shots playing darkly on Bruce's reputation. They were police 'crime scene' photographs, taken by the LAPD homicide department after they entered Bruce's apartment and discovered his corpse in the bathroom. Ronnie later heard that Spector bought them from the sheriff's department for $5,000; it is also said that Spector, in turn, sold just one of the shots for use in the final moments of the 1974 Bruce bio-pic *Lenny*, and recouped all that he spent on the original photos.

'Lenny died of an overdose of mediocrity, an overdose of abuse, an overdose of misunderstanding and, most of all, an overdose of Police,' Spector reiterated a decade later. 'They made Lenny Quasimodo. They turned him into the Hunchback.'

Philles, too, was dead – or, at least, ebbing away. As much out of habit as anything else, the label continued releasing new singles, but Spector himself had little involvement in them, probably no more than simply a grunt of agreement. A Righteous Brothers out-take, taking on the old 'White Cliffs Of Dover' chestnut, was hauled from the vault in mid-summer, to be followed by what proved the last-ever Ronettes single, Jeff Barry and Ellie Greenwich's 'I Can Hear Music'. Tellingly, Jeff Barry handled the session and took the production credit.

Spector was absent, too, from the next release, Ike and Tina Turner's 'A Man Is A Man Is A Man'. Again a solo Tina was showcased, but this time under the aegis of producer Bob Crewe. Spector never formally closed Philles, but it was clear that the label was moribund; even his announcement, early in 1967, that he had signed Ike and Tina Turner directly to the label, and would be following through with a brand new single in the spring, was in fact succeeded by nothing more than a release for one of the songs he'd recorded with Tina a full year before. And then, when both 'I'll Never Need More Than This' and, later in the year, 'A Love Like Yours' passed by unnoticed, Philles quietly closed its doors.

Spector, however, was not idling. He made a cheerful guest appearance at a Rock 'n' Roll Conference staged at Mills College in Oakland, California – scarcely the kind of event where one would expect to find a demoralised recluse holding forth. And, though there is probably no truth in the pervasive legends that Spector took to making walk-on appearances in such TV shows as *Mission Impossible* and *Mannix*, he did pen the theme to comedienne Lucille Ball's *Lucy Goes To London* television special, broadcast in America on 17 October 1966; and, exactly one year later, on 17 October 1967, he showed up in an episode of *I Dream Of Jeannie*, alongside Monkees songwriters Bobby Hart and, renewing an acquaintanceship that dated back to Spector's days producing Curtis Lee, Tommy Boyce. 'Jeannie The Hip Hippie' found Jeannie (Barbara Eden) taking over the management of a pop group and utilising her powers to make them famous.

Spector could, perhaps, have done with some of her spellbinding on *The Last American* front. After so promising a start, the project was now barely inching along, devouring monies that Spector, apparently, had yet to pay — somewhere in the region of a million dollars. The probability of the entire project stalling was growing more and more realistic, with Spector only adding to the movie's problems by maintaining an absolutely hands-off distance from the actual production. On one notorious occasion, at one of the increasingly regular meetings that tried to salvage the situation, Spector spent the entire discussion with his nose buried in a book on breeding St

Bernard dogs. At other conferences, he might as well have been a fly on a very distant wall for all he brought to the discussions.

Finally Hopper had had enough. He launched legal action against Spector, demanding that the producer put his money where his mouth had been. Screenwriter Steven Stern then weighed in, with his own demands for the advance that Spector had promised him – Spector ultimately agreed to settle out of court, a total payment of $600,000, but he clearly retained some influence over the production. Even with a change of screenwriter, as Stern's *The Last American* transformed into Terry Southern, Fonda and Hopper's *Easy Rider*, Spector received his cameo appearance, sitting in the back of his own Rolls-Royce, registration PHIL 500 (his driver, Max, sat in the front), silently making a drug deal with the movie's two anti-heroes.

Spector and Ronnie were married at Beverly Hills City Hall on 14 April 1968. As with his marriage to Annette, it was a tiny ceremony – Bennett's mother was the only guest; Spector's own mother was not even told of the event until after the fact. Spector's best man was driver Max's brother Serge; his wife Terry was matron of honour. And again there was no honeymoon, although the couple did spend the evening with the rest of the wedding party, attending a Mahalia Jackson concert.

From the outset, Ronnie knew that this was unlikely to be a fairy-tale wedding. Though she never discovered much about her husband's previous match, still she knew him well enough to understand that one needed the patience of a saint and the understanding of a martyr to weather all the storms that were inevitably going to fly her way.

Nevertheless, Spector seemed determined to make this match work from the outset. There would be eruptions (according to Ronnie, there was a major fight on their wedding night itself) but, with the end of his active involvement in *The Last American*, and with Philles barely even existing in name alone, Spector genuinely believed he would have the time now to actually make a life with his wife. The only cloud on the horizon was, would the life that he wanted for her dovetail with that which she envisioned?

Ronnie's career, too, had ground to a standstill of sorts. It matters little whether Spector was too jealous to actually let her out of his sight, or if he simply believed, old-fashionedly, that his wife's place was by his side. Either way, she said, he withdrew her not only from The Ronettes, but from any kind of social interplay whatsoever.

He even seemed to hold himself back from her. When they were together, unless an argument was brewing, they got along fine. But he was as likely to while the day away shut up in his study playing records – Wagner was an especial favourite, while pop was virtually outlawed. Other times, he would spend hours playing pool, either practising on his own or arranging extravagant all-night tournaments to which he invited some of LA's most legendary pool hall hustlers.

Yet though he was often thoughtless, he was rarely heartless. Even in the thick of another screaming battle, Ronnie never believed for a moment that he did not love her. Phil made her feel like she was the only girl in the world, she wrote. Unfortunately, as far as he was concerned, she *was* the only girl in the world. And he never let her forget that fact.

In her autobiography, Ronnie described herself as a prisoner in her own home – a luxurious home, admittedly, and one that was packed with so many comforts that Spector himself could not understand why she could ever want to leave its safety. Unfortunately, that meant he also failed to understand that his wife was not like him; that she did not revel in her own company, or that of a handful of hand-picked friends. Crushed and claustrophobic, she went days without seeing anyone apart from the servants Spector had engaged; went days without even seeing the sun, as Spector kept the windows drawn and darkened. There was nothing for her to do around the house; if she even thought of busying herself with a simple chore, a servant would swoop to take over from her.

She wondered, sometimes, how Spector himself was able to deal with the inactivity. He had always been what people might call reclusive, but he had always been so active as well. Only slowly did she grasp the kind of things that kept him busy. The care that he lavished upon the construction of a virtual fortress around the house; the attention he gave to the five guard dogs he had now obtained, a Russian wolfhound, a pair of Borzois, a couple of German shepherds; and the deliberation with which he delightedly began cultivating precisely the kind of image that the media had already conferred upon him, he was as methodical with these things as he had ever been with his music...maybe even more so.

Since his earliest days of success, close to a decade before, Spector had grown accustomed to seeing himself described as an eccentric. Okay then, if it was an eccentric that they wanted, it was an eccentric they would get. And he pulled it off so successfully that, when the cult trash-movie director Russ

Meyer, shooting *Beyond The Valley Of The Dolls* in 1969, was searching for a model for the record producer character Ronnie Barzell, he needed look no further than Phil Spector.

The massive dogs, the barbed wire fence, the intercoms in every room, the secrecy that surrounded his every move. If Spector could not shape the outside world to his precise requirements, he could at least do it to his own. 'Whenever a reporter came to interview him,' Ronnie wrote, 'he made sure [the dogs] were sitting on the living room sofa. The reporter would take [one] look...think Phil was a little nuts, and he'd put that in his article. And Phil loved it.'

It was difficult not to imagine Spector sitting up late at nights, pondering his next unaccountable quirk, while Ronnie herself swiftly grew wearily accustomed to watching *Citizen Kane* with him. Part of her was repulsed by the knowledge that her own life was being inexorably sucked into a re-enactment of that movie. But she could not help but be impressed by the style with which Spector was orchestrating that enactment.

Even amid so much craziness, he remained capable of surprising her with the most unexpected gestures. For her 25th birthday, 10 August 1968, apparently in absolute defiance of her own belief that she was never allowed out of his sight, he bought her a car, complete with an inflatable replica of himself to sit beside her, so she would never appear alone when she was out driving. And, early in the new year of 1969, he brought her a new song that he wanted her to record.

Spector wrote 'You Came, You Saw, You Conquered' with Toni Wine and Irwin Levine, a magnificent number that he was certain would not simply relaunch Ronnie's career (at least until he had second thoughts about that), but would also inaugurate a new golden age for Phil Spector himself.

Quietly, without even a whisper in the trade papers, he had negotiated a new deal with Herb Alpert and Jerry Moss, whose A&M label was now ranked among the heaviest hitters on the West Coast, six years after its founders joined forces to head up a self-avowedly middle of the road pop label. According to legend, their combined resources when they set out amounted to just a few hundred dollars – and 27 years later, when they sold the label to the giant Polygram record group, it was worth around half a billion dollars.

Since his days alongside Lou Adler in A&R at Doré, Alpert had all but abandoned hopes of making a successful career in music when he met Jerry

Moss, at that time a freelance promotions man who also dabbled in record production. Their first collaboration came when Alpert played trumpet on a session organized by Moss during 1961. By early 1962, they'd launched their own label, Carnival, debuting with a 45 release credited to Dore Alpert, 'Tell It To The Birds' – almost immediately, the Dot label purchased the rights to the single for $750, which the duo ploughed into setting up their own recording studio in Alpert's garage.

Their first recording there was 'Lonely Bull', a mariachi-style instrumental credited to Herb Alpert and the Tijuana Brass. It was originally to be released on Carnival; however, learning of another label with the same name, Alpert and Moss renamed their concern A&M (from their initials).

Released in October 1962, 'Lonely Bull' was a massive hit, prompting an immediate LP of the same name and igniting a period of massive chart success for Alpert and his band – at one point in 1966, Alpert had five albums in the US Top 20 simultaneously, while 1968 brought a worldwide No 1 with 'This Guy's In Love With You'.

A&M moved from Alpert's garage to new offices on Sunset Boulevard in early 1963, before taking over the Charlie Chaplin movie studio on Sunset and La Brea in late 1966. The label's roster expanded to match its growth. Adhering to Alpert's own stranglehold on adult listening tastes, early recruits included the Baja Marimba Band (formed by Julius Wechter, a former member of Martin Denny's band), Sergio Mendes, Chris Montez, Claudine Longet, The Sandpipers, We Five and Evie Sands.

By 1967, however, Moss was opening A&M's doors to the rock market, signing both home-grown acts and concluding licensing deals with the British labels Regal Zonophone and Island. Over the next three years, A&M would become the US home for such British stars as Procol Harum, Joe Cocker, The Move, Spooky Tooth, Fairport Convention, Free, Jimmy Cliff, Cat Stevens, The Strawbs and Humble Pie, while domestic recruits included Phil Ochs, organ virtuoso Lee Michaels, and country rockers Dillard and Clark and the Flying Burrito Brothers. A&M was also behind one of the most unconventional live successes of the age, Joe Cocker and former Spector sideman Leon Russell's legendary Mad Dogs And Englishmen outing.

Phil Spector was to be one of the jewels in this new crown, although the relationship got off to a distinctly rocky start when he arrived at A&M's expensively appointed studios – such a far cry from the surroundings to which he was accustomed – and found himself wholly discomforted by the modern equipment. He quickly found his way around it, of course; learned to bend it to his will, and 'You Came, You Saw, You Conquered' was completed in a matter of days. A&M scheduled its release for March 1969, and began looking forward to the master's next contribution.

He discovered precisely what they were hoping for in The Checkmates Ltd, a strong soul band led by vocalists Sonny Charles and Bobby Stevens. They'd been playing around the soul circuit for years, but had never made an impression – they were simply too pure, too soulful and too wary of musical gimmickry to have caught any passing mogul's eye. Spector, however, saw them opening for Ella Fitzgerald in 1968, loved them and quickly brought them into the A&M deal.

'Love Is All I Have To Give' a song Spector co-wrote with Nino Tempo's sister April Stevens, was their first release, on the same day as Ronnie's 'You Came, You Saw, You Conquered'. It was a tentative effort, designed more to test the waters than announce a new superstar. In the meantime, Toni Wine and Irwin Levine, authors of Ronnie's single, were set to work coming up with a suitable song for the group's next release...they delivered 'Black Pearl', a luscious ballad with a hookline to die for and a featherlight production that effortlessly confirmed that the old Wall of Sound was as much ancient history for Spector as it was for anyone else. 'Black Pearl', a Top 30 American hit that spring, brought Spector howling into the modern era, and work on a Checkmates Ltd album only emphasised his return to action.

Still throwing musical caution to the wind, bending rules that the A&M studio staffers had deemed as inviolate as those he had shattered in the past, Spector transformed that workaday soul band into a thing of modernistic beauty, capable of anything and afraid of nothing. He took Creedence Clearwater Revival's 'Proud Mary' and lay down a version that even Ike and Tina Turner could only try to emulate (their recording of the song would follow more than a year later); he took a sampling of songs from the hit musical *Hair* and wove a symphony from them. But even as he worked, he could see The Checkmates Ltd crumble.

For the release of 'Black Pearl', Spector had the idea of singling out Sonny Charles, whose lead vocal carried the song, as a frontman of sorts, billing the group as Sonny Charles And The Checkmates in the knowledge that it would give the media a single source with which to identify. Other groups of the era, The Delfonics, The Tams and so on, were successful enough in their own way, but they were absolutely anonymous, and came across that way in both print and performance. Spector hoped that focusing attention on Charles would bring the rest of the band to prominence as well.

But he completely misread the group. Once Charles was brought to the fore co-vocalist Bobby Stevens began demanding a share of the spotlight, and Spector knew the rest of the band would be issuing their own demands. With just a handful of tracks completed for the LP, Spector handed production to arranger Perry Botkin Jr, and turned his back on The Checkmates Ltd.

Hopes of a new beginning with A&M, too, were surrendered. He would complete just one further project for the label, licensing them the tapes to the all-but-unissued Ike and Tina Turner album, and securing an endorsement from Beatle George Harrison, to splash across the cover. This time, however, he was neither turning his back on stardom, nor plunging into a new eccentric pastime. Rather, he had just been granted one of his lifelong ambitions, and he intended devoting as much time as he could to it – his month-old son, Donté Philip Spector.

Throughout their first year of married life, the most serious cloud on the Spector family's horizon was the absence of children. Both Spector and Ronnie desperately wanted to start a family but, try as they might, she simply could not get pregnant. Their thoughts began to turn towards adoption, a scheme that Ronnie put into operation in March 1969. Watching a TV documentary on LA's 'unwanted babies', she fell so in love with one of the baby boys highlighted in the programme that she leaped into the car and drove immediately to the adoption agency.

The paperwork was set in motion that same afternoon – when her husband returned home later that day, it was to learn that, pending the necessary formalities, their first child would arrive within the month. Donté Philip Spector was announced to the world via a birth announcement that Spector himself designed. The boy was described, of course, as 'a Veronica and Phil Spector production', but fans who thought that might prove his only masterpiece that year were soon to discover their mistake.

10 We All Shine On

In November 1969, *Rolling Stone* published a transcript of Jan Wenner's interview with Phil Spector, earlier in the season, and found itself acting as an ambassador between the producer and his immediate future.

Spector was musing over the artists he'd most like to work with: Janis Joplin ('[she] leaves a lot to be desired, recording-wise'), Mick Jagger ('could be a lot of fun'), Bob Dylan ('I'd do a Dylan Opera with him. I'd produce him. He's never been produced'). And The Beatles.

The group had long been a prime objective for Spector. Back in 1964, talking to the London *Evening Standard*, he admitted, 'I would love to have a crack at recording that group.' He had not, however, seen or spoken to the band in years, and when Wenner asked how he viewed the current state of the band, apparently torn by division over every aspect of their career, Spector merely mused, 'I haven't spoken to John Lennon in some time, so I don't know where he's at now. But I think, without question, he is the leader of that group, and he makes the decisions. I'd like to know how The Beatles feel about him and what he is going through. I almost get the feeling that they want to help him, but I don't think they really can, because he's always way ahead of them.'

The reasons for his concern were apparent everywhere. Over the past year, particularly since Yoko Ono arrived on the scene, Lennon had seemed almost directionless, foundering across the world of pop, rock, art and experimentation, apparently without any sense whatsoever of what he intended doing once he got there. Yoko's presence, of course, played a part in his apparent confusion, and Spector spoke for many observers when he remarked, 'I have a feeling that [she] may not be the greatest influence on him'; the soon-to-be second Mrs Lennon was herself an established avant-garde artist, and it was the sometimes grating collision between her physical and visual works and Lennon's musical activities that played loudest across the records that the pair made together.

What, however, could Spector do that could maybe uncork whichever genies were so tightly packed inside the Lennon psyche? Wenner never asked (or, at least, never published) that question, and Spector never answered it. But Lennon, a devout *Rolling Stone* reader in his own right, heard it asked anyway, and wondered himself what the answer might be. He had already affirmed, years before, that 'if [The Beatles] ever used any [producer] besides George Martin, it would be Phil' and, in meetings now with The Beatles' manager, Allen Klein, Spector's name came up in conversation.

Klein was himself a formidable ally for the Beatle. An accountant by trade, a shrewd entrepreneur by vocation, in over a decade on the New York music scene, Klein had wrangled some of the toughest deals ever seen from the parsimonious record labels of the day, upping artist royalties by unheard of percentages and safeguarding his clients with the tenacity of a she-wolf. Yet he trod on a lot of toes as he did so and, for every artist who, like Lennon, saw Klein as the answer to many of their problems, there was another who regarded him as the worst news in the world.

But through it all, Klein was also a music fan and, while his detractors complain that he had surrounded himself with some of the most lucrative artist catalogues in the entire music industry (Sam Cooke, The Animals, Herman's Hermits, The Rolling Stones and, now, The Beatles), he had also surrounded himself with some of the best. And he wanted the best for those artists. So, when Lennon mused aloud on the possibility of The Beatles working with Phil Spector, Klein leaped into action.

The group was in shreds, but one final project remained incomplete. The *Get Back/Let It Be* documentary film and album that The Beatles had recorded close to a year before, still lay in a heap of tapes in Abbey Road Studios. Over the intervening months, engineer Glyn Johns, regular producer George Martin, EMI staffer Malcolm Davies and John Lennon himself had each tried to cull a workable album from the mountain of music. But, no matter how the tapes were manipulated, consensus proved impossible to arrive at. It didn't help, of course, that The Beatles themselves were splintering, as John Lennon announced to his bandmates he was leaving, then McCartney told the world that *he* was. Even in the rare moments of unity that did arise during the group's last year together, the stark simplicity of the *Let It Be* material divided the quartet like no issue ever had.

But the solution to that division was to prove even more calamitous. George Martin told *Rolling Stone*, 'it was always understood that the album would be nothing like The Beatles had done before. It would be honest, no overdubbing, no editing, truly live.' The very suggestion that Phil Spector be brought in to make something out of the tapes, he continued, 'contradicted everything'. But it also completed everything.

The problems with the original tapes were only compounded by the group's most recent album release, *Abbey Road*. In terms of actual recording, that album represented the final LP The Beatles would make together and it was a masterpiece. By comparison, *Get Back* simply sounded unfinished. Allan Steckler, over at Klein's ABKCo organisation, told Beatles historian Bruce Spitzer, 'The Beatles had shown a marked progression in their writing, playing and production values. *Get Back* was a drastic throwback, particularly when compared to *Abbey Road*.' Klein agreed.

Lennon was not immediately convinced that Spector was the right man for this particular job. He loved Spector's old records, of course he did. And they'd always got on well on the occasions that they met. But he, too, wondered whether Spector's methods might not prove the absolute corollary of everything that the *Get Back* project was meant to represent. Still, four sets of ears had already failed to make anything out of the tapes; maybe it would be fifth time lucky. His only request to Klein was that he be allowed to stage a trial run, by recruiting Spector to produce his own next single, the Plastic Ono Band's 'Instant Karma'.

By late January 1970, all of the pieces were in place and Spector was flying to London, booking in at the Inn On The Park hotel with his bodyguard, George Brand, installed in the room next door. Just one day had been set aside to record the single, but Spector was not going to be rushed. By the time he arrived at Abbey Road, Lennon and his band – George Harrison, bassist Klaus Voorman and drummer Alan White – had been waiting for him for an hour. Neither was any time wasted on introductions once he arrived. George Harrison biographer Simon Leng quotes Voorman recalling, 'we cut the song and it was great, but there was this little guy walking around with "PS" on his shirt and I was thinking "who is this guy?" I had no idea who he was.'

Lennon knew. Spector told *Rolling Stone*, 'when we went into the studio to do "Instant Karma!", John was afraid to sing. He loved Ronnie's voice, and he wanted to be able to do that. He wanted the tremolo – he wanted all

The Teddy Bears: Phil Spector,
Annette Kleinbard and
Marshall Lieb

Love and the ladies: Phil Spector and The Ronettes, 1964

'Looking more like an act than the acts themselves.' Phil Spector and The Rolling Stones

Lenny Bruce in pensive mode, 1964

The three wise men of rock 'n' roll: Phil Spector salutes Andrew Loog Oldham and Keith Richards

Before they lost that lovin' feeling: Phil Spector and the Righteous Brothers, 1965

The Crystals, shortly after their departure from Philles

Ike and Tina Turner: sex
and sex and rock 'n' roll

All he ever wanted was
to be free: Phil Spector
in *Easy Rider*, 1969

Phil Spector, George
Harrison and Apple
Records' Peter Bennett
during the *All Things Must
Pass* sessions, 30 October
1970

Portrait of the artist as mid-'70s
cool dude

John Lennon and Yoko Ono with the Elephant's Memory Band, 1971

Last breaths of a ladies'
man: Leonard Cohen

After the end of the century: the Ramones in 1981

Phil Spector and Dion DiMucci
with '80s singing star Patti
Smyth

Phil Spector and Atlantic
Records chief Ahmet Ertegun at
the Rock 'n' Roll Hall of Fame,
1989

Phil Spector with BB King at the 1997 Brit Awards

Daughter Nicole joins Phil Spector at the 1997 Brit Awards

Umbrella at the ready, Phil Spector prepares to celebrate winning back the rights to 'To Know Him Is To Love Him' in London, 1997

Starsailor at the 2001 *Q* Awards

that stuff. When he came in [the control room], and I put the tape on, he said, 'It's just like Sun Records'.

Voorman continued oblivious to Spector's identity even as the session progressed, and the stranger's own most peculiar working methods began to take shape. 'Every tape recorder from EMI was rolled into that studio,' the bassist continued, while the recording process itself was like none the musicians had ever experienced before. At one point, Spector asked drummer Alan White to hit his tom-toms as hard as he could, having first muffled them with a bath towel. He had Lennon and White playing opposite ends of the piano simultaneously. And everything was being recorded at ear-splitting volume, so loud that Spector himself was forced to resort to sign language when he needed to communicate with anyone else in the room.

Most of his gestures were self-explanatory. To raise or lower the volume on a particular instrument, for instance, he'd pretend to be playing it, then he'd point up or down. But what did he mean when he stuck out his tongue, and started slapping it? It took a while but finally the musicians figured it out. More reverb, of course.

Finally, the playback started. Voorman continued, 'it was just incredible. It was ridiculously loud, but also there was the ringing of all these instruments and the way the song had such motion. And I knew immediately who he was...Phil Spector.'

Already a ricochetting riot of echoing percussion, thundering around Lennon's most colossal chorus ever, 'Instant Karma' could have been even grander – Spector begged Lennon to let him take the tapes back the LA to add violins and a few extra frills. Lennon refused, but Spector had the last laugh regardless. While the British release featured Lennon's own approved final mix, Spector secretly tweaked the US master after all – 'the only time anyone's done *that*,' Lennon told Richard Williams. 'He put a cleaner version out without tellin' me.'

But Lennon didn't mind. 'Instant Karma' was released the following month and became Lennon's biggest hit yet, the first solo Beatles record ever to sell a million copies. Phil Spector had passed the audition. He could begin work on the *Let It Be* tapes immediately.

The idea of combining the world's greatest band with the world's greatest producer was scarcely one that would fill the average listener with dread. No matter that Spector himself had been brushed aside in the commercial eye almost as thoroughly as every other producer and performer of the pre-

Beatles age; no matter that he had not actually produced anything that most folk could name in close to three years. Phil Spector and his Wall of Sound remained the ideal to which any number of young musicians and producers aspired as the 1960s dribbled to an end, just as The Beatles' arsenal of accomplishments remained the acid test for musician who considered they had a career worth pursuing.

Neither was Spector under any illusions as to what he was letting himself in for. The time he'd spent with Lennon while they were cutting 'Instant Karma' had already acquainted him with the precise state of The Beatles, both as a band and as a recording act. The band had broken up in all but name and public perception, and their last will and testament was a pile of taped jams and studio knockabouts, laced with multiple tapes of the handful of worthwhile songs that they'd eked out of the group's disintegration.

The Beatles did not need a producer, they needed a salvage company, and Spector was under no illusions about that, either. Whether he turned in the greatest record in the world, or the worst piece of rubbish ever, he would never please all the people that The Beatles had hitherto pleased all the time – not because they disliked what he did, but because Beatlepeople were a clannish crowd. They didn't want outsiders messing with their moptops, and Spector was an outsider. 'He knew he couldn't win,' said George Harrison. 'So he just made up his mind not to lose.'

Spector himself was especially bullish. He told *Melody Maker* journalist Richard Williams, 'it was no favour to me to give me George Martin's job because I don't consider [him to be] in [the same] league as me. He's an arranger, that's all.' The tapes he had to work with, Spector raged, had been left 'in a deplorable condition', while the band themselves were beyond caring. Spector himself asked whether any of The Beatles wanted to join him in the studio. 'No. They didn't care.' John Lennon admitted as much. 'The tapes were so lousy and bad, none of us would go near them to touch them. They'd been lying around for six months. None of us could face remixing them, it was terrifying.'

Buried deep within the bowels of The Beatles' Apple building on Savile Row, London, Spector spent much of February and March 1970 playing through the tapes, intent upon finding the jewels that he believed must have been secreted somewhere within. His presence in the UK was top secret – many of Spector's English friends insist that they did not even know he was in the country, while other friends in America simply assumed he'd gone to ground somewhere. Finally, however, he arrived at Abbey Road Studios to begin work on Monday 23 March – the same week, ironically, that it became apparent that The Beatles' latest single, the George Martin-produced 'Let It Be', was *not* going to top the British chart. Having entered the listings at No 2, it had now dropped to No 3 and, the following week, would dip one place further. Ruling the roost in its place was actor Lee Marvin's 'Wanderin' Star' and, if there were not portents to be derived from that happenstance, then the world is a lot less interesting place than it ought to be.

Ushered into Studio Four at Abbey Road Studios, with engineer Peter Bown and, dropping by from time to time, Allen Klein and George Harrison, Spector already knew the songs that he was required to work on. Past attempts at compiling an album, and synchronizing it with the intended movie, had already narrowed the track selection down to a dozen or so songs, and those are the ones Spector concentrated on.

He would pull occasional other songs into contention – early on in the process, he turned his attention to Paul McCartney's 'Teddy Boy', oblivious to the fact that McCartney himself was in Studio Three, working on his first solo album and planning to include that same song. When he did discover that, Spector returned The Beatles' take to the archive.

Spector worked on his remixes for five days; on the sixth (coincidentally, April Fool's Day), he finally brought in the orchestra and choir that would be splashed so lavishly across 'The Long And Winding Road', 'I Me Mine' and 'Across The Universe' – the three most impressive and, ultimately, contentious tracks on the entire album. Neither did he scrimp on the size of the orchestra. Under the guidance of Richard Hewson, orchestral arranger for Paul McCartney's production of Mary Hopkins' chart-topping 'Those Were The Days', 18 violins, 14 vocalists, 4 violas, 4 cellos, 3 trombones and 3 trumpets were augmented by 1 live Beatle, drummer Ringo Starr – a total cost to EMI of £1,126, 5 shillings [£1,126.25].

With Spector having now taken over Studio One, the musicians were booked to perform on just two songs – upon their arrival at the studio, however, Spector blithely handed them the parts for all three. Peter Bown told Beatles' historian Mark Lewisohn, 'out of the blue he distributed these extra parts, without intimating that there would be any extra payment'.

The engineer had already warned Spector that there was no way he'd be able to get away with the stunt, and Bown was correct. As one, the orchestra stood up and walked out, and Bown quickly followed them. He'd worked with many of the musicians before and knew that Spector would try to use that relationship as leverage.

'I went into the control room, put a wedge under the door and tried to keep out of it.' At home he took the phone off the hook – and the moment he replaced the receiver, it rang. 'Spector was on the line, asking me to return to the studio and continue. The musicians got their extra payment.'

Neither were Spector's problems limited to the musicians' wallets. The perceived limitations of Abbey Road also drove him to distraction, as he demanded the same sonic niceties from Studio One as he was used to receiving at home. Technical engineer Brian Gibson told Lewisohn, 'he wanted to hear [the recording] while it was being recorded, *exactly* the way it would sound when finished, with all the tape echo, plate echo, chamber echo, all the effects. This was horrendously difficult in Studio One which is, technically, quite primitive.'

In front of the assembled masses, Spector grew more and more frustrated, screaming out demands. '[He] was on the point of throwing a big wobbly – "I wanna hear this! I wanna hear that! I must have this!"' Finally, Ringo Starr walked across and took him to one side. 'Look, they can't do that. They're doing the best they can. Just cool it.' Spector 'cooled it', but he still avenged himself on 'The Long And Winding Road', the song that was causing so much heartache. There were not enough tracks on the tape for him to overdub the full orchestra, so he freed one up by erasing one of Paul McCartney's vocals.

The 2 April marked the final day of the sessions, as Spector bestowed a final mix upon the previous day's labours, and then sank into welcome, and drink-sodden, exhaustion. He had seldom drunk much in the past but now, there always seemed to be a bottle of Courvoisier handy, and it would be emptying faster every day. But, of course, he was not to be allowed to rest. He had completed his task. Now the world was waiting to judge it.

McCartney's broadsides were the most powerful, dismissing all that Spector had wrought with a vehemence that time has done nothing to diminish. 'The album was finished a year ago,' he told London's *Evening Standard* newspaper on 21 April 1970, 'but, a few months ago, [Spector] was called in...to tidy up a few of the tracks.' Tidying naturally became remodelling, and McCartney could scarcely conceal his incredulity. 'A few weeks ago, I was sent a remixed version of my song 'The Long And Winding Road', with harps, horns, an orchestra and women's choir added. No one had asked me what I thought. I couldn't believe it.' Forgetting such past insertions as Lennon's wife Yoko ('Bungalow Bill'), and his own spouse, Linda (on 'Let It Be' itself), he insisted, 'I would never have female voices on a Beatles record.'

The plot sickened as he read a note from Klein that accompanied the tape. He thought the changes were 'necessary', and McCartney raged, 'I don't blame Phil Spector for doing it, but it goes to show that it's no good me sitting here thinking I'm in control, because obviously I'm not.' At the time of the interview, he'd written back to Klein asking that some of the alternations be revised. 'But I haven't received an answer yet.'

Neither was he going to. '[Phil] was given the shittiest load of badly recorded shit with a lousy feeling to it ever, and he made something of it,' Lennon told *Rolling Stone* the following year, and fellow Beatles George Harrison and Ringo Starr agreed. Less than a month after McCartney first aired his own grievances with the process, what proved to be The Beatles' final album release, *Let It Be*, was released throughout the world exactly as Spector had left it, and McCartney would never forgive it for its faults (although, when it won a Best LP Grammy the following year, he personally accepted the award.)

Even as Lennon and Spector publicly insisted that McCartney hadn't simply approved the mixes, but that he'd also sent Spector a telegram affirming that fact, McCartney added the revision of 'The Long And Winding Road' to the legal battery with which he was dissolving The Beatles, pointing to it as evidence of how his erstwhile bandmates were trying to destroy his reputation.

Speaking in The Beatles' *Anthology* volume a full 30 years on, on the eve of releasing the pre-Spector mix for the first time, McCartney lamented, 'I heard the Spector version again recently, and it sounded terrible.' Others were equally scathing. 'I cannot bring myself to listen to the Phil Spector version of the album,' Glyn Johns said in a BBC interview in 1981. 'I heard a few bars of it once and was totally disgusted, and I think it's an absolute load of garbage.' He readily confessed, of course, that 'obviously I'm biased'. But still he was adamant, 'Spector did the most atrocious job, just utter puke.'

In fact, shorn of its most contentious overdubs, Spector's vision of *Let It Be* was scarcely the overblown conceit that sundry sticky-beak histories have since painted it. Retaining Glyn Johns' original notion of presenting the experience as 'live in the studio', but replacing several of the performances he had isolated with other versions of the same songs, Spector peppered the album with various off-the-cuff commentaries and introductions, opening with Lennon's announcement of 'I dig a pygmy,' on the cusp of 'Two Of Us'.

He ditched a lacklustre take of Harrison's 'For You Blue' in favour of a vibrantly overdubbed version that Harrison himself preferred, and threw out a rough studio run-through of 'Dig A Pony', replacing it with the powerful version recorded on the Apple Studios roof on 30 January. And, in every instance, Spector's choice can not be faulted. Neither can his production – unless one disapproves of crisp guitars, clean vocals and audible lyrics.

Two other rooftop performances, 'I've Got A Feeling' and 'One After 909' opened side two of the album and Spector allowed both to stand on their own merits, simply tweaking the instrumentation somewhat to bring out nuances that earlier mixes completely overlooked, while 'Get Back' possibly proved even rougher than Johns intended, as Spector returned to the original single, then added not only a snatch of studio tomfoolery and tuning, but also brought up Billy Preston's electric piano, to give the impression of an entirely different rendition of the song.

The album version of 'Let It Be', too, returned to the previously released version, but again, Spector was not content to let it stand as was. Having drenched the drums with echo ('he wanted tape echo on *everything*,' Peter Bown recalled), he added an angrily distorted Harrison guitar solo, turned up the brass, tacked on an additional chorus and left even Lennon to reflect, later, that Spector went somewhat over the top – 'a little fruity' – on that one.

Nevertheless, John Lennon joined George Harrison in offering Spector's methods the clearest applause, as both promptly turned to him to help them with their own next projects – solo debuts from two of the most famous band members in the world.

On 27 May, six weeks after Spector finished work on *Let It Be*, and even as the entire planet was now gathering around to find out what he'd made of it, he was back at Apple, listening while Harrison played through an apparently endless selection of the songs he'd written during the recent Beatle years, including a handful that Spector recognised from the *Get Back* tapes – the epic 'Isn't It A Pity', the plaintive 'All Things Must Pass', the grinding 'Wah Wah' and the Dylan co-write 'I'd Have You Anytime'.

It was a pleasant afternoon and an instructive one, for both men – three months later, with the actual recording sessions in full flight, Spector wrote

Harrison a letter confirming thoughts that he'd had on that first May afternoon: 'I think you should spend whatever time you are going to on performances so that they are the very best that you can do…that will make the remixing of the album that much easier. I really feel that your voice has got to be heard throughout the album, so that the greatness of the songs can really come through.' For an artist like Harrison, to whom insecurity was all but second nature, such words would have shaken away any number of panics and dreads.

The sessions for the album were vast – as vast, in fact, as the album itself would turn out to be. Harrison's reputation as the Quiet Beatle had always irked him; at a stroke, the 23 songs that comprised *All Things Must Pass* would double the number of Harrisongs available to the general public.

Anything up to 15 musicians were found littering the studio at any one time – Ringo Starr, Eric Clapton, Ginger Baker, Jim Price, Jim Gordon, Carl Radle, Dave Mason, Pete Drake, Bobby Whitlock, Billy Preston, Klaus Voorman, Gary Wright, Gary Brooker, Alan White and the members of Badfinger all trooped through the sessions, together with a revolving door of friends and passers-by, any and many of whom were roped into one song or another. Phil Collins, drummer with little-known London prog merchants Flaming Youth, could dine out on tales of his uncredited conga playing on 'The Art Of Dying', and he is surely not alone in claiming such a distinction. And, overseeing them all, Spector sometimes sat, sometimes crouched in the control room, one eye on the equipment, one hand on the Courvoisier…'he was hitting [it] pretty hard, and this was like early afternoon,' Badfinger's Joey Molland reflected. '[But] he was still Phil Spector as far as I was concerned – the sound was incredible.'

Harrison detailed the sessions themselves. 'Some of [them] were very long in the preparation of the sound and the arrangements had, at times, various percussion players, sometimes two or three, two drummers, four or five acoustic guitars, two pianos and even two basses on one of the tracks.' The songs would then be performed as many times as Spector deemed necessary, until every arrangement was in place and the producer was satisfied with the sound. Then he'd call for one final take, record it live, and that would be it.

Though he rarely ventured outside of the control room, Spector's very presence commanded a degree of formality that surprised a lot of Harrison's guests. Past sessions that he and they had passed through were marked by an atmosphere as relaxed as Harrison himself appeared to be. Spector, however, had no time for relaxation. Exasperated when string arranger John Barham failed to get precisely the results he wanted, Spector simply strode out and gave one of Britain's premier arrangers a lesson in conducting, in full view of the orchestra.

'There were blow-ups,' the keyboard player Tony Ashton later acknowledged. 'Phil would go off on one, screaming and yelling at people if things didn't go according to how he wanted them. But what producer doesn't? Compared with some of the lunatics I've worked with, he was almost laid-back.' Spector, too, admitted that there were moments of supreme frustration, such as recording the slide guitar on 'My Sweet Lord'. '[George] did 90 fucking versions of it. Then he had to do 90 more with a bottleneck. Then he brought Eric Clapton in to do another 90.' But still Harrison marvelled that Spector was a lot easier to work with than he had been led to believe by hearsay. Spector had a job of work to do and, so long as everybody let him do it, he was happy.

As the sessions drifted on, however, Spector's attention appeared to be wandering. Either that, or he simply wasn't looking where he was going. Klaus Voorman smiled, 'George was doing some overdubs, Phil came in and was completely drunk and just fell over backwards...in the Apple control room. I think he broke his arm.' The German bassist insisted that Spector 'sort of disappeared' after that, 'and George [assisted by Alan Parsons] finished the album'.

Several of the musicians involved confessed that Spector's departure came as something of a relief; admitted that when they wanted to hear the Wall of Sound, they dug out an old Ronettes record. Listening, however, as Spector layered instrument upon instrument, chord upon chord, transforming a simple note into a blistering cacophony, they could not help but be impressed. The actual recording was monotony personified. But the end result took your ears off.

It needed to. Throughout 1970, all post-Beatle eyes were on Lennon and McCartney, with Harrison and Starr widely regarded as mere sideshows alongside the main attraction. Even EMI apparently wondered how they could even hope to compete with the proven masters – Ringo was simply a singing drummer, while George had barely contributed more than a couple of songs to any Fabs album you could name. The announcement, in mid-year, that his solo debut was to be spread across six full sides of vinyl, led a scarcely credulous media to just two conclusions. Either he'd devoted his entire career to date to stockpiling songs for some future rainy day; or, he'd spent a lot longer jamming with his heavyweight friends than anyone could have guessed. The result, November's *All Things Must Pass*, did not contradict either prediction.

Two full LPs-worth of conventional numbers were followed by a third disc of superstar jams. But, at its heart, *All Things Must Pass* was an album of songs, and absolutely marvellous songs at that, possessed by an honesty, a simplicity and, above all, a resonance which neither Paul's just-released *McCartney* nor Lennon's forthcoming *Plastic Ono Band* even hinted towards. Those albums, classics though they certainly are, were more concerned with establishing their sires as songwriters in their own right, the irrevocable sundering of the best-known double act in music history. *All Things Must Pass*, on the other hand, gave the impression that it simply didn't care what people thought. And that was its magic.

'Beware Of Darkness' and 'Art Of Dying', respectively opening and closing the album's second platter, rate among the finest compositions of Harrison's entire career, while the utterly buoyant, and heroically guitar-laden 'What Is Life' not only brought its maker a US Top 10 hit in February, 1971, it returned to chart duty the following year when Olivia Newton-John sent a truly lovely cover into the UK Top 20. She had, of course, already scored with a similarly superb version of another *All Things* highlight, Dylan's 'If Not For You', and she made it no secret that her take was wholly modelled on Harrison's arrangement. (Dylan himself never truly got to grips with what remains one of his most affecting love songs.)

Spector's departure from the studio was only temporary. On 26 September, as Harrison put the finishing touches to *All Things Must Pass*, Spector was back at Abbey Road with John Lennon, to begin work on *his* solo debut.

Lennon began working towards the album back in June while undergoing treatment with primal therapist Dr Arthur Janov in LA. He and Yoko spent some of their time in the city as guests at the Spector mansion and, recording demos around his sessions with Janov, Lennon had amassed a remarkable selection of songs, few of which owed much to anything he had attempted with The Beatles – there were moments on the *White Album*, perhaps, but the new material was very much a fresh frontier. Indeed, *John Lennon/Plastic Ono Band* has been described as one of the most pain-filled albums ever made, a cathartic scream that set to music all that Lennon learned from Janov. For Spector, however, such internal anguish mattered little.

'What John needed was an editor,' Spector told *Rolling Stone* in 2000. 'That's what The Beatles would do, they'd edit each other.' As solo artists, they no longer had that luxury… 'John couldn't turn to Paul and say, "What do you think here?" So I filled that gap. [And] John did do that – "What do you think of this?" "What do you think of that?" Which meant to me that he was used to asking, that he liked feedback. We worked well that way.'

Ray Coleman, author of the best-selling *Lennon* biography, later described *John Lennon/Plastic Ono Band* as the sparsest sounding record ever to bear Spector's name, and both artist and producer acknowledged that, for anybody seeking the Wall of Sound within its grooves, they would need first to reaffirm precisely what they meant by the term. Rather than building up the instrumentation, Spector stripped it down. Individual strings and keys can be heard being plucked and played – and yet, the sound remains enormous.

It is when you hear Lennon's original demos for the songs that you realise just what the American contributed to the sessions. The bare ballad of 'Mother', with Lennon's voice straining for notes it has no hope of hitting, while the bass and drums stroll bored behind it, is forced to deploy distorted guitars and a virtual jam bang before it picks up any speed whatsoever. Spector dispensed with all of that; rather, restating all that he told Harrison during the *All Things Must Pass* sessions, Spector pushed Lennon to concentrate on the performance alone – then left the song at that. Later, of course, he added a tolling bell to the song's intro, and that might have been icing the cake a little. But Spector knew, the album was going to be picked to pieces by every critic in the world no matter what they did to it. So he decided to hand it to them in pieces in the first place, and let them figure out how to handle it.

But it is warmth, not weight that is stripped from the music; expertise, not energy that is torn from the playing. Lennon brought in no more than three additional musicians for the majority of the album, bassist Klaus Voorman, pianist Billy Preston and the ever-reliable Ringo Starr, relying on himself, Yoko and Spector to bang, thump and bash merrily around them. Spector discovered that when it was time to record the piano solo during 'Love'. Lennon expected him to play it, and the producer remembered, 'it took twenty takes. I made a million mistakes'.

He had memorized the part, and he knew it perfectly. But the moment the red light went on, and he saw John and Yoko watching from the control room, his nerve went. Finally, Lennon's voice crackled over the intercom. 'You don't like being on the other side of the goddamn fookin' glass, do ya? Well, now you know what it's like to be an artist.'

But, of course, it was as producer that he excelled, as Yoko affirmed. 'He's a very sensitive and talented producer, and he knew how to accommodate John's wishes. He just walked in when we were doing "God". And we weren't doing "God" [the way it appears on the album] at all. And he just said "now, what about Billy Preston?" And we said "okay, well let's try". And Billy did such a brilliant, brilliant piano. I mean, you can never think of "God" without Billy's piano playing there. [But] that was Phil's idea. He just walked in, listened to it and said "What about it?" And that's how he just made that track shine.'

The album was completed in under three weeks. On 27 October, John and Yoko left London for New York, the following day Spector and George Harrison followed them there, to wrap up *All Things Must Pass* in time for its 30 November release date. *John Lennon/Plastic Ono Band* would join it on the shelves less than a fortnight later.

11 Sometime In New York City

Spector was back in London at the beginning of February 1971, again aligned with Harrison, this time to record a new single for wife Ronnie.

It was Harrison who supplied the song, the winsome 'Try Some Buy Some', although Ronnie herself didn't know that as she flew into London with her mother and, leaving his governess Mrs Taylor behind, three-year-old Donté. All she had been told was, she'd been given a contract with Apple Records, that her husband was waiting at the Inn at the Park hotel for her arrival and that she was due at Abbey Road on the day after her arrival to begin rehearsing with Harrison, Leon Russell and Badfinger's Pete Ham.

She didn't recognise Harrison when she arrived at the studio – she thought he was one of the studio engineers. Neither was she over-enamoured by the song, confessing to its author that she didn't understand a single word of the lyrics, and being utterly taken aback when he confessed that he didn't, either. Spector himself, however, had no concern for such details. Neither was he worried when it became apparent that his arrangement was pitched in a completely different key to any that Ronnie could comfortably reach. 'Just reach a little,' he told her. 'I know you can hit these notes.'

Finally Harrison came to the rescue, scything out the lyrics that were pitched too high, while Spector paced impatiently around the studio...he continued pacing, too, as Ronnie delivered what he determined would be the final take. Her suggestion that she try re-recording the song with a little vibrato was brushed aside with a dismissive sneer. 'Forget the vibrato. Vibrato is sixties. This is 1971.'

Such an eye for chronological detail did not, however, prevent Spector and Harrison themselves from indulging in some romping reminiscences. With the tapes still rolling, and Ronnie singing happily along beside them, the pair picked up a couple of acoustic guitars and began jamming back and forth through their own favourite oldies – 'The Great Pretender', 'That'll Be The Day', 'I'll Be Your Baby Tonight…'.

Spector flashed on an old Arthur Alexander lyric – '"now, you tell me…" what is that song?' Harrison flashed back the answer – '"You Better Move On"', then began strumming the chords to his own 'Let It Down', while singing 'The Hokey Cokey' over the top. Spector countered with 'Blue Bird Over The Mountain'; Harrison lashed into a light-hearted 'Ob-La-Di Ob-La-Da' – never his favourite Beatles song. The session (or, at least, the tape) concluded with Harrison singing George Formby, leaving Spector baffled by the lyrics of 'Leaning On A Lamp-post'; Harrison convulsed with laughter.

The party continued as they turned their attention to the intended B-side to 'Try Some Buy Some'. Harrison had another song for Ronnie to try, the '60s-inflected 'You', while Spector brought in a new Toni Wine number, 'Loverley Laddy Day', and the team were still hard at work when it became apparent that this session, at least, was not to go according to plan. At 9pm, the studio door burst open and in marched John Lennon and a crowd of friends saying, 'We're here to make a record with Ronnie Ronette.'

Spector was furious, but said little. Instead, he allowed the gatecrashers to entertain themselves for a while, added to the festivities by ordering take-away meals all round from a nearby Indian restaurant; and, when Lennon finally asked what they were going to record, Spector announced, 'Tandoori Chicken' – a song that he and Harrison proceeded to 'write' on the spot.

'Tandoori Chicken' was simplicity itself, a great Carl Perkins rock 'n' roll guitar chug from Harrison, and a lyric no more demanding than the constant repetition of the title. It was scarcely the kind of recording that either he or Ronnie would ever be proud of, but it reasserted his command in front of Lennon and his cronies; and re-established his cool at a time he almost lost it. But when the ensuing single sank without trace, Spector wasn't simply unsurprised. He scarcely even noticed.

Ronnie, on the other hand, was stunned. Over the past couple of years, Spector's golden touch had flown back into reach, and 'Try Some Buy Some' was as exquisite as anything he had cut with John or George. Indeed, asked in 1999 to comment upon five favourite recordings from her entire catalogue, she reflected, 'the record was done to make me happy, and it did. It might not have been made for the right reasons, but it's a good record.' (Her other selections were 1977's 'Say Goodbye To Hollywood', the 1987 hit 'Take Me Home Tonight' and the then-current 'She Talks To Rainbows', plus one other song from the Phil Spector canon, 'Be My Baby': 'I was like the happiest 17, 18-year-old girl you'd ever want to know, to have a No 1 record all over the world, I loved it so much, the sweat and the tears and the sex appeal, everything').

Neither, though it sold next to nothing, were the song's qualities lost on other artists. Harrison himself re-recorded 'Try Some Buy Some' for 1973s *Living In The Material World* album, and 30 years later, David Bowie wrapped himself around it, admitting 'I always thought [the song] was totally neglected.'

Ronnie's reunion with Spector was brief. No sooner was the single completed than she was flying back to California; and, while he would follow her, his own career insisted he spend much of his time in either London or New York. He had now been appointed Apple Records' Head of A&R, responsible for selecting new releases on the label, on top of his production duties. John and Yoko's next single, 'Power To The People', and another Lennon project, the Elastic Oz Band's 'Do The Oz', raising funds for the legally beleaguered underground magazine *Oz*, were both Spector productions during the first half of 1971.

He also went into the studio with Derek And The Dominoes, the semi-anonymous super-sessionman group that Eric Clapton pieced together as he attempted to bounce back from his experiences with Cream and Blind Faith. Clapton had been desperate to work with Spector – indeed, when George Harrison first approached him about appearing alongside the rest of the newly formed Dominoes on *All Things Must Pass*, Clapton agreed only if Harrison could convince Spector to return the favour.

When it came down to the actual recording, however, Clapton found himself wishing he'd simply kept his mouth shut. Sequestered in Apple Studios, the team completed two songs, 'Tell The Truth' and 'Roll It Over', for release as a single in September, but even before the record was pressed, the Dominoes were assailed by doubts. The song was too fast, the mix was too full and the ending was too abrupt.

In fact, the two songs pack a ragged promise that the Dominoes' subsequent work, with Spector's old rival Tom Dowd, was simply too well-mannered to match, as Spector exercised the same jam band textures that, two years later, he would graft onto the Lennons' *Sometime In New York City* masterpiece. Replaying 'Tell The Truth' and 'Roll It Over' in the light of what the group would go on to accomplish, one can only regret that the same combination never turned its hands to 'Layla'. Instead, while 'Tell The Truth' would be released as Derek And The Dominoes' first single in September 1971, it was withdrawn almost immediately, victim of what the official announcement insisted was the band members' 'increasing dissatisfaction with the record'.

June, meanwhile, saw Lennon begin work on his next studio album at the home studio he had installed in his sprawling white mansion, Tittenhurst Park, and Spector was again in attendance. The producer laughed at the memory. 'Everybody had been saying, "If Spector gets involved, it's going to take six years to finish." We finished the whole album in seven days.' In fact it took a little longer than that – ten days at Tittenhurst, followed by another three at the Record Plant in New York. But one week...two weeks...still it was a remarkable rate of speed, and one that Spector ascribed wholly to the fact that 'we knew what we were going to do. We knew it was going to be a Beatle-like album.'

John Lennon/Plastic Ono Band had been well received, but scarcely the commercial smash that McCartney's *McCartney* and Harrison's triple album had proven. It was time, all agreed, to pull something commercial out of the hat – to prove Lennon could do it, to prove Spector could do it and to prove that, compared to John, Paul and George *couldn't* do it. Spector understood from the outset that his brief was to find hits, and he knew Lennon would provide them the first time he heard what became 'Imagine'. Lennon had little more in place than the piano part and a few lyrics gleaned from Yoko's *Grapefruit* poetry book, but Spector was sold. 'Just write it, it's right,' he told him – and, of course, he was correct.

Again, Lennon recruited the minimum of musicians to accompany him – drummer Alan White, bassist Klaus Voorman, Beatle George and pianist Nicky Hopkins. 'The first time I met Spector,' Hopkins laughed years later, 'He was in a suit and tie, shades, cigarette, very neat, very quiet. This is the madman? This is the legendary weirdo? Even when he said "hello", I couldn't hear him. And the last time I saw him, he was the same – and every time in between as well. He got things done but I don't know how, because you scarcely knew he was there.'

It was John and, occasionally, Yoko who ran the sessions. When 'How Do You Sleep?', Lennon's self-confessedly 'nasty' open letter to McCartney, failed to gel, it was Yoko who complained that the band was improvising too much, rather than getting down to the nitty-gritty of Lennon's riff; when the engineer was having trouble finding the right spot on the tape for Lennon and, alongside him at the microphone, Spector, to drop in the harmonies during 'Oh Yoko', it was Lennon who barked impatiently. And, during that same performance, when Spector proved to be as nervous about singing as he was about playing the piano last time around, it was Yoko who called down the required reassurance – 'don't be afraid, Phil, just sing into the mike'.

'I think deep down, Phil was *at ease* with John,' Hopkins continued. 'He knew him, he trusted him, he trusted his judgement. If John brought in a musician, it was because he knew that musician would bring something to the session, and Spector respected that. The same when he worked with George. You read these stories about Spector in the studio with other people and you think "fuck, what a monster, I could never work with someone like that." Then you talk to people who were on George's album, or the people who were on John's...the first ones, anyway...and we'll all tell you the same thing. "Oh, that little guy who sat in the corner chain-smoking? Yeah, he seemed okay."'

Spector did assert himself when the occasion demanded, however, including at least one occasion when Harrison asked that he be allowed to try another run through a guitar solo. The song in question was either the Nixon-flaying 'Gimme Some Truth' or 'How Do You Sleep?' – solos that Lennon was already convinced were 'the best he's ever fucking played in his life. He'd never get that feeling again.' George Harrison, on the other hand, was convinced that he'd only just begun cooking. Finally, Spector stepped in, a silent observer who might not even have been paying attention to the conversation beforehand but who, by directing his comments at Lennon alone, had obviously been listening very carefully indeed. Fearing a repeat of the 'My Sweet Lord' debacle, 90 tries, then 90 more, he simply said, 'it's great, John,' before adding – as if it were Lennon who was demanding a retake – 'just leave it as it is'. *Imagine*, as the finished long-player was titled, would emerge the most perfectly played, perfectly realised album of John Lennon's entire career.

With the mixing of *Imagine* complete, Spector finally made his way back to Ronnie in Los Angeles in late June, although it was not home thoughts that drew him back. George Harrison and Klaus Voorman had themselves recently flown into the city to record what Harrison, at least, believed to be the most momentous single of his life, 'Bangla-Desh'. Spector, of course, would be producing.

Now cast in history as rock's first ever charity recording, predating Band Aid by a full 13 years, 'Bangla-Desh' was the first shot in a two prong effort to raise awareness and, more importantly, money for the infant nation of Bangladesh, scene of one of the worst famines in recent years. The single was not, initially, greeted with the magnanimity it merited. A simplistic lyric included one couplet (rhyming 'Bangla-Desh' with 'such a mess') that would subsequently be condemned as the worst lyric ever penned by a member of The Beatles; while the song itself was generally rubbished by people who failed to see beyond Harrison's own (admittedly increasingly tireless) fascination with the Indian sub-continent.

Of course, that did not prevent many of the same people from turning out in droves to support the Concert for Bangla-Desh that followed the single's release in August, a then-unprecedented star-studded event that drew Bob Dylan (making his first American concert appearance in six years), Eric Clapton, Leon Russell, Badfinger, Ravi Shankar and more onto the Madison Square Garden stage, and presented Spector with the chance to produce an album for the benefit of by far the biggest audience that had ever awaited such a recording.

He succeeded – *The Concert For Bangla-Desh* topped the UK chart and won a Grammy as 1972s Album of the Year, Spector's first and only nod from that august committee…but he also failed. The ensuing album sounds atrocious, muted and muddy, and even loses vocals and instruments as the discs meander on. Spector himself was certainly unhappy with the end result, pointing to the maddening haste with which he'd been asked to complete the project, only for the release to then be tangled up in tape of a different kind, as Harrison found himself fighting with Apple's distributors, Capitol, over whether or not they should contribute their profits to the cause as well. Harrison thought they should; they weren't so certain.

Work began on *The Concert For Bangla-Desh* album the day after the show itself – with a scheduled release date just two weeks hence, Spector and Harrison worked flat out every night for the next week, before Capitol threw their own spoke into the works. Spector, however, scarcely had time for regrets. On 31 August, John and Yoko flew into New York, this time for keeps. '[We] were forever coming and going…so we finally decided it would be cheaper and more functional to actually live here,' Lennon announced as they took up residence on the 12th floor of the St Regis Hotel. 'So that's what we did.'

Lennon was already planning the duo's next project, an album that would document the city into which he was now leaping so wholeheartedly, and Spector was once again to take the helm. Most of their time together was spent at the hotel, going over songs; only once were the three seen together in public, when Spector was among the guests at the opening of Yoko's latest art exhibition, the ten-year retrospective *This is Not Here*, at the Everson Museum on 9 October.

Of course it was also John's 31st birthday and, following the opening, a group of friends joined him at a restaurant for dinner. In that 2000 *Rolling Stone* interview, Spector remembered how 'one of the violin players heard John was there, so he sent for the other violinists, and they came up to John's table and, as a tribute, they played "Yesterday"'.

Lennon was furious. 'John was like, "I didn't write that fucking thing. I hate that fucking song"'. Spector, on the other hand, found the entire thing hilarious. Had The Beatles not spent their entire career behind the solid front of Lennon *and* McCartney? Would Yoko Ono, decades later, not refuse McCartney's request that that one song be reassigned to McCartney and Lennon? He'd asked to be associated with the song, and now he'd got it. 'He was pissed off!'

At the same time, Lennon was also revelling in the attention that his presence in the city had aroused. From the world of alternative politics, Jerry Rubin, head of the Yippies movement whose 'power to the people' mantra had already been borrowed for a Plastic Ono Band single, met the couple and talked earnestly of his plans to lead a movement dedicated to change in America; by the end of the evening, Rubin had been appointed the Lennons' 'political advisor'. From the world of traditional showbiz, actors Fred Astaire and Jack Palance, and the network TV chatshow host Dick Cavett, all visited the Lennons' hotel suite; and, in the studio, the Lennons and Spector were preparing to record what would, in simple sonic terms, become their greatest ever accomplishment, the festive hymn 'Happy Xmas (War Is Over)'.

The song made both men laugh. Lennon himself insisted, 'I wanted to make one Christmas record with you, Phil, because it would've fucking killed me not to.' And the first time he played the song to Spector, a few evenings before the session, it was almost as if he was daring the producer to 'name that tune'. Spector got it in one – the tune was a little slower, the melody a little fussier. But it was still 'I Love How You Love Me'.

Recorded over the last four days of October at the Record Plant studios, 'Happy Xmas' reunited the trio with the rhythm section soul of the *Imagine* band – Nicky Hopkins, Jim Keltner and Klaus Voorman – plus Spector's own specific demand, a breathtaking five guitarists ('Hugh, Stu, Bob, Chris and Teddy,' Hopkins laughed. 'It sounded like the theme from *Trumpton*') and, on the final day, the 30-strong children's Harlem Community Choir, complete with their mothers. 'It was a lovely session,' said Hopkins. 'The song was so unlike anything either John or Yoko had done before, but the first time that John sang it to us, you just knew it was going to become one of *those* records, the ones that get pulled out every Christmas for ever more.'

Spector was scampering around as excitedly as the kids. 'I'd never seen him so animated,' Hopkins continued. 'I think...I was talking about it later with, I think it was Jim [Keltner], and we decided that it was the first time in a long time that he was actually able to pull all his old tricks out of the box for a record, and – with the song going on around him, it must have been like Christmas was already there.' The memory of Spector demanding fresh flavours for his sonic pudding – 'More percussion! Bells! Celeste! Chimes!' – is one that Hopkins never forgot. 'I look back on that session and it was one of the most joyful I ever did. Oh, and the photographs they took at the end of it...'

With the recording complete, John and Yoko, Spector, the musicians, the choir, the engineers, even the studio secretaries and watching journalist Richard Williams, were gathered around the plastic Christmas tree that John had erected in the studio. Photos were taken, a short film was shot, and when everybody spontaneously burst into choruses of 'Merry Christmas', their salutations were recorded and added to the record.

Reinvigorated by New York and the new company he was keeping, John was writing at a furious pace. 'Happy Xmas, War Is Over' itself was written, recorded and released as a single within a matter of weeks; 'Luck Of The Irish', 'Call My Name', 'Free The People' and 'Angela' were all demoed to varying states of completion around the same time. 'Woman Is The Nigger Of The World', a song John had been carrying around since 1969, when Yoko made that same remark in an interview with *NOVA* magazine, was dusted down; while 'Attica State' was dashed off within days of the September 1971 riots at the upstate New York gaol that left 129 prisoners and guards dead or injured.

Only one obstacle stood in his way – the authorities' refusal to grant him an American work permit. Already regarded with some suspicion by an administration that was growing increasingly wary of 'pop' music's subversive effects on American youth, Lennon's own case was further prejudiced by the company that he and Yoko were very publicly keeping. Rubin and the Yippies were only the tip of the iceberg. Their highly publicised support for jailed White Panthers leader John Sinclair also counted against them, while even their choice of backing musicians, Elephant's Memory, had had their own run-in with the FBI in the recent past.

Now the same bureau was on the Lennons' case, and the operatives assigned to the pair could scarcely believe their luck. Barely a single demonstration took place without John and Yoko turning up to support it, from a Free John Sinclair concert in Detroit, to a Transit Workers Union rally outside the BOAC airline offices in Manhattan. The pair were even associating themselves with known and suspected IRA sympathisers, while sessions for the new album, already titled *Sometime In New York City*, were littered with songs that oozed subversive sentiment. In January, US Immigration informed the Lennons that their application for work permits had been turned down. Weeks later, a recently applied extension to John's visitors' visa was revoked.

A series of appeals allowed Lennon to fight immediate deportation, and he was eventually granted the full residency that he sought. But, as the battle raged on, he made no secret of his belief that the 'deportation proceedings… are politically motivated' and it quickly became apparent that a lot of other people agreed with him. Over the next three years, a growing tide of both public and media sympathy rose up around the Lennons' plight, but it was Spector who led the chorus. Speaking with the *LA Times*' Robert Hilburn in 1972, he lashed out at what was then an almost embarrassing silence from the entertainment industry, demanding to know 'where is Lennon's own generation? Where are all the rock stars who owe so much to Lennon's influence? Where are all the people whose lives were so enriched by The Beatles' music? Why aren't they demanding that this outrage be stopped?'

In the midst of so much external excitement, *Sometime In New York City* arrived to an almost muted reception as the critics and, it seemed, the public struggled to wrap their heads around Lennon's latest warren of thoughts and concerns. They failed. Press response to the album was unfeasibly cruel, all the more so since the unanimously praised *Imagine* had convinced even

Lennon's traditional detractors that he was finally regaining control of the talent which recent events ('Revolution No 9', the *Unfinished Music/ Wedding Album* triptych, 'Yoko') suggested was seriously off-kilter.

Rolling Stone, possibly still smarting over Lennon's brusque response to the re-publication of his 1970 interview as a book, called the album 'embarrassingly puerile and witless'; *Melody Maker* sneered 'cheap rhetoric with appallingly bad lyrics'; while even the FBI got in on the slaughter, as one of their operatives noted in the Lennon's file that while this new material 'probably will become a million seller...it is lacking Lennon's usual standards'. Sales of *Sometime In New York City* faltered just inside the Top 50 in the US, just outside the Top 10 in Britain.

It mattered not that this new release contained the most focused example yet of John and Yoko's musical compatibility; nor that in the clash of Spector's perfection and Elephant's Memory chaos, Lennon had finally alchemised his own rawness; nor even that the same songs (with different lyrics), could have been described among his most memorable melodies in years. The album was savaged, the Lennons were ridiculed and Spector, as co-producer, was informed, once again, that he'd 'lost it'. History, of course, has more than mitigated his work on the album (the thud of percussion and sax that brings to life the opening 'Woman Is The Nigger Of The World' remains an exhilaratingly heart stopping moment). But at the time, contemporary ears deemed his broad sweeps of sound as unpalatable as the songwriting they embellished.

Neither would there be any going back. It was clear, not only from the mauling that *Sometime In New York City* received, but from other portents too, that Spector's days within rock's most inviolate inner sanctum were drawing to a close. George Harrison had already announced his decision to fly solo across his own next album, *Living In The Material World*, while Lennon's other activities in recent months suggested that his own need for Spector's guiding hand was over. Even as *Sometime In New York City* came together, Lennon was busy producing an album for New York street musician David Peel, *The Pope Smokes Dope* – and Peel enthused, 'John was an excellent producer. He had that Phil Spector Wall of Sound down pat, with everything exaggerated. We had six guitars and ten congas. He was deadly serious, but he knew how to have fun.'

So did Spector. But sometimes, he wondered just exactly what he had to do to enjoy it.

12 Games Of Death

Away from the studio for the first time in almost two-and-one-half years, Spector had no alternative but to turn his attention back to his domestic life, and the awareness that it had shattered.

He had money, that was not an issue. An audit of his accounts the following year, undertaken in Ronnie's name, unearthed community property of at least $225,000, while the royalties from the Lennon and Harrison albums alone amounted to over $375,366. But Spector needed more than cash. He needed security and activity as well, and both were suddenly in very short supply.

His marriage was crumbling, as he and Ronnie fought over the most insignificant freedoms, and she took an ever more pathetic refuge in drinking as the only escape from what she regarded, more than ever, as imprisonment. Finally in August 1971, Ronnie entered rehab at Saint Francis' Hospital, in an attempt to overcome her increasing reliance on alcohol, and even that became a battleground of sorts. Ten days in, a few weeks out...it became a routine that she herself considered heavenly. 'When things got bad at home,' she wrote later, 'I'd get raging drunk, pass out and then spend ten days in rehab.'

Spector loathed the situation and took to describing the marital home as a halfway house. More than once he found himself desperately pleading with Ronnie to try and give their marriage a chance; equally desperately, he struggled to find new ways of occupying his wife's time and attention, seemingly unable to comprehend that the one thing that might remedy everything was no further away than at the end of the driveway – and the beginning of the outside world.

In December 1971, he and Ronnie adopted two more children, six-year-old twins Louis and Gary. According to Ronnie herself, she knew nothing about the adoption until Spector and George Brand arrived at the sanatorium to take her home from her latest bout of treatment. Driving home, the limo took an unfamiliar detour but, when she asked where they were going, Spector simply smiled and said 'the playground'. Then, once they arrived, he pointed out two blonde boys playing on the swings. 'They're up for adoption. I wanted you to check them out before they saw us. That way they won't get hurt if we decide not to take them'.

Ronnie tried to remain non-committal. The children were adorable, she murmured, but her mind was already racing. She knew precisely what Spector was planning, and she could already predict the outcome of it – two more lives lost within the hell-hole of their home. She was surprised that Spector did not demand more of a response from her, but gratified. It meant that she would have more time in which to work out how to tell him that the ploy was not going to work. Except she didn't have any time at all. Louis and Gary were already at the house when they arrived, together with the people from the adoption agency. 'I set everything up while you were in the hospital,' Spector smiled. 'Merry Christmas.'

By the New Year, Ronnie had added weekly visits to Alcoholics Anonymous to her schedule, admitting that she originally attended as much to escape from the house, as for any benefits that the meetings themselves might provide. As time passed, however, she came to view the organisation not as a respite from her marriage, but as a means of escape. She had somehow convinced herself that, if she drank enough, her husband would eventually grow disgusted enough to simply throw her out. Regular AA meetings had now taught her that would never happen. The only way Ronnie was going to get out of the marriage was under her own steam. And, on 12 June 1972, she did that.

Three days earlier, after another argument, Spector had exiled Ronnie from the bedroom, sending her to sleep instead in the guest apartment where her mother, Beatrice, was now living. That night, while Ronnie was at AA, Spector drank his way through his own favourite tipple, a bottle of crème de menthe, then locked the entire house up tightly. When she returned at 10pm, it was her mother who quietly let her in through the kitchen door. Barely was she inside the house, however, than Spector appeared on the staircase, demanding to know where she'd been; and what could be so fascinating that she felt no compunction over ignoring her family for the sake of it. A boyfriend, perhaps?

He leaped at her; they struggled, Spector pinning her to the floor and screaming in her face. Frantically Beatrice Bennett leaped onto his back and began beating him, herself shrieking wildly; as he rose to face her, the two women grasped one another and fled through a doorway, Beatrice blocking Spector's way as he flew in pursuit. 'Take one more step and I'll tear that wig right off your skinny little head.'

Spector stopped moving, but his mouth continued working. In the court papers she filed days later, Ronnie related, '[he] came to my mother's room, told me I should get a lawyer to get a divorce'; in her autobiography *Be My Baby*, however, she paints a far more chilling picture of the events of that night. 'If that bitch tries to walk out on me, I'll have her killed the minute she steps outside the gates,' he snarled. 'I've already got her coffin. It's solid gold and it's got a glass top, so I can keep my eye on her after she's dead. I'll show it to you. It's right downstairs.'

The two women walked away and left him raving; the following morning, abandoning everything she owned – her pocketbook, her credit cards, her shoes, her son – Ronnie and Beatrice stole out of the house into the dawn…and then ran towards Wilshire Boulevard, and the law offices of Stein and Jaffe. It was Jay Stein who served Spector with the divorce papers a few days later. Spector responded by packing Ronnie an overnight bag of things she might need – three shirts, a pair of pants and a set of women's underwear that she had never seen before.

Stein booked her into the Beverly Crest hotel; he also arranged a restraining order to prevent Spector from approaching her. Unfortunately, the order did not extend to phone calls, nor to emissaries. Spector rang constantly and Ronnie quickly learned never to accept his calls. But she suspected nothing when George Brand showed up, accompanied by another man whom she assumed was one of Spector's lawyers.

Only when the stranger walked to the telephone, dialled a number and then handed the phone to Ronnie did she discover who he really was. Spector was on the other end of the phone, explaining first, that Brand's companion was a hit man; then, that if Ronnie didn't sign the contract he had with him, granting Spector complete custody of Louis and Gary, he'd already been paid to kill her. She signed and Gary later admitted, 'all I know about when she left is…when she left'. So far as he was concerned, George Brand's family – with whom all three children spent much of their time – offered far more of a home than their 'mother' ever did.

The divorce proceedings commenced that summer, with the court documents quickly providing a damning dossier of Spector's treatment of his wife. Ronnie's testimony included allegations of both physical and verbal intimidation and, when Spector's attorney, Jay Cooper, tried to turn her alcohol problems against her, she hit back with the insistence that drink was the only effective way 'to shut out his continuous stream of shrieking'.

Spector himself said little in court, preferring to display his contempt for the proceedings by toying with every order that the court handed down. When he was ordered to pay Ronnie's hotel bills, he made sure that the payments were as late as possible. When she was granted visitation rights with Donté, he gnawed away at her allotted time. And, when the court determined that she was entitled to temporary support for $1,200 a month, he despatched a Brinks armoured car to her lawyers' offices to make the first payment in nickels – 24,000 five cent pieces.

The phone calls never ceased. In court, Ronnie supplied several of the hotel's operators to testify that Spector threatened them when they refused to patch his calls through to her room. He trailed Stein's car as the lawyer drove Ronnie away from the court house every evening, yet there were other times when he seemed so pathetic, so heartbroken, that she could almost believe that she really was the guilty party, punishing him for misdeeds that he wasn't even aware of. On one occasion, she wrote, he looked like nothing so much as 'a sad-eyed dog that had been kicked once too often'. On another, he pursued her from the courthouse, begging 'Veronica! Don't leave me! Don't do this to me.' He sounded, she said, 'like some kind of human fire siren'.

But when Spector had warned her, long before, that she would never be able to survive a divorce without going nuts, he knew what he was talking about. And, when Beatrice announced, after three months of daily trips to the court house, that she was returning to New York to visit Ronnie's sister Estelle and her newly born daughter...Beatrice's first grand-daughter...it was as if Spector instinctively knew that that moment had arrived.

Beatrice's plane had been airborne for just two hours when the phone in Ronnie's hotel room rang. Shattered by the departure of the one person she was convinced she could rely upon, Ronnie answered. It was Spector, and he knew precisely what to say. As far as Ronnie was concerned, her own mother had just deserted her. Now Spector was accusing her of doing the self-same thing to her own children.

She hung up the phone, poured a glass of vodka and lit a Marlboro. The next thing she knew, she was lying in a hospital bed, after being pulled from a fiercely blazing hotel room. Drunk, she had fallen asleep with her cigarette still burning.

Jay Stein had already spoken to Beatrice; Ronnie was to be placed on the first plane to New York. The lawyers would handle the divorce from hereon in, and so they did. Although the court action would drag on until February 1974; and though the final divorce settlement was considerably less than Stein and Jaffe had hoped for ($50,000 in community property, and monthly payments of $2,500 for three years); finally Ronnie was free.

The on-going divorce was not the only trauma Spector underwent as the early–mid 1970s drifted past. On 20 July 1973, his friend Bruce Lee, the martial arts expert, died while shooting his latest movie, *Game Of Death*. Spector was devastated. Lee had spent some months living at Collina Drive, training with Spector's bodyguard of the time, Mike Stone; Spector, in turn, had helped raise financing for what was to become Lee's breakout movie, *Enter The Dragon*.

Now he was gone, and Spector was convinced that the official explanation, a brain edema brought on by an allergic reaction to an analgesic he was taking, covered up a rat's nest of darker happenstance. Everywhere fans gathered to discuss Lee's untimely passing, whispered rumours of conspiracy abounded and, just as Lenny Bruce's death had convinced Spector to erect ever greater security measures around his home, so Lee's passing, too, persuaded him that no celebrity was truly safe, unless he himself made certain of it. The workmen were back at the mansion that summer.

Neither had Spector been able to settle to any worthwhile work. By October 1973, he had scarcely seen the inside of a studio in close to 18 months. A brief reunion with Larry Levine saw him hack out a clutch of instrumental backing tracks, but he had no idea what he intended doing with them, and no singer in mind to voice them. He was, simply, killing time. That month, however, he received a surprise phone call. John Lennon was in Los Angeles and he was looking for a good time. That good time would eventually last for close to two years, and pass into history as Lennon's Long Weekend. On that same figurative timescale, Spector would only be around for the first few hours of that span. But the events that unfolded were to have repercussions that resounded long after Lennon's other activities were forgotten.

John Lennon's Lost Weekend, 18 months wildcatting through the bowels of showbiz sleaze, is one of *the* great tales of rock 'n' roll excess, indulged in by one of the greatest excesses in rock 'n' roll history. No matter that the most scintillating retelling is to be found within Albert Goldman's gruelling masterpiece of axe-grinding malice, *The Lives Of John Lennon*; nor, as countless subsequent biographies have it, that the entire escapade has since been reduced to a couple of paragraphs of Hard Love therapy, cunningly perpetrated by his briefly estranged wife Yoko. If the Lost Weekend had never existed, history would have had to invent one – and who better to enjoy it than Beatle John?

Lennon travelled light to LA, accompanied only by girlfriend May Pang and a couple of suitcases. He wasn't sure what he wanted to do, but he knew that this was where he wanted to do it, thousands of miles from New York and Yoko, in a city that styled itself the ultimate playground for the rich and famous. Lennon, of course, was both and the whole city, or at least that narrow band of Hollywood nightclubs where he'd be spending most of his time, was a spiritual pick-me-up that never let you down again. There, he could reinvent himself, by escaping from whatever else he'd become.

Lennon's latest album, *Mind Games*, was on the verge of release; his next, a tribute to the rock 'n' roll records he'd loved as a kid, was in the planning stages already. Both were a long way away from the albums he'd made in the past, but all Lennon needed to do was convince people that this latest change was an honest one, that he wasn't going to go back to bed or wrap his wife up in a bag anymore.

Spector was the obvious choice to produce the oldies album; indeed, Lennon told *Melody Maker*'s Chris Charlesworth, 'Phil and I have been threatening to do this for years. I want to go in and sing "ooh-eee-baby" type songs that are meaningless, for a change. Whenever I'm in the studio, between takes, I mess around with oldies. I even used to do it in The Beatles days, so now I'm finally getting around to doing a *John Lennon Sings The Oldies* album. I hope people won't think I've run out of ideas, but sod it. I just want to do it.'

Lennon had only been in town a few days when the pair met to discuss the project, and he had just one piece of advice for the producer. Don't treat him like a Beatle, don't treat him like an artist. 'I just wanna be Ronnie Ronette.' Spector would have carte blanche on the sessions – aside from the handful of songs that Lennon had already determined he would be singing,

Spector could choose the material, book the studio, hire the musicians, map the arrangements. Lennon would simply turn up and sing.

In 1980, reflecting upon the albums he'd made with Spector earlier in the decade, Lennon remarked, 'if you play [them] and you play [his own] work, you see there's a vast difference. We never gave him his head, we didn't let him go free on it. We used his amazing ear for pop music and sound without it becoming "Spector". You know, thousands of castanets.' This time around, however, that's all he wanted. Thousands and thousands of castanets.

The *Rock 'n' Roll* album was born of various influences but, perhaps most pressing of them all was Lennon's need to discharge a legal obligation that had been dogging him for the past three years. Writing 'Come Together' for The Beatles' *Abbey Road*, he had lifted lyrics from Chuck Berry's 'You Can't Catch Me', a blatant tribute that the song's publisher, Maurice Levy, was swift to pick up on. Legal action was threatened, but the pair finally reached what seemed a most amicable settlement. Lennon would record and release three songs whose publishing rights were also owned by Levy: 'Angel Baby', 'Ya Ya' and 'You Can't Catch Me' itself.

He made a similar deal with Spector. For all his recent problems, Spector was unsure about returning to the studio with Lennon, even after John promised him total control. When the talk turned to songs, however, three more were instantly taken care of – Lennon would turn in covers of 'Be My Baby' and (a suitably reworded) 'To Know Her Is To Love Her', together with a new Lennon/Spector co-write, the reflective 'Here We Go Again'.

Spector booked the sessions into A&M's Studio A on La Brea, and set about gathering the cream of local musicianship to his side. When Lennon and May Pang arrived at the first day's recording, they were astonished to count no less than 28 musicians filing in around them, old-time Spector veterans like Leon Russell, Hal Blaine, Jeff Barry, Nino Tempo, Dr John and Barney Kessel and his sons David and Danny; new faces like Steve Cropper, José Feliciano and Jesse Ed Davis. If there was an instrument worth recording, Spector had found someone to play it. And if it was *really* worth recording, he'd found two people. Hal Blaine recalled, 'a new Wall of Sound was assembled at A&M. We were in the big studio and the lot was buzzing.'

When Harry Nilsson arrived in LA a few days later, he found himself touring every club and bar in town looking for a single face that he recognised. 'And there was nobody there. I started studio hopping in case there was somebody around who was alive, and the last stop on the list was

A&M. I saw this guy I knew; I said "what are you working on?"; he said "John and Phil" – Lennon and Spector. So I said "where are they?"; he said "in that room", and there was every friend I'd ever had in that room.'

Most of the time, said Nilsson, everybody just sat around waiting. Work did get done, of course, but 'work' for Spector meant making certain that every individual player's sound was correct, before he called for the one take that would nail the song down. And that process could take hours. Surreptitiously at first, but with ever-increasing abandon as the sessions dragged on, the idle musicians began seeking out ever new and exciting diversions, to keep themselves busy while they awaited their turn.

Taking their lead from Spector and Lennon, both of whom were seldom more than a few paces away from a bottle (Lennon was mixing Courvoisier and Remy Martin; Spector remained on the crème de menthe), the sessions swiftly degenerated into a showbiz party, with a stream of guests constantly dropping by to add their own magic to the mixture.

Spector himself was not averse to some tomfoolery. In keeping with his own interpretation of the on-going party, he took to arriving at the studio in virtual fancy dress. One day he was a karate instructor, another time a doctor. Nilsson remembered arriving there one evening and being struck by the sight of a cowboy in full western regalia standing where Spector normally prowled, and waving a pistol above his head. 'It took a moment before I realised it was Phil. And the pistol *was* loaded.'

'We could have gotten into a lot of serious trouble,' Spector smiled, years later. 'Harry Nilsson...I loved him dearly, but there were a lot of drugs going down. I mean, we'd be in a convenience store, a 7-Eleven or whatever, and Harry would say, "Let's try to stick it up, just to see what happens." "What? Are you fucking crazy?" Coke makes you do those kinds of things. We could have gotten killed.'

There were other incidents. One rumour saw Spector being ejected from a Bobby Bland show at the Whisky A Go Go, after spending the entire evening screaming abuse at the opening Dixie Hummingbirds; another found him turning up at the Record Plant West to berate Stevie Wonder for hijacking an engineer that Spector himself wanted, heightening the dramatic effect for the gathered onlookers by pulling a gun on Wonder as he did so.

Mostly, however, Spector's attention was solely one-dimensional. Occasionally, he grew impatient with the activity around him – one night, he was so exasperated with Lennon's behaviour that he had someone tie him to a chair. 'John told me about it,' Nilsson laughed. 'He managed to squeeze out of the chair and dialled a friend who came to get him through a window.'

But, as the evenings wore on and the moods grew looser, Spector found himself spending as much time shooing revellers away from the equipment as he did manipulating it himself. The gun that had hitherto been merely a part of his costume now began appearing more regularly, lying on the control desk within an easy arm's reach. He never intended using it, but the mere sight of it was often sufficient to deter the latest batch of would-be boarders.

Larry Levine, engineering the sessions, was equally nervous. 'I know that Phil would never hurt anyone on purpose,' he said during 2003. 'But there was always the chance of an accident and, when a guy's been drinking, his reflexes are not as sharp. So it always frightened me whenever I would see that –[not] from the standpoint, as I said, of him being angry enough to shoot someone, but just the fact that the game he was playing was too dangerous.'

Nevertheless, the sessions were getting completely out of hand. Every day when Spector arrived at the A&M lot, he would be greeted by another battery of complaints from the studio manager – rooms were damaged, equipment was broken. Someone had filled the mixing desk with alcohol. The hallways and elevators were littered with piss and shit. Each time, Spector issued another reassurance that it would never happen again, that he would find out who was responsible and make sure they paid for the damage – and, each time, his attempts to smoke out the perpetrators ended in failure. Finally, A&M cracked. Spector was told to take his circus somewhere else.

In later years, as the story of the sessions was transmuted into rock 'n' roll legend, the occasional participant would step forward to acknowledge that Spector was the last person who should have been blamed for the carnage. Much of the damage was done by people he'd never seen before, friends of a friend of a friend of one of the musicians, who'd heard there were wild times to be had, and set about having them in Studio A. Had he only voiced his own complaints to the powers that mattered at A&M – label head Herb Alpert, for example – he might at least have gained a stay of execution; might even have been granted a few extra studio security men.

Spector, however, remained silent. He had booked the session, he was in charge of it. If anything good came out of the proceedings, he would be the one who took the credit; it only followed, therefore, that if anything bad emerged, he must take the blame. Dutifully, he packed up his equipment and relocated the sessions to the Record Plant West.

For a day or so, it seemed as though the change of venue might have shaken the party-goers off the trail. Soon enough, though, they were back; soon enough, too, Spector had his gun out once again. 'It was the first time in my life that I ever felt sorry for a producer,' Dr John told Albert Goldman. 'There was nothin' that Spector could do.' Some nights, Spector would try and ration Lennon's drinking, only to discover that Lennon had already got tanked on the way to the studio and had more booze stashed somewhere else in the building. Other nights, he would delegate someone to keep an eye on the singer, at which point Lennon would refuse to even open his mouth. 'The cat wouldn't cut till he had his taste,' Dr John continued. 'But when he had his taste, he *couldn't* cut.'

Prior to recording what would ultimately emerge a beautiful version of Lloyd Price's 'Just Because', a song Lennon insisted he only tackled because Spector had asked him to, the pair worked out a spoken-word passage that would fit cosily over the instrumental mid-section. Standing at the microphone, however, a drunken Lennon launched off in another direction entirely. 'I want to take all the new singers, Carole and that other one, Nipples, I wanna take them and hold them tight, all them people that James Taylor had...I wanna suck their nipples.' And the only warning he gave Spector was an innocent request at the beginning of the take, 'You don't mind if I change the lyrics, then?' Spector smiled indulgently at the end of the passage, and vowed to try again another time.

On another occasion, an unfinished version of the old Ronettes classic 'Be My Baby', lacking backing vocals and the final mix-down punch that characterise the (ultimately) released take, finds Lennon unleashing both an absurd cod falsetto and his sexiest teen idol coaxing...which in turn degenerates into the amped-up howlings of a frustrated teenager.

Outside of the studio, too, Lennon behaved like a spoiled child. One night, Spector is said to have invited him to stay over at the mansion, then found himself forced to lock the singer in the bedroom, after an evening of drinking transformed Lennon into a rampaging violent slob. Another night, after Lennon took up residence in producer Lou Adler's house, the singer supposedly worked himself into such a state that Spector and George Brand wound up tying him to a bed frame, the only thing they could think of that might calm him down. They were wrong. No sooner were their backs turned than Lennon broke free and stormed through the house, demolishing his host's furniture, smashing the gold records that lined the home's walls and tearing a chandelier from the ceiling. And the next day, when he turned up at the studio – on time as always – he didn't remember a thing.

Back at the Record Plant Spector tried rewarding Lennon for good behaviour. 'He won't let me do "Be Bop A Lula"', the singer moaned to anyone who would listen. Spector, who was still trying to complete another song entirely, leaned forward. 'I won't let you do anything till you get this. Then you can do "Be Bop A Lula".'

'And "Send Me Some Loving"?'

'You can do anything you wanna do, Johnny.'

'After this?'

'Yes, after this. You can even do "Johnny B Goode"…and I wish you would.'

He would continue wishing. Every moment that they spent in the Record Plant, another temper would fray, another slight would be thrown, another instrument would be broken. During one particularly fraught take of 'Angel Baby', with Spector already wrestling with the problem of an especially noisome bird that had taken up residence outside the studio window, Lennon suddenly erupted with a furious 'shut up, you fucking…' – aimed at Spector, not the bird. Then, when Spector admonished him for continuing his count-in after the band started playing, Lennon's muttered 'no wonder Ronnie…' drew first silence, and then a strained laugh.

Finally, Spector had had enough. He sat and took the best that Lennon could throw at him, and the worst that the hangers-on could unleash. But his patience was now exhausted. Something was said, or done or implied, and *that was it*. He drew his gun, raised it above his head and fired.

The report was deafening, shocked the room to silence and left Lennon clutching his ears in pain. It was minutes before the singer was finally able to speak, and try to defuse the situation with at least a flash of wit: 'Listen Phil, if you're goin' to kill me, kill me. But don't fuck with me ears. I need 'em.'

Spector was unsympathetic. Even at the outset of the session, he had sensed that no lasting good would come from rekindling his partnership with Lennon; that, no less than The Beatles situation, he was being called in for salvage, not a celebration. Lennon was in a bad way, adrift from both Yoko and his own once-inviolate critical and commercial bases, and deeply troubled by their absence. Yes, the *Rock 'n' Roll* album was a sound concept – both Bryan Ferry and David Bowie, young bucks who long ago overtook Lennon in the critical estimation, had made similar gestures of their own in recent years. But it could also be regarded as a cheat, the last resort of the songwriter who had stopped writing songs, with the recruitment and surrendering of all power to Spector no less an admission of defeat than the track listing. You can hide an awful lot behind a wall of sound.

That Spector was willing to go along with the subterfuge was another matter entirely. Desperate to work on a project that would bring him back into the public eye, he had accepted the commission because he knew he could do it. But, with that knowledge came the awareness that he was being brought on board *not* to show what he could do, but to reiterate what he had already done. Just as Lennon had sang these same numbers years ago, so Spector had twiddled these same knobs. The musicians and the technology might have moved on but, when you came down to brass tacks, the songs remained the same.

Still Spector might have forgiven Lennon all of his excesses, but for one final incident. In late November 1973, Spector was called back to the court house for one more round with Ronnie, as they tried to thrash out the divorce settlement. It was Ronnie's first trip back to LA since she had fled to New York and she was dreading it. Spector, on the other hand, had all reason to feel confident. John Lennon had agreed to act as a character reference for him.

Unfortunately, Lennon saw little that would make him want to discharge that duty. The moment Ronnie entered the room, Spector lost all control, shouting and swearing at her. The judge called for order; Spector railed on. He was threatened with a charge of contempt, but did not even appear to hear it. Lennon, seated alongside him, tried to intervene and calm him down; Spector shrugged off his arm and continued his tirade. 'Phil wouldn't shut up until the bailiff physically dragged him out of the court room,' Ronnie wrote. 'John just watched the whole thing and shook his head. He glanced over to me and mouthed the words "Good luck".' Then he left the room.

Spector was mortified. After all he had put up with from Lennon over the past two months, this was how he was repaid. Lennon, of all people, knew how important Ronnie was to him; Lennon, of all people, knew how emotions can sometimes get the better of someone. Returning to the studio that evening, Spector picked up the master tapes that contained every note they'd recorded and drove home. The following day, when Lennon arrived at the studio, the room was empty. There was no Spector – which was a relief; but there were no tapes, either.

Occasionally, according to Albert Goldman, Spector would call Lennon to deliver news of some great calamity – 'the studio's burned down' or the like. There was another lengthy period of silence during which, Spector later claimed, he was working his way through a massive pile of tapes that he'd been entrusted by President Nixon – the Watergate scandal was breaking, and the tapes were the source of such breathless media speculation that there were even rumours of Warner Brothers releasing them commercially – with Spector in charge of editing and production. The producer finally broke cover to call Lennon and announce, 'the house is surrounded by helicopters. They're trying to get the tapes!'

For the most part, however, calls to the mansion went unanswered, or were picked up by strangers who could not disturb Mr Spector. Visitors to the mansion, too, were ignored or, again, sent on their way by whoever answered the door. Spector himself hadn't simply gone to ground. So far as Lennon was concerned, he had vanished off the face of the planet.

It would be another two months before he was finally given any explanation for Spector's disappearance. Calling the mansion one more time, in March 1974, Lennon was stunned to be informed that Spector was dead. He had been killed in an accident in his beloved Rolls-Royce, hurled through the windscreen after jamming on the breaks to avoid something in the road. Aside from multiple head, face and body injuries, he had also been seriously burned. Lennon didn't believe a word of it.

Over the next four months, both Lennon and Al Coury, Capitol Records' promo man, continued trying to prise the missing masters out of Spector. Lennon had little hope of success – 'those tapes are fucking gone,' he was to tell Coury. But Coury had other ideas. News of the car accident notwithstanding, Spector had been far from idle over the past few months, inking a deal with Warner Brothers Records that would see him take control of his own record label for the first time since the demise of Philles, almost a decade before.

Capitol now weighed into that arrangement, putting pressure on Warners to cough up the costs of the John Lennon sessions – a claim that Warners, naturally, disputed. A week later, on 14 June, a lorry load of 24-inch master tapes was delivered to Capitol, with only one condition attached to the return. Spector demanded $90,000 for the tapes, plus a 3 per cent royalty on every one of his tracks that was used on the finished LP. He was also retaining two of the recordings for his own undisclosed purposes.

Lennon's delight in retrieving the tapes was shortlived. 'Out of the eight [songs that we completed], there were only four or five that were worth using. The sessions had 28 guys playing live and a lot of them were out of tune, which is too much even for rock 'n' roll.' It would be another year, and a barrage of further problems, before *Rock 'n' Roll* finally reached the stores and Lennon laughed, 'I've never been so long on an album in my life. It [took even] longer than *Sgt Pepper*!'

He admitted, however, that the blame for the delay did not ultimately lie with Spector. Lennon averred, 'Phil was fantastic.' It was Lennon himself who 'got madder and madder [until] it ended up breaking down and falling apart.' It was Lennon, too, who would plunge into exile, and exist in mere rumour for much of the next four years. At the close of 'Just Because', 'Doctor Winston O'Boogie' bids 'farewell from the Record Plant West' and, in one of last interviews he would ever do, with *Rolling Stone* in November 1980, he admitted that he really was saying goodbye to the music industry.

13 'Nothing Frightens Me'

John Lennon's suspicions were misplaced. Phil Spector *was* involved in a car accident and, though he wasn't dead, he *was* seriously injured. Rushed to the UCLA Medical Center that night of 31 March 1974 (not 'on or around February 10', as a painfully confused report in *Rolling Stone* had it), he was so badly torn and broken that, had the Chief Casualty Officer not detected a faint but stubborn pulse, he might even have been labelled Dead On Arrival, and packed off to the morgue. As it was, the *New Musical Express* reported, Spector received 380 stitches in his face, 480 in the back of his head and the doctors still didn't expect him to pull through.

In fact he might not have, had he not struggled into consciousness long enough to hear one of the nurses telling Nino Tempo, the first of his friends to race to his bedside, that it looked as though Mr Spector was going to die. According to English journalist Roy Carr, Spector sprung upright at those words and uttered his first coherent sentence since he arrived at the hospital. 'Bullshit! Bull! Shit!'

Spector spent much of that first night in surgery; and the next three days on the critical list. But, when another magazine tried to investigate reports that Phil Spector was hanging between life and death, the reporter assigned to the task was unable to ferret out any but the scantiest details of the incident. So he ran instead with a speculation Spector was simply undergoing a hair transplant. After a decade of toupees, after all, it made sense that he would take advantage of this latest advance in male vanity treatment. Spector obviously enjoyed the story, as well. When he was finally discharged from hospital, his hair was sprayed a garish silver and gold.

The rumour mill span into overdrive. Though he scarcely left the house during the weeks he spent recuperating from the accident, curiosity in his activities was at an all-time high. Half-remembered incidents from years past suddenly resurfaced as current happenings, and fresh sightings of 'Crazy Phil' were literally dripping off the Hollywood grapevine. The entire city, it seemed, was on permanent look out for the metallic-topped, holster-bearing madman that the best of the legends now portrayed him to be. 'The thing that disturbs me,' Spector mused as he contemplated the mass of newsprint that he was still capable of generating, 'is that almost everything written about me is in the form of an obituary. People write about me as though I was dead. Hell knows where they get their facts!'

In his 1976 interview with the *New Musical Express*, he railed, 'it doesn't matter that I carry a gun, have bodyguards or live in a fortified mansion. When I go into a recording studio, I make Art and I changed rock 'n' roll into a form of Art. I gave it credence.' And, crucially, he was doing so again, as he devoted the weeks he was forced to spend healing himself to ensuring that his latest project, the Warner-Spector label, hit the ground running.

The creation of the label was a triumph for both Spector and for Mo Ostin, the Warners head who personally negotiated it. A long-time admirer of Spector, of course, Ostin was also absolutely nonplussed by the growing industry sense that Spector was somehow becoming untouchable.

The John Lennon *Rock 'n' Roll* album had yet to be released, but privately circulating tapes of the Spector sessions were themselves the talk of the town. According to one of so many rumours, Spector ran off a bunch of cassette tapes of Lennon's most drunken moments, for distribution among the musicians who witnessed them. Of course they circulated further than those corners, and the tapes did indeed show Lennon in belligerently incoherent light. But they also proved that Phil Spector was a long way from losing his magic touch – even when the entire world was tumbling into chaos around him.

In conversation, too, Ostin quickly learned that Spector was far from the deranged lunatic portrayed by the streetwise tittle-tattle. The giant crucifix that hung around his neck, he explained, was there for protection – he'd just seen the movie *The Exorcist*, and he wasn't afraid to admit, in common with a massive proportion of the rest of its audience, that it had scared him shitless. The hair colour was a little more outrageous, he admitted, but it detracted people's attention away from what his head really looked like – the network of scars and stitches that were the legacy of the motor accident. And the guns? In 1974, a little under half the households in America owned at least one gun, and half of them had probably shown it to people, waved it around, had some fun with their friends. If that made Spector a madman, at least he was in regular company.

He acknowledged that his behaviour might have seemed a little strange in the recent past, particularly in the high-rolling months around the *Rock 'n' Roll* sessions, when he, Lennon and Nilsson, and anyone else who tagged along, revelled in their celebrity on the Hollywood club circuit. But he was also adamant that 'it didn't take extraordinary strength for me to change the way I was. What I was doing just had to stop. It isn't hard to see that, especially after you've gone through a couple of windshields at high speeds.' He told writer and friend Harvey Kubernik, 'I have to admit that I did enjoy it to a certain extent – being rich, a millionaire in his mansion, and dressing up like Batman. But now I can see beyond that, and see just how unhealthy and unproductive it became. I'm ready for anything now. Nothing frightens me. I feel I can do more now than I could ever do before. I feel extremely ready musically. I'm more comfortable, more relaxed, more together. I understand what I want to do, and I'm going to do it. It's time to get serious again.'

His musical instincts were bubbling. He'd done his time at the top of the pile; now he wanted to return to what he was really good at, nurturing new talent, relaunching old and, in between times, restoring to circulation the very best of the music he had made in the past, which now exchanged hands for extortionate prices on the burgeoning oldies collectors market.

His business acumen remained as focused as ever. With his newly acquired manager Marty Machat at his side, Spector managed to thrash out a deal with Warners that was the envy of the entire industry, one that allowed him to produce all the records he wanted to, but only having to release the ones he saw fit to. It was real artistic freedom, and Spector intended taking every advantage of it.

Cher was to be his first subject. Although the former Philles backing singer was in no way struggling (her most recent single, 'Dark Lady', topped the American chart in March 1974), storm clouds were nevertheless gathering around her. Her divorce from Sonny Bono was making more headlines than her music ever had, and the couple's inevitable decision that they would no longer be able to continue working together had dealt a death blow to *The Sonny And Cher Comedy Hour*, the 60-minute TV variety show that they had co-presented since August, 1971. The final episode was screened in May 1974.

Spector's most recent encounter with Cher had not, apparently, been especially pretty. She was one of the myriad passers-by who dropped by the John Lennon sessions, although not necessarily to party. Rather, she appeared while Spector was putting the finishing touches to an old Holland, Dozier, Holland cover that Lennon had eyes for (and which Spector had previously cut with Ike and Tina Turner), 'A Love Like Yours (Don't Come Knocking Every Day)', and immediately began badgering Spector to allow her to voice it. He refused, growing angrier and angrier as she wheedled on, before Cher finally flounced away.

Now, however, he had reconsidered. Notwithstanding his conviction that Harry Nilsson was one of the prime architects of the Lennon's sessions' demise, Spector had a well-practised eye for a priceless pun, and 'Nilsonny And Cher' was simply too good to pass up. Contacting the singer, he arranged for him to duet with Cher on the eventually unused 'A Love Like Yours' backing track. Two further recordings followed, a deliciously slowed down version of 'Baby, I Love You', and a song Spector wrote with April Stevens and Nino Tempo, the so-darkly textured 'A Woman's Story' – the lament, he explained to anyone who asked, of a down-on-her-luck prostitute.

All three songs were destined to raise Cher's musical profile high above the somewhat lacklustre MOR she'd recently been tackling. The reading of 'Baby I Love You', in particular, was sensational, hauntedly delicate acoustic and slide guitars punctuated by a veritable heartbeat of a drum, and Cher's voice absolutely disembodied from all the innocence and exaltation of the song's original incarnation as Spector transformed one of his greatest teenage anthems into a declaration of adult emotion.

Yet neither of the singles Spector culled from the sessions moved off the shelves, as Cher's manager, David Geffen, exacted revenge for an incident that occurred between Spector and himself, during the session itself – and which ended, according to witnesses, with Spector physically decking the entrepreneur. According to Spector, Geffen 'pulled some strings' and had 'A Woman's Story' dropped by some of America's most important radio stations.

There would be battles, too, with Dion's manager, Zach Glickman, as Spector's vision of his next collaboration arose a vast, dark and almost brutal beast that Glickman (not without reason, as it transpired) was convinced would do absolutely nothing for his client. The fact that the album, *Born To Be With You*, has since become ranked among Spector's most resonant triumphs, and certainly stands among his most influential '70s recordings, would have been immaterial in 1974, when the only bottom line that mattered was instant success and gratification. Glickman was convinced that *Born To Be With You* was never going to provide either and Spector, enraged by the businessman's attitude, ultimately did his utmost to make sure that those fears came true.

Dion DiMucci is frequently described in rock history as another artist who entered the 1970s distinctly down on his luck, a relic of the late '50s doo-wop explosion who had clung on to a record deal despite so many subsequent changes in taste and fashion. In fact, he had already proven himself a master of reinvention, first overcoming the departure of his famed backing group, The Belmonts, to score another three years of hits; then by re-emerging from four years in the wilderness with the 1968 smash hit 'Abraham, Martin and John'.

Since that time, he had scored with a distinctly personalised reinvention of Jimi Hendrix's 'Purple Haze', and his own confessional 'Your Own Back Yard', and while the early 1970s had seen the chart positions ebb away, still Dion could be ranked among his era's greatest survivors – a tag with which Spector could certainly identify. Indeed, he and Dion were practically contemporaries; not only did they both score their first hits in 1958, but they were born just a year, and a few miles, apart in the Bronx.

Still, Dion could not help but be stunned by his own first meeting with Spector, after arriving at the mansion to begin discussing the record. Ushered into the room where Spector awaited, he found it lit by just one light bulb, while his host lurked in the shadows, circling the singer and spilling out a virtual stream-of-consciousness babble that, only later, resolved itself into one of the song lyrics that Dion would be singing on the album: 'only you know what you have been through, only you know where you have been to...and I'm gonna be there, too.' He meant it, as well. 'Despite [our] similar backgrounds,' Spector wrote in the finished album's sleeve notes, '[we] never really knew each other until we worked on this album. [But] today, in the truest sense of the word, Dion is a brother...'

Just as he had with the John Lennon sessions, Spector intended pulling out all the stops for the Dion album, both old and new. Returning to his old stomping grounds at Gold Star's studio A, and recalling Stan Ross to the mixing desk for the first time since they recorded the Paris Sisters together in 1962, Spector then set about compiling a line-up that made the 28-strong Lennon outfit look like a slimline scratch band. No fewer than 40 players were assembled to accompany Dion: a dozen guitarists, seven percussionists, five pianists were drawn from as far around his own career as he could reach. Hal Blaine, Jim Keltner, Klaus Voorman, Jesse Ed Davis, Jeff Barry, Nino Tempo all played on the record; Cher and Sonny dropped by (separately) to visit Spector and Dion; and, watching awestricken from the control room, a pair of East Coast musicians who'd dropped into Los Angeles on the crest of their own wave, Bruce Springsteen and Miami Van Zandt.

Journalist Robert Hilburn brought them to the studio, aware that the New Jersey songsmith and his own producer, Jon Landau, were so deeply in thrall to the Wall of Sound that even Spector would not resist quipping, 'if you wanted to steal my sound, you should have got me to do it'. There were no hard feelings, though; instead, Spector set about showing the upstart how it was done, before inviting Springsteen to leap into action for the recording of Spector's latest Jeff Barry co-write 'Baby, Let's Stick Together'.

That song would emerge one of the most viscerally powerful performances of the entire session. A full-blown return to the thunderclaps of old was built around a drum sound that moved mountains, while the echo that drapes Dion's vocal is almost heart-rending. Which might explain why Spector ultimately decided to cut the song from the finished album. Its thoroughbred party-time punch was absolutely out of place alongside the remainder of the record, and 'Baby, Let's Stick Together' was ultimately released only as a blink-and-you'll-miss-it UK single during 1976.

Compared with some of Spector's other 1970s sessions, the Dion recordings passed by with very little untoward excitement. Indeed, Dion's own strongest memory of the period appears to be the absolute nightmare Spector endured after George Brand suffered a heart attack in the studio. The entire session halted as Brand was raced to the hospital – there, Spector produced a bag stuffed with cash, slapped it onto a desk and demanded the best treatment that the hospital could provide. (Following his heart attack, Brand retired as Spector's bodyguard. His replacement was a former LAPD detective-sergeant, Jay Romaine.)

Born To Be With You wasn't simply a fabulously crafted album, it was also a powerfully reactive one. The previous year, Dave Edmunds scored a massive British hit with his own version of the Don Robertson-composed title track, enacted to the Welsh multi-instrumentalist's own absolutely note-perfect recreation of the Wall of Sound – one that made Landau and Springsteen's attempts look positively anaemic by comparison.

Torn between admiration and disdain at Edmunds' accomplishment, Spector accepted his 'Born To Be With You' as a benchmark, then set himself the task of hurtling over it. Backwards. Where Edmunds translated the song into an ode to joy, Spector recast it as a veritable dirge, slowed down even in comparison with Cher's 'Baby I Love You' (not at all coincidentally, another song that Edmunds had handled) and bristling with a despondency that would set the stage for the entire album.

Seven songs were completed, including dramatic retreads of Barry Mann and Cynthia Weil's 'Make The Woman Love Me', two Gerry Goffin/Spector compositions, 'Only You Know' and 'In And Out Of Shadows', and a couple of Spector/Dion collaborations, 'Good Lovin' Man' and 'He's Got The Whole World In His Hands', And the darkness didn't lift once.

The inclusion of the five-year-old 'Your Own Backyard' (one of two non-Spector productions featured on the finished album) added to the aura of introspective gloom that permeated the music, and that is where Zach Glickman stepped in, demanding that Spector surrender the finished tapes to him – presumably in the hope that some joy might be salvaged from the sound. Spector, of course, refused.

Dion shared his manager's reservations with the sessions, both at the time and a quarter of a century on, when he was asked to comment upon the album's most recent reissue. 'I don't think we ever really finished that,' he told the *Daily Telegraph*'s Tom Cox. 'It kind of majored on the minors. A lot of the focus went on the showbusiness thing and not enough went on the music.' It shocked him to discover that names as far apart as Bobby Gillespie, Jason Pierce and Pete Townshend have pronounced *Born To Be With You* one of the finest albums ever made; and it disturbed him that a record he did not even consider finished should be rated so far above music that he poured his life and soul into.

'I know how it works – there has to be a captain. Phil and I did have a few conversations, though. We didn't exactly fall out. But, when we were recording "Born to Be with You" [itself], Phil said, "Get out there and run something, we'll see what we can do." I ran through it, and he kept it – as the final version! I said, "Phil, I was just doing a sketch".'

On another occasion, Dion explained, 'Working with Phil Spector could be exciting, frustrating, even a little sad at times. He's a real artist and one who liked to surround himself with a spectacle, but it seemed to me that he was afraid of failure. He's got the image of a genius and that puts a lot of pressure on him, always trying to outdo his last masterpiece.' To which Spector could only respond, wasn't that what he was hired to do? If all these people wanted was the same old same-old, they should have gone to Landau or Edmunds. Instead, they came to him. And he gave them what they wanted.

Still, if they didn't like it... Spector sprang into action. He'd recently arranged for Dion to appear on *American Bandstand*, the top-rated music programme on American television, to promote the album's first single, 'Make The Woman Love Me'. One call to the show's host, Dick Clark, took that opportunity out of the equation.

Next, taking advantage of that most treasured clause in the Warner Brothers contract, that the label would only release the records that Spector wanted them to put out, he withdrew *Born To Be With You* from the schedule. The album would not see release for close to another year, by which time Spector and Marty Machat had poked another hole into their relationship with Warners, and worked out a new deal with the UK label Polydor. Henceforth, a new label, Phil Spector International Records, would feed Britain's own on-going love of the Wall of Sound, and would reward that country for its loyalty with an exclusive release for *Born To Be With You*. There would be no American appearance whatsoever for the album.

An oft-times seemingly interminable delay accompanied Spector's next collaboration as well, a reunion with Darlene Love that Love herself knew nothing about until it was too late. She had recently signed with Gamble and Huff, the architects behind the Philadelphia soul sound that so dominated the charts of the early 1970s. Deep within the contract, however, a clause gave their Philadelphia International label the right to sell on her contract should another producer or company make a reasonable offer for it. Love had not paid much attention to the clause; nor would she have, had Gamble and Huff not acted upon it in early 1974. They sold her back to Phil Spector.

Spector didn't, initially, act upon his coup. Eventually, however, Love was recalled to sing backing on the Cher and Dion projects and, soon after, was recruited to work on material for a movie project he was involved in, director Taylor Hackford's aptly-titled rock 'n' roll Svengali epic *The Idolmaker*.

Little came of it – Spector didn't like the songs the movie backers intended to use; they, in turn, were underwhelmed by the amount of time he spent getting back to them. Finally, he was dismissed from the project (Jeff Barry replaced him, and the movie went on to be nominated for a Golden Globe Best Musical) and he turned his attention towards a Darlene Love single.

Composed by Barry Mann and Cynthia Weil, 'Lord If You're A Woman' was intended as the first step towards a full Love album. Unfortunately, it was not to be. Love herself was seven months pregnant at the time, and Spector, she remembered, seemed more interested in entertaining the various guests who dropped by the studio, Cher and John Lennon among them, than in Love's own performance. When the session wrapped up a couple of hours later, there was no discussion of a return date; in fact, the single itself would not see the daylight for another three years.

So far, then, Warner-Spector had proved little more than a holding operation, allowing Spector to find his way back into the musical mainstream (as opposed to a Beatle-oid backwater) without putting much more than his time and expertise at stake. To confirm what a few media observers were already describing as his 'comeback', however, he needed more than a succession of golden oldies.

North Carolina country singer-songwriter Danny Potter had already been recruited to the label (as its third signing, after Cher and Dion); although his sole single, 'Standing In The Sunshine', was produced by Harry Hindel. The label's first releases of 1975, therefore, were to debut brand new talent on the Warner-Spector label, singer Jerri Bo Keno and the disco band Calhoon.

Originally from Long Island, Calhoon relocated to Fort Lauderdale in 1974, when they were offered a spot as house band at the disco Rumbottoms. From all accounts, Spector himself had little interest in the band's admittedly generic disco recordings, simply setting up the studio and then handing the production credits to engineer Walt Kahn, the local DJ who first brought the group to his attention. Neither of the band's singles sold very much, and Calhoon quietly disappeared back to whence they came from.

Jerri Bo Keno attracted more attention, both from Spector and the public at large. A New Yorker, she had been working the local disco scene for a year or so before signing with Spector, and was the recipient of one of the most remarkable records Spector ever made, a full-blooded Wall of Sound symphony that clicked with a demonic disco rhythm. 'Here It Comes (And Here I Go)', written by Spector and Jeff Barry, was a sadly apt title, however. Though the single was selected to launch the UK Phil Spector International label that spring, 1975, it was utterly overwhelmed by the clutch of reissued oldies with which the label hit the stores that same day, and Jerri Bo would never be heard of again.

Spector's next recruit was one of his most surprising. Mark Stein was the former frontman with Vanilla Fudge, the leviathan American heavy rock band whose attempts to clash pop sensibilities with classical orchestration led to, depending upon one's tastes, some of the most exhilarating, or ponderous, recordings of the entire progressive rock boom. The Fudge had long since broken up and Stein had remained more or less out of sight for some five years by this time.

His reappearance under Spector's aegis was not likely to alter that scenario. Released only in the UK, Stein's alarmingly bombastic version of 'The Long And Winding Road' had been recorded a full three years before with producer Shel Talmy at the helm, and it sank without trace. To anybody keeping track of either the Warner-Spector or Phil Spector International labels' output, the comeback was rapidly developing into a calamity.

A reissue for an album of smooth instrumentals by Barney Kessel, 1966s *On Fire* was utterly unremarkable, while the attractive proposition of pairing Spector with LA scenester Kim Fowley, 'Give It To Me', was, according to Fowley himself, shattered when Spector simply walked out of the studio, having first locked the doors and set off the fire alarm. By early 1976, he had abandoned both Warner-Spector and Phil Spector International in much the same way. In July, Spector hauled a clutch of archived Philles-era recordings out of the vault in the form of the rarities collection *Rare Masters*; by early 1977, Warner-Spector had folded. Phil Spector International would follow soon after.

Spector's own attention to detail was not helped by the tragedies that seemed to be piling up around him. In the course of just six weeks in the spring of 1975, two of his closest friends, DJ Tom Donahue and writer Ralph Gleason passed away. Could anybody really be surprised if his record label was suffering?

All the same, he remained capable of pulling off the occasional master-stroke. In February 1976, Spector shocked a lot of people by agreeing to an interview with journalist Roy Carr, of the weekly *New Musical Express*. Carr was involved in the first preparatory stages of a proposed movie of Spector's life and, spread over two issues (three weeks apart) of the paper, the piece was a masterpiece, from both men's point of view. Spector even agreed to pose for the *NME*'s cover photograph, wire-haired and wart-hog moustached, staring through the side window of the Roller, and the muzzle of a handgun as unwavering as his eyes.

Spector gave an absolutely virtuoso performance for the Englishman's microphone. He knew what was expected from him, and he had no intention of disappointing anyone.

According to Carr, they were in mid-conversation when Spector suddenly rose and left the room. When he returned, he was stripped to the waist, and playing an accordion. On another occasion, as talk veered towards the new generation of producers for whom nothing but the kitchen sink was good enough, Spector announced he intended challenging 'those six record producers who think they're the best' to a contest – 'and I'll show them who really *is* the best…the greatest.'

Richard Wagner lived in his mind, he explained, and he reflected on his involvement with The Beatles by remarking, 'there wasn't a day, an hour, a moment when they were in the recording studio…that I didn't influence The Beatles, that I didn't work for them, that I didn't aid them, love them and give my all to them.' The insinuation that, long before *Let It Be*, it was he, and not George Martin, who nursed The Beatles into prominence was obvious, and Spector clearly enjoyed milking Carr's disbelief. 'When someone gave Phil Spector the job of making four stars out of one group, he did it. But let's leave [The Beatles production credits as they are]. We certainly don't want to change the record or shatter any illusions, do we?'

Yet amid the fanciful anecdotes and brutal *braggadocio*, Spector opened up in ways that utterly twisted the popular perception of the man. He spoke bitterly of the deaths that had assailed him, and hinted at the blame that was still to be apportioned.

He discussed his renowned preoccupation of guns, and calmly pointed out the occasions, in the last few years, in the same American city, that other so-called celebrities might have been glad to have had a firearm to hand – the abduction of heiress Patti Hearst, the Mansonite slaying of actress Sharon Tate, and so forth: 'it's better to have a gun and not need one, than to need a gun and not have one'. Neither were these the ramblings of a paranoiac. Celebrities were becoming more vulnerable – in late 1976 in Jamaica, Bob Marley only narrowly escaped death after armed intruders broke into his home; in 1977 in London, Sex Pistol Johnny Rotten was deliberately targeted by a gang of razor-toting thugs and in 1980 in New York City, John Lennon was murdered by a demented fan. No one can say if things might have turned out differently if Lennon or the watching Yoko had been armed. But they could scarcely have turned out worse.

Spector held forth on the popular perception of his lifestyle, and revealed that it meant nothing to him. 'If people think I'm crazy, perhaps it's better that way. I don't really care anymore.' And he explained what he did when he wasn't being a record producer – raising three young (and, as Carr pointed out, 'dearly loved') children, a full-time occupation that son Gary recalled in a posting on the Spectropop website in January 2000: 'he had a family that cared about him, and wanted him to be part of their lives'. That feeling, Spector assured Carr, was very much a mutual one. The only subject Spector didn't elaborate on was his own future plans. But they, too, were in hand.

Among manager Marty Machat's other clients was the Canadian singer-songwriter Leonard Cohen, widely regarded as being among the few people in the music industry who could (and did) give Spector a run for his money in the reclusive stakes.

Close to three years had passed since Cohen's last album, *New Skin For Old Ceremony*, but the bard was finally keen to get back to work. He was also interested in breaking out of the folky cult confines in which he had hitherto dwelt, in an attempt to embrace a wider audience. Whether or not Phil Spector was the person with whom he could make that attempt appears not to have crossed anybody's mind. Machat and his wife Ariel arranged a meeting, and the pair, Spector and Cohen, appeared in full agreement of at least two things. They both wanted to make a record, and both liked a drink.

The pair had, in fact, already met once before, back in 1974 during Cohen's two-night residency at the LA Troubadour. Machat brought Spector along to watch and, straight after the second show, Spector announced an informal reception for the singer back at the mansion. Now Cohen was back in town, this time for a longer stay, and Machat quickly put the pair in touch.

Cohen detailed the genesis of the project. '[It] was a very curious time in my life because I was at a very low point, my family was breaking up. I was living in Los Angeles which was a foreign city to me, and I'd lost control, as I say, of my family, of my work, and my life. It was a very, very dark period.'

Their first meeting did not, initially, promise to dispel that darkness. In 1978, Cohen told *Rolling Stone*, 'Our mutual lawyer brought me over to Phil's house one evening, and it was tedious. It really was too dreary inside that dark, cold house in Hollywood.' So what if the house was always alive with voices, from the servants to the bodyguards and, of course, the children? Spector himself spent much of his time simply drifting around alone – which meant, when he did have visitors, he would do everything in his power to keep them there, simply for the company. Unfortunately, those visitors rarely saw it the same way. When Cohen eventually asked to be allowed out, Spector flatly refused.

Joey Ramone, a later visitor to the mansion, knew how he felt. 'When you went there, you were there; you can't get out until he's ready to let you out, and he's never ready. He didn't have company too often and I guess he likes to keep you around. You'd say 'well, Phil, it's time for us to go now,' and he'd disappear. Then he'd come back and he'd want to show you his terrarium, or some of the hideous-looking things he had in there.'

Cohen certainly felt trapped. Finally, he turned to Spector and told him, 'rather than watch you shout at your servants, let's do something more interesting'. He suggested they try writing a song together, sitting down at the piano to see what might come out – and once they began playing, the entire timbre of the evening altered. They started out hammering through an ad-hoc rearrangement of Patti Page's 'I Went To Your Wedding'; and, by the following morning, they had two wholly new songs complete.

Over the next three weeks, the pair wrote no less than 15 songs together, Cohen providing the lyrics, Spector setting them to music, and both of them growing drunker by the minute. Following the album's release, long-time Cohen fans would complain of the almost boozy sexuality of the songs, the lyrics' attention to the most intimate of carnal details and the brutal voyeurism that replaced Cohen's traditionally lighter touch – as if the man who once rhymed 'four poster bed' with 'giving me head' was any stranger whatsoever to explicitness.

Cohen, however, was unbowed by such criticisms – he later described those same lyrics among his own personal favourites, while the writing process itself was 'refreshing'; even 'fun'. He grew accustomed to Spector's habit of changing his clothes three or four times a day; he even got used to the fact that Spector always carried a gun, and admired the eye for detail that ensured the weapon always matched the outfit of the moment.

More disconcerting was Spector's latest trick, stripping and reassembling a firearm with military speed and precision. Sometimes he would time himself with cold deliberation; other times, he seemed almost distracted, ripping and rebuilding the weapon with the casual attention other people pay to drumming on the table with their fingertips. Anybody in the room at the same time would be tensing themselves for the surely inevitable accident, one eye on the gun, the other on the nearest convenient bolthole.

Cohen continued, 'I was flipped out at the time and he certainly was flipped out. My "flipped out" was...withdrawal and melancholy, and his was megalomania and insanity, and the kind of devotion to armaments, to weapons that was really intolerable. With Phil, especially in the state that he found himself – which was post-Wagnerian, I would say Hitlerian – the atmosphere was one of guns. I mean, that's really what was going on, guns. The music was subsidiary, an enterprise. People were armed to the teeth, all his friends, his bodyguards, and everybody was drunk, or intoxicated on other items, so you were slipping over bullets, and you were biting into revolvers in your hamburger. There were guns everywhere.'

His unease shifted up a notch once the sessions relocated to Gold Star studios. 'It was clear that he was an eccentric,' Cohen reflected, 'but I didn't know that he was mad. Phil was beyond control.'

Once again, Spector surrounded himself with the musicians and staff he knew best – the Kessels, Jesse Ed Davis, Hal Blaine, Jim Keltner, Nino Tempo, engineers Larry Levine and Stan Ross – and those that they recommended to him. But the mood seemed grim from the outset, a cloud of ill temper that settled over everybody in the room, and ensured that everyone would feel Spector's wrath at some point or another. One particular incident, however, remained in Cohen's mind long after.

They were recording 'Fingerprints' at the time, and fiddle player Bobby Bruce was adding his part when Spector suddenly barked for him to stop playing, tore into a vitriolic condemnation of the way Bruce was playing, then walked into the studio and drew his gun. Cohen recalled, 'now, [Bruce] was a country boy, and he knew a lot about guns. He just put his fiddle in his case and walked out. That was the last we'd see of him.' It was also the end of the session. The other musicians were so shaken that not one of them wanted to spend another minute in the room with Spector in that mood.

Spector demanded perfection from the musicians, but also spontaneity. At one session, having driven the band for hours through their parts, he gathered them together for the final take – and snatched away their charts. If they didn't know it by now, he told them, they'd never learn it. Another number, the nine-minute 'Death Of A Ladies Man', was recorded at 2.30am, again after hours of exhausting rehearsal. 'Working with Phil,' Cohen said, 'I've found that some of his musical treatments are very...er...*foreign* to me. I mean, I've rarely worked in a live room that contains 25 musicians, including two drummers, three bassists, and *six* guitars.'

Such vast orchestrations had their place, however. Listening to the performances as the tapes mounted up, there were moments where the sessions seemed destined to fulfill all of Marty and Ariel Machat's dreams of opening Cohen to a wider audience – indeed, as Spector told the *LA Phonograph*, midway through the sessions, 'We've made some great fu-in' music on this album.' The brawling 'Memories' bowls along, an echo-laden vaudeville drinking song that invites everyone who hears it to join in with the so-perfectly timed refrain of 'won't you let me see…your naked body' – 'this isn't punk rock,' Spector screamed, as Cohen settled at the microphone, one evening. 'This is Rock Punk!'

'Iodine' swings on one of Nino Tempo's most seductive rhythm arrangements, while Steve Douglas' sax squalls behind Cohen and singer Ronee Blakley's rambunctious duet; and anybody looking for a dance smash to sidle wholly out of left-field could turn to 'Don't Go Home With Your Hard-on', a number that not only captured precisely the funky energies that Spector had been searching for the previous year, but which also roped Bob Dylan and Allen Ginsberg into its rambunctious backing chorus. Hal Blaine laughed, 'they couldn't quite get the hang of coming in at the right places, so Phil asked me to conduct the chorus on the overdubs.'

Earlier in the year, Cohen had joined Dylan aboard his on-going Rolling Thunder Revue tour (Ginsberg and Blakley were also part of the circus); now Dylan was returning the favour and Doc Pomus, one of Spector's own guests at the sessions, instantly recognised the look of absolute delight on Spector's face when Dylan walked in. 'Phil was on his best behaviour that evening. He'd never forgotten about the Dylan Opera, and I don't think Bobby [Dylan] had either. You could see Phil's mind working – "play my cards right, and who knows what might develop".'

Unfortunately, nothing did. If Dylan and Spector exchanged more than a handful of words, nobody thought to listen in and, when he and Ginsberg left the studio at the end of the session, they would never return.

Some nights, Cohen found himself wishing he could do the same. His own attempts to take Spector aside to discuss even the most trifling matter were either ignored or rudely brushed aside. What had started out as a collaboration – the meeting, as Cohen put it, of 'an Olympian and crippled nature' had been transformed into a malignant dictatorship, and the occasional affectionate overture that Spector directed towards the increasingly enraged Cohen was scarcely designed to lighten the tension. One evening, Spector swung over to Cohen with a bottle of Manischewitz kosher red wine in one hand, and a gun in the other, draped an arm around the singer's shoulder and shoved the barrel of the gun into his neck. 'Leonard, I love you,' he said. Cohen simply replied, 'I hope you do, Phil.'

In fact, Cohen was convinced that the opposite was true. 'I think that, in the final moment, Phil couldn't resist annihilating me. I don't think he can tolerate any other shadows in his darkness' – and, as if any final confirmation of that was required, it was delivered when it came time to mix the album and neither Spector nor the master tapes were anywhere to be found.

Days of anxiety passed before Spector delivered what his own contract stated was the album's final state and, when he played back the tapes, Cohen was horrified. 'He had taken the guts out of the record,' Cohen told *Rolling Stone*, but the telegram he sent to Spector, asking that he give the album another go, was ignored. Finally, Cohen agreed to write the album off as 'an experiment that failed'; trust that his fans would be able to pick out its 'real energizing capacities' and allowed it to be released as Spector left it.

'I could have delayed its release. But I couldn't have forced Phil back in the studio, and it might have taken another year.' When *Death Of A Ladies Man* was released to universal confusion and not a little condemnation in January 1978, Cohen told the same magazine, 'I would also like him to pick up *Rolling Stone* one day, and see that he was urged to reconsider his approach to recording by a man who knows him well and who has suffered because of his failure to allow things to breathe.'

Death Of A Ladies Man would prove to be Leonard Cohen's final album for more than five years.

14 Phil @ The Whisky

'This isn't Punk Rock, this is Rock Punk!'

Spector's bellowed declaration in the midst of the Leonard Cohen sessions was more than a simple play on words. As 1976 turned into 1977, Los Angeles had been absolutely smitten with a fascination for the latest musical force to arise out of rock 'n' roll's underbelly – local New York and London predilections that rapidly became an international preoccupation.

Much of punk rock's appeal passed Spector by. He appreciated the energy and intent that lay at the movement's core, but the sheer rush of bludgeoning amateurism that accompanied them was far, far from his own vision of what music represented. With one exception.

Late in 1976, New York's Ramones paid their first ever visit to LA, on a wave of media interest and audience identification. By the time they returned the following February, with Debbie Harry's Blondie as support, the entire pop glitterati was dressing up and turning out to fete them.

Though they played at speeds hitherto unknown in rock 'n' pop, the Ramones were tailor-made for the Sunshine State. Their lyrical fascinations were drawn straight from an idealised '50s comic book world of sausage-noshing Germans, three-headed baby freak shows and Cold War paranoia, and their musical influences were pure Beach Boys-out-of-the-Brill Building, a point that was evidenced every time they swung into another of the arsenal of '60s covers that peppered their set ('California Sun' and 'Do You Wanna Dance' were both early entrants); or ripped into one of their own self-composed paeans to an age gone by – 'Babysitter', 'I Remember You', 'Sheena is A Punk Rocker' and 'Swallow My Pride'.

In her poem 'Phil @ The Whisky', Patti Smith namechecked the spellbound stars who packed the Whisky floor for the first night of the Ramones' residency: 'Darlene Love was in the audience, Bruce Springsteen was in the audience.' Dan and David Kessel were in the audience as well; they had spent that same day in the studio with the Ramones themselves, producing them as backing musicians on a projected single by DJ Rodney Bingenheimer.

The brothers were utterly blown away by the experience, and were convinced that Spector would share their enthusiasm. According to Joey Ramone, 'Dave [Kessel] came backstage at the Whisky and said they were going to try and have Phil come down the following night. We were – "yeah, great…"; we never imagined that he'd actually come. You know all the stories about him at that time, how he stayed in his house with the curtains drawn and the lights out, playing the same Johnny Cash album over and over again, then sending the bodyguards out for a pizza. But the next night, in walk Dan and Dave and right behind them…the first thing Phil said to us was, "my bodyguards wanna fight your bodyguards". And we were – "sorry, we don't have any".'

According to bassist Dee Dee Ramone, Spector arrived at the show in his Batman garb (so much for having put such disguises behind him!), topped off with a Mephistophelean beard and aviator shades, 'the crown prince of darkness himself'. He also invited the band back to the mansion – and that, according to Joey, was an experience in itself. Past the barbed wire, past all the warning signs – '"beware of the dog", "beware of the big dog," "achtung minefield"…there were electric fences with all these dead, fried insects hanging off them, and when you went into the kitchen, there was a monster St Bernard living in one of the closets. You opened the door to get something and out leaped this huge dog…'

The visit grew more surreal. The *New Musical Express*'s Roy Carr, himself visiting Spector once again, detailed what happened when Spector stepped up to Dee Dee and challenged him to a fight, dancing the Ali shuffle around the bemused Bruddah. '"Hey man," pleads a panic-stricken Dee Dee Ramone. "If ya hit me, I ain't gonna hit ya back. I've got too much respect for ya! Anyway, I don't know how many armed bodyguards ya got hidden in the kitchen who'll come bursting through the door with their guns blazin' if I do!"'

Spector had not invited the band back simply to freak them out, however. He also had a business proposition for them. Warner-Spector was still functioning (just) as a record label, and Spector spoke of prising the group away from Sire and signing them direct to his company – pointing out, as he did so, that it would be difficult for any label to do a worse job for them than

Sire had managed. He asked how many records they'd sold so far – the band members didn't have a clue, but Spector had the numbers to hand already, and they weren't pretty. Still the Ramones demurred. Even the offer of a $200,000 advance – cash, on the spot – could not sway them, but Spector was not going to give up so easily.

The Ramones were just releasing their second album, *The Ramones Leave Home*, at the time; over the next two years, they would cut two more, *Rocket To Russia* and *Road To Ruin*. Spector listened to each in turn and, every time, his response was the same. Joey continued, 'his shtick was, "do you wanna make a good album with whoever, or do you wanna make a great one with me?" And finally...I wanted to do it from the start, but the rest of the group weren't sure. But, around the time of *Road To Ruin*...we'd just recorded "Needles And Pins", [written by] Jack Nitzsche and Sonny Bono, and that was about as close as you could get to Phil Spector without actually going with him. So I said "what about it?" and the others were – "okay". So that's when Phil went to Seymour Stein [head of the band's label, Sire] and said he was going to do it.'

Ed Stasium, the Ramones' long-serving engineer/producer, agreed. 'Phil always wanted to produce the Ramones, ever since he saw them at The Whisky years before. He was bugging Seymour, "I wanna produce the Ramones, I wanna produce the Ramones."' Stein, of course, knew Spector from his own days in the New York scene of the early 1960s, and he knew the pitfalls that awaited the Ramones if and when they actually entered the studio with him. He was also aware, however, that Spector's pledge that this record 'was going to be the biggest record ever made, even bigger than *Hotel California*,' as Stasium recalls, was no idle boast. If any modern musical marriage could be described as 'made in Heaven', the union of the Ramones and Tycoon of Teen was it.

Still, Stein opted to tread carefully, first suggesting to Spector that he try working with another of Sire's power-pop punk hopefuls, the Boston-based Paley Brothers team of Andy and Jonathan Paley.

Their debut LP, *The Paley Brothers*, proved their own love of the Spector sound. Recorded in Santa Monica early in 1978 with producer Earle Mankey, its widescreen-bright pop exploded into orbit with 'Tell Me Tonight', a song dominated by percussion straight from the Wall of Sound. Spector was certainly enthused, booking time at Gold Star studios, hauling in the usual mass of musicians to cut at least a handful of tracks with them.

Sadly, it was not to be. Although they certainly completed one song, a reworking of the Dion single 'Baby Let's Stick Together' (described by Jonathan Paley as 'the best thing Spector has done since his heyday in the '60s), the Paleys themselves were on the point of breaking up. The fruits of their studio labours were archived and Spector turned his attention back towards the Ramones.

The band were in LA putting the finishing touches to the soundtrack for their forthcoming *Rock 'n' Roll High School* movie at the time, and Spector arranged to meet them at what Dee Dee, in his *Poison Heart* autobiography, described as 'an out of the way rehearsal studio in Hollywood somewhere. We were halfway through [a] song [when] Phil appeared and walked confidently to the center of the empty room, placed his briefcase in an open position and, as there was no chair, crouched on the floor, peering at us from behind the briefcase.'

The band peered back, utterly perplexed. 'I don't know what Phil was doing behind his briefcase, but something seemed very suspicious to me about this type of behaviour,' Dee Dee wrote. But their fears were completely misplaced. The moment they finished the song, Spector stood and walked over, to congratulate them on how great they sounded.

As usual, Spector booked into Gold Star studios, although his usual battalion of session musicians was distinctly absent – only saxophonist Steve Douglas and keyboard player Barry Goldberg received the traditional phone calls from Spector's personal secretary, Donna Sekulidis. Larry Levine was there in his customary role of engineer, but Spector also allowed the group to supply their own 'musical director', Ed Stasium.

If the absence of his usual multitude of musicians proved that Spector respected the Ramones' own integrity as a band, however, they swiftly learned that their own working methods were far, far away from any that Spector would countenance.

At a total cost of over $200,000, the album took close to four months to complete – months that ground past at less than snail's pace, as the constant repetition ground the band's own nerves to shreds. Dee Dee mourned, 'we had been working at least 14 or 15 hours a day for 13 days straight, and we still hadn't recorded one note of music.' Joey, meanwhile, joked that Spector 'spent longer trying to get Johnny's guitar sound for 'Rock 'n' Roll High School' than we spent making the entire first album'...anything up to eight hours, according to different accounts of the session, although all are in accordance on the manner in which the process came to an end. Johnny Ramone walked out and, when Spector demanded he come back this instant, the guitarist simply shrugged. 'What you gonna do? Shoot me?'

'I think a lot of the stuff about Spector and the guns was blown out of proportion,' Joey Ramone reflected. 'Yes, there were guns around, and there was the famous incident where he and Dee Dee got into some kind of argument, which ended with Phil pulling out a revolver and pointing it at him. But we all had images to keep up, you know what I'm saying? We were the Ramones, "da bruddahs," leather jackets...he was Phil Spector, genius, madman, gun-waver.'

Spector's confrontation with Dee Dee Ramone, the band's bassist, is, indeed, famous, passing into Spector folklore almost before the album was complete, and becoming hopelessly muddled in the process. Dee Dee, however, clarified at least the rudiments of the moment in his own autobiography, *Poison Heart*. The band were visiting the mansion at the time, but Joey alone seems to have merited Spector's attention. 'He left me, John and Marc (drummer Marky Ramone) downstairs in the piano room, while he took Joey upstairs for a private conference.' Three hours later... 'I was getting restless, [so] I got up off the couch and tried to find Phil and Joey. Phil must have thought I was an intruder – the next thing I knew, [he] appeared at the top of the staircase, shouting and waving a pistol.'

As Dee Dee stood frozen to the spot, Spector went through his stripping and reassembling motions 'in two seconds flat', never taking his eye off the bassist. Dee Dee, however, was unimpressed. 'Phil, I don't know what your fucking problem is, but I've had it. I'm going back to the hotel.'

Spector sneered. 'You're not going anywhere, Dee Dee.' 'He levelled the gun at my heart, then motioned for me and the rest of the band to get back in the piano room.' Then, with everybody sitting docilely on the sofa, he sat down at the piano 'and made us listen to him play "Baby I Love You" until well after 4.30 in the morning'.

'Baby I Love You' was one of two of his own songs that Spector brought to the session, alongside the old Bob B Soxx number 'Not Too Young To Get Married'. His insistence that the group record one or other ('Baby I Love You' won through) was one that Johnny, Dee Dee and Marky instantly recoiled from, but Spector told them not to worry. He had no intention of recording it with them. This was for Joey alone and, across countless hours of rehearsal, with a makeshift Wrecking Crew combo (Jim Keltner and the

Kessels joined Goldberg and Douglas) magically appearing in the room, Spector not only turned the musical clock back 20 years, he reinvented Joey as well, transforming him from the beanpole colossus that fired a thousand punkers' dreams, into everything that Spector himself had perceived the Ramones to be when he first clapped eyes on them.

'I think…people have said that Phil didn't really want to work with the rest of the group, that I was the one he was interested in,' Joey said later. 'I dunno – it's difficult for me to talk about, because we were a band, we were a package, and the idea of someone trying to isolate any of us was something that simply didn't cross my mind. I probably spent more time with Phil than the others, but that's because we had more to talk about. The rest of the group weren't fans, not like I was, and I think Phil sensed that. Also, because I was the singer, and he had very firm ideas of how he wanted the record to sound…I remember he told me once that I was the new Dion DiMucci, he played me the album he did with Dion and said "this is what I want you to sound like".

'Of course, when we did "Baby I Love You", it didn't sound anything like the Dion album, it was completely up…the complete opposite. And it didn't sound anything like the Ramones, either, which is what really pissed off the others. There was talk that we should release it as a Joey Ramone solo single, but I didn't want that because of…what I just told you, about us being a band, a package. But did it fit on a Ramones album? I dunno. It went on a Ramones album, though, and it was our biggest ever hit.'

'The thing was, Phil had never worked with a band before,' Joey told journalist Jaan Uhelszki. 'His artists were more of his own conception. Phil liked to dominate and manipulate, so it was a little strange. But I felt like I was performing for the master. He's a passionate, high-drama person. I still admire him – but, during his episodes, nobody was enjoying any of it. We were all pissed off with his drinking, his antics, high drama and the insanity.'

The band members learned to dread the moment that the control room door creaked quietly open, and one of Spector's own staff entered with a tray of little white cups, each one filled to the brim with Manischewitz. He'd sink a few, averred Joey, 'then he'd start banging on the floor and screaming: "piss, shit, fuck, fuck, shit, piss". He would just go on. He started freaking out, and there would be no reason to go on any longer with the session.'

On other occasions, the arrival of a stranger in the studio – anyone from a messenger boy to a receptionist, or even a Ramones roadie that Spector didn't immediately recognise – could bring work to a screeching halt while the producer determined whether the newcomer was any kind of threat, while there was another crisis when Larry Levine went home one evening, and was rushed to the hospital with a heart attack. It was his second in six years and Levine himself knew that his own smoking was to blame.

Spector, however, convinced himself that he was responsible, and sank into a depression that, according to Joey, 'might have sunk the album there and then. He felt so guilty...I asked him if he'd heard how Larry was doing, or if he was going to visit him, and...he never went. He was sure that Larry would reach up from his sick bed and throttle him..."you did this to me, you bastard!" So he got drunk again.'

End Of The Century – Spector dreamed up the title – was finally completed in September 1979, for release the following January and, in truth, failed to live up to the potential of the union that created it. Certainly no other single track worked as well as 'Baby, I Love You', although there were several others that at least tried – the rollicking thump of 'Do You Remember Rock 'n' Roll Radio' would not have sounded out of place on *The Big TNT Show*; 'Danny Says' emerged one of the hauntingly bitter-sweet buzzsaw ballads with which the group had excelled since their debut album and 'I'm Affected' brooded over a soundtrack that could have been diverted from a '60s cop show.

A remake of 'Rock 'n' Roll High School', too, was thrilling. Too many of the other songs, however, seemed little more than rewrites or parodies of past Ramonic glories, fatal flaws that all the production magic in the world could not remedy, and it was ironic that the glories that should have been *End Of The Century*'s for the taking were to remain untapped for another 16 years, until Joey Ramone himself sidled into the producer's chair to oversee Ronnie Spector's *She Talks To Rainbows* comeback EP.

Ronnie recalled, 'I did a record called "Baby I Love You" in the '60s, and Joey rerecorded it with the Ramones in the '80s, and I went to one of his video shoots. I didn't hear from him for a while, but one night, my [second] husband and I were sitting around talking, and he'd been listening to cassettes in his car and he heard a Ramones song called "She Talks To Rainbows". He said "you gotta hear this song, it's so much like you". And I loved it, so I rang Joey up, we met up at this club the following night, and I just said "Joey, you gotta give me that song." And from there, we just picked up more material, we collaborated together and it was so natural."

Five tracks made it onto the EP – a Ramones cover, a Beach Boys song, a duet with Joey, an old Ronettes number and, surprising everyone who heard it, a Johnny Thunders cover. 'One night Joey and I were sitting around talking about songs which might work for this record, and he played me "You Can't Put Your Arms Around A Memory", and I said "that is so right, that is so me, I love this song." At that time, my mother was in a nursing home and I knew she didn't have much longer, so with that happening, "You Can't Put Your Arms Around A Memory" was – boom, that's the song.

'I'd never heard it before. But I've lived it! With my career, my past life is like a memory, my ex-husband [Spector], those old records, it's like a memory and people are still trying to put their arms around me, thinking I'm maybe still the little girl, 17-years-old from Spanish Harlem, who sang "Be My Baby" in 1963. But it's been over for decades, and "Memory", it says that in the lyrics. There's a lot of reasons why I love doing "You Can't Put Your Arms Around A Memory", but the main reason is, because it's true. You can't. And though people might think the '60s were my time, they weren't. The '60s are so old and I feel so brand new.'

She Talks To Rainbows would be greeted among Ronnie's finest recordings since, indeed, the '60s, but her collaboration with Joey, so promising across those five songs, was not to last. Stricken for the past eight years with non-Hodgkins Lymphoma, the singer passed away on 15 April 2001. The Ramones themselves had been out of commission for five years by then, but Joey never balked at recalling their proudest moments. And for him, the chance to work with Phil Spector was equalled only by the thrill of working with Ronnie.

'If you ask me what the best record I've made is, I'd have to say it's *She Talks To Rainbows*, because it's everything that *End Of The Century* could have been' he said in 1999. 'And if you ask about the Ramones, *End Of The Century* had to be...if not the best record, it was the culmination of everything. It was why you joined a band in the first place – get past the chicks, the fame, all that stuff and you're in a band because you want to make music that matters to people, that actually sits in history and says "I exist".

'That's what *End Of The Century* does. It doesn't matter if people know it because it's a Ramones record that happened to be produced by Phil Spector, or a Phil Spector record that happened to be by the Ramones. They know it, and I don't think you can say that about many of our albums...the first two, maybe. But, as far as I'm concerned, *End Of The Century* is the one that matters.'

Yet he shrouded his enthusiasm with one lasting caveat. 'Phil's contract with us was actually for two albums. We were going to do *End Of The Century*, tour, and then go back in the studio with him for another one. But I am so glad that we didn't!'

15 Silence Becomes Me

The Ramones and the Paley Brothers were not the only members of the so-called New Wave to catch Spector's eye as the 1970s wound down. When French producer Marc Zermati travelled to LA to record with The Flaming Groovies, he was astonished when Spector dropped by the studio one day, to visit one of the sound engineers – and even more astonished when Spector extended an invitation for Zermati and the band to drop by the mansion one evening. Upon arrival, however, they got no further than the front door. According to the bodyguard who answered the door, then took their names back to Spector, the producer was adamant that he'd never heard of them.

But if Spector turned away The Flaming Groovies, he would soon discover how it felt when the boot was on the other foot. Having first seen Blondie when they opened for the Ramones at the Whisky in February 1977, Spector kept tabs on them as well, watching while they transformed themselves from a competent garage band with a pronounced debt to the Shangri-Las, to the most vividly updated recreation of the girl group sound of old. Debbie Harry's voice especially appealed, a gum-chewing, finger-popping street-savvy yammer that swung straight out of the Lower East Side. The group's records, however, only hinted at the majesty that she ought to have been capable of and Spector was convinced that she was worth far more. His overtures towards the group were never to be reciprocated. Spector's interest was flattering, Harry later mused. But his reputation wasn't.

End Of The Century brought the Ramones the biggest record they ever would score, a No 44 hit in America, No 14 in Britain; 'Baby I Love You' proved that, in sonic terms, every last iota of Spector's fabled passion and brilliance was still firing on all cylinders. But the horror stories that leaked out of the sessions – the guns, the drink, the $200,000 that it cost to complete the album, the three separate remixes that Spector put the record through –

were more than enough to scare Blondie off, together with any other band who might have otherwise coveted a taste of the magic. At the end of December 1979, Spector turned in the final mixes of *End Of The Century* to Sire, and regarding his own contributions to the next two decades, its title couldn't have been more apt. For him, it was indeed the end of the century.

It was time to drift once again – into solitude, into legend, into the kind of notoriety that only a true icon can embrace. The public eye, after all, feasts only upon what it sees and, when an artist or an idol fades from everyday sight, then the tiniest snatch of information becomes a tale to consume many acres of newsprint.

Towards the end of the year, it was reported that Jack Nitzsche had shown up on Collina Drive, hoping to drown his sorrows with Spector. It had been a rough year for him – having just broken up with girlfriend Carrie Snodgrass, Nitzsche was then arrested after breaking into her home and assaulting her at gunpoint – according to Snodgrass, he kicked and beat her, raped her with the barrel of his gun and then threatened to shoot both her and her child. He was sentenced to three years probation, but the harsher punishment was the way in which so many old friends began avoiding him, whispering behind their hands, not even waiting until his back was turned.

Spector was not among them, but he seemed to join in anyway. All three of the children – 10-year-old Donté, 13-year-old Gary and Louis, were in the house at the time and, as Spector looked out of the upstairs window at this unexpected visitor, he could not help but wonder who was really standing in the driveway – an old friend he had not seen in years...they'd not worked together since the Ike and Tina sessions in 1966? Or the madman whose last reported project was threatening to shoot a child, while fucking his ex-girlfriend with a loaded gun? Spector drew his own revolver and ordered the intruder off the grounds.

He and Nitzsche would soon be meeting again under more personable circumstances, and remained friends for the remainder of the arranger's life (he died from cardiac arrest on 25 August 2000). For now, however, Spector's treatment of his old friend was added to the long litany of his other incomprehensible acts – by many of the same people who would have responded in precisely the same fashion.

Donté himself would not remain Spector's responsibility for long. Just weeks later after the Nitzsche incident, on 23 January 1980, the boy showed up at the West Hollywood police precinct to report losing his bicycle. It was past 10pm and the duty officer asked the boy whether his parents knew that he was out so late. Donté said no...he'd run away from home that morning and had no intention of ever going back.

The police called Spector and received no reply. Their next call was to the LA County Department of Juvenile Correction, who in turn contacted Ronnie in New York. She was on the next flight out to LA, where her lawyer, Jay Stein, had already begun piecing together what had happened. According to what Stein told her, Donté ran away because his father wasn't feeding him. Spector would set the boy chores and, if he didn't complete them, he would be sent to bed without supper.

The twins suffered just as much. Locked in separate rooms by their governess every night, the boys had no freedom whatsoever – they were even transported to school by armed guards. But, as Ronnie put it, being older 'they were a little better equipped to deal with Phil's weirdness'. They were better, too, she presumed, at handling his bouts of depression, rage and irrationality, although it would be almost another quarter of a century before Donté and Gary, at least, stepped forth to reveal what they described as the full horror of their childhood.

In 2003, during the weeks that followed Lana Clarkson's death, newspapers around the world carried interviews with the pair, in which years of pain and abuse were, apparently, finally uncaged. 'For years, we were just caged animals to be let out for Dad's amusement,' Donté – now 33 years old – told Britain's *Mail on Sunday* newspaper in 2003. From the age of nine, he was reported as saying, his father used to force him into performing simulated intercourse with his latest girlfriend.

More controversially, Gary, now 36, was said to have made similar allegations. Three years earlier, in his posting on the Spectropop website, Gary had spoken out in noble defense of Spector, acknowledging his 'faults' but insisting, 'I just like to try and help others see him from another side to all the stories... He was not a people person...[but] he shows in his own way that he cares. I will always love my father, flaws and all.'

Now, according to the American *Dateline* programme, he had gone public with memories of how he was 'blindfolded and sexually molested. Dad would say, "You're going to meet someone," and it would be a "learning experience."' When the website www.spectormurdercase.com repeated these claims, however, Gary was quick to issue a denial. 'I was never brought into any room with unknown women and I was never forced.' In another posting, he remarked, simply, 'Our life was rough at time[s]. [But] we don't need reporters making it sound even worse for the sake of ratings.'

Nevertheless, in 1980, Jay Stein told Ronnie that he was amazed none of the boys had run away from home any earlier. Even more amazing, given the cage in which they were apparently imprisoned, was the fact that one of them was able to get away at all.

With Donté being held at a children's home in Baldwin Hills, and Spector himself apparently completely uninterested in the boy's welfare, Ronnie immediately launched a new custody battle. It was expensive and arduous but this time, she triumphed – igniting, for herself, a whole basketful of troubles as she tried to learn to live with a boy 'whose only role model had been Phil Spector. I couldn't believe how much Donté took after his father,' she told in her autobiography. Nor would she ever come to terms with that likeness. In argument after argument, she would see her ex-husband peering out from behind the boy's eyes, but still she was devastated when, having gone back to California for a week's holiday with a friend, Donté announced that he would not be returning to New York. He went to live, instead, with Grandmother Bertha.

If Spector appeared unaffected by the loss of his youngest son at the beginning of the year, he was to be shattered by the death of one of his oldest friends, at the end of it. On 8 December 1980, John Lennon was murdered outside his home at the Dakota Hotel. Though seven years had passed since Lennon and Spector last worked together, they had remained in contact regardless, and Phil was devastated by the news.

Spector was at home when he heard. 'I got a call,' he told *Rolling Stone* and, two decades after the slaying, he remained livid. '[It] never should have happened. John didn't believe in any kind of security. I don't know whether it was New York, or just not being a Beatle and not being under scrutiny anymore, but I guess in his last years he became much more trusting, much more carefree. He'd stop and talk to people, and a lot of them were like the nut who killed him – 'You wrote that song about me.' Who wants to talk to those people? But it kind of shows you, while they hated being The Beatles, they also missed it. They missed the adoration. John missed that rapport.'

Spector called Yoko as soon as he could get through, and pledged to help her in any way that he could. She took him up on his offer in the early years. They had never got on that well with one another but, united in grief for the slain Lennon, they suddenly found that they had a closer bond than they could ever have imagined. As Ono began preparing for her own first album without Lennon by her side, she instinctively reached out to Spector to oversee the proceedings.

He flew to New York, but it was to be a shortlived collaboration. With the basic tracks for what became *Season Of Glass* completed, Ono had a change of heart on the nature of the album – Spector, of course, had aimed for a full sound, one that matched and occasionally threatened to outdo the full-blooded rush that was 'Walking On Thin Ice', the astonishing track that she and Lennon had completed on the night of his murder. Ono, however, pulled back. Assuring Spector that his co-production credit would not be altered, she gently removed him from the project and completed the album herself. As an extra thank you to Spector, she later presented him with one of Lennon's guitars.

Spector returned to California. Living now with girlfriend Janice Savala, a former secretary at Screen Gems, he threw himself into domesticity. Though even Spector's own children would never know if the couple actually married, the twins Nicole and Philip were born in 1983 and, again, Spector was living the kind of life of quiet domesticity that any proud new father might hope he could.

Of course, the world promptly turned his silence into a fresh wall of reclusive withdrawal, completely unaware of the heartbreaking tragedy that was taking place behind the mansion walls. Phil Jr was diagnosed with leukemia and would spend much of his young life undergoing painful treatment and chemotherapy. It was to no avail. Aged just nine years old, Phil Jr slipped out of this world with as little public fanfare as he slipped in; even among Spector's greatest fans, his short life was a secret – not because Spector and Janice had anything to hide, but because they had no need to tell. The supermarket tabloid-style magazines whose entire circulation is based around the lives, deaths and heartaches of its celebrity subjects would *not* be selling the Spectors' suffering. So they sold his silence instead.

In 1983, British television's Channel 4 commissioned film-maker Binia Tymieniecka to produce an hour-long documentary on Spector, drawing comments from as far afield as Ronnie Spector, and Ramones Dee Dee and Johnny, but receiving no co-operation whatsoever from Spector himself. The result was a programme that brought little fresh fact to the table, but certainly reinforced the image – a point that Ronnie, in particular, seemed intent on driving home: 'I think Phil was a very normal person at the beginning of his career. But as time went on, they started writing about him being a genius. And he said, "Yeah, I am a genius." And then they would say, "He's the mad genius." And so he became the mad genius.'

Yet, though he went out of his way not to broadcast the fact, the genius was by no means silent. When the Gold Star studios were destroyed by fire in March 1984, Spector was one of the multitude who drove past the site in the days that followed, to mourn the loss of one of his most cherished icons, and console David Gold and Stan Ross, still at the helm of the establishment.

Under happier circumstances, Doc Pomus was just one of Spector's old associates who grew accustomed to receiving late night telephone calls demanding that he abandon everything and throw himself wholeheartedly into some new, percolating masterpiece. 'He'd get you all worked up, as excited as he was, and then you'd never hear from him again.'

Busying himself around Phil Jr's treatment, and the entire family's battle against the boy's illness, the schemes tended to revolve around unknown artists whom Spector claimed to have 'discovered', although Pomus suspected that most didn't exist. 'He was just testing people to find out where their loyalties lay. That way, if something *did* happen, he'd know he had people he could rely upon.'

In fact, Spector would probably have already moved on to another idea. Unlike many of his contemporaries and, indeed, the majority of his disciples, Spector remained in full control of the vast majority of his back catalogue as a producer, with full and final control over everything from reissue rights (which, for now, remained tightly guarded) to the use of his music in movies and commercials. Early in the decade, that latter provision was scarcely called upon – movie soundtracks remained largely bound up in specially commissioned scores; advertisers were still scouring the self-contained world of music libraries for music to move more washing powder with.

Recently, however, that situation had changed radically. From granting such permissions maybe once or twice a year (in 1979, 'Da Doo Ron Ron' and 'Be My Baby' were licensed for the Who's *Quadrophenia* movie, and that was a good year), suddenly Hollywood was gagging for nostalgia-jerking oldies with which to fill its films, and Spector was frequently pleased to oblige; or, just as frequently, pleased not to.

'I spent six months trying to get the rights to "Be My Baby" for a movie,' one producer remembered, 'and I didn't get anywhere at all. Then, a couple of months later, I tried again for another film – and the agreement was on my desk within a week. Someone told me later that he made his decisions completely at random; one day he'd say yes to everything, the next, he'd say no, and the day after that, he wouldn't say anything and just let you dangle. And once he'd made his decision, that was it. You could come back to him every day for the rest of your life, and the answer would never change.'

1986, however, saw Spector issue what would prove to be the most lucrative license of his career (and, for close to 15 years, one of the most troublesome), when he allowed The Ronettes' 'Be My Baby' to be featured in the upcoming Patrick Swayze vehicle *Dirty Dancing*, destined to become one of the highest grossing movies of the decade. The soundtrack album alone was enormous – spending 18 weeks at No 1 in the US, it sold over 11 million copies, but it was Spector who banked the millions of dollars that the song earned. The Ronettes had signed their own rights away back in 1963, in return for a lump sum of $14,482.

In many ways, it was a phenomenal stroke of luck. That same year, Spector also licensed The Ronettes' '(The Best Part Of) Breaking Up', The Crystals' 'Da Doo Ron Ron' and Darlene Love's 'Wait Till My Bobby Gets Home' to the latest of the Hollywood Brat Pack movies, Robert Downey Jr and Molly Ringwald's *The Pick-up Artist*. But, while *Dirty Dancing* was to prove the biggest hit of 1987, *The Pick-Up Artist* emerged one of the biggest flops.

If Spector's attentions seemed to have returned once again to his back catalogue, however, he was still open to new projects and ideas. 1986 also saw him approached with a new recording proposition, as Danny Davis – the former promo man at Philles – settled in at a new label, the LA-based Columbia affiliate Private I Records.

Private I had recently picked up singer La Toya Jackson, the eldest of the daughters in the famous singing clan, but one of the last to blossom as a performer. Since making her singing debut with her brothers' Jackson Five combo in the late 1970s, she had cut three albums for two major labels, none of which had made any serious impression whatsoever – the first two, *La Toya Jackson* and *My Special Love*, gnawed the lower end of the Top 200 chart; the third, *Heart Don't Lie*, didn't even get that far.

Now Private I were trying to relaunch her and Davis, who had remained in at least loose contact with Spector over the years, thought it might be worth putting the pair together – if nothing else, he reasoned, brother Michael's mega-stardom might at least pique Spector's attention. In fact,

Spector didn't even need that carrot. Hankering to get back to work, he agreed to meet with Jackson and, apparently, was utterly charmed by her.

Jackson, too, was thrilled. In her autobiography *La Toya*, she enthused about the prospect: 'of course I was aware of Phil's many million-selling records in the early 1960s...he was a legend with a capital L, so I looked forward to meeting with him.'

En route to the mansion, Davis tried to fill Jackson in on what to expect – 'he told me how some people found [him] a little bit...well, strange. "But you and Phil should get along fine," he assured me.' Neither was she overly concerned as they journeyed through the electric fence and over the speed bumps, past the sign that warned 'you are here at your own risk', and she caught her first glimpse of the mansion itself, 'an imposing Italian-style structure that would have made a great horror movie set'.

That first meeting was brief, but seemed to go well. No sooner had she returned home than Spector rang and asked her to return the following day, without the chaperone. They'd get a lot more accomplished that way.

As it turned out, they accomplished nothing. According to Jackson, Spector kept her waiting for some 90 minutes before finally appearing, to greet her with one question – 'would you like to go to the Bates Motel?' She looked back at him uncomprehendingly, and he repeated the question. 'I want to take you to the Bates Motel. I have the key to room No 1. I own the key to the Bates Motel.' Still no reaction, and it dawned on him that Jackson didn't have a clue what he was talking about. 'What's the matter?' he finally shrugged. 'Haven't you ever seen *Psycho*?'

She'd failed the first test, and soon she would fail the second, staring helplessly at him as he sat down at a piano and began to hammer out 'a discordant melody I'd never heard before.'

'Sing!' he commanded.

'I don't know the melody...'

'SING!'

So she sang, following the words on a piece of sheet music he handed her, while Spector accompanied her with a screaming tirade against her brother Michael. He pulled her onto the piano bench and continued his crashing on the keys – then suddenly he leaped up, announced he was sick of her, sick of Michael, sick of everything and left the room.

Jackson turned to leave, but found that the doors were locked. Periodically, Spector would reappear and each time, he had adopted the persona of another character: a slurring drunk, a suave city slicker, a hip record executive. She told him she needed to leave for a meeting; he told her the meeting had been cancelled. 'You're staying here for two weeks straight and I'm not letting you out of this house until we get this album completed.'

According to her autobiography, it was four hours before Spector finally relented and allowed Jackson to leave, making her way back to her home in Encino to discover he'd spent a good part of the evening on the phone to her parents, issuing a barrage of threats and insults that culminated with Spector and Jackson's father taking turns to threaten one another with violence.

'I'm coming over there to blow your brains out,' screamed Spector.

'I'm coming up there to blow your brains out,' countered Jackson.

'Oh yeah? I'll be waiting for you with my Magnum. You just dare come over here.' And so on. Needless to say, Spector and La Toya Jackson never did get into the studio together.

Neither did anything come from another project that, initially, bode well for both Spector and the artist concerned. In 1987, with the English electronics band Depeche Mode rising fast on the American dance circuit, Seymour Stein, whose Sire label distributed the quartet's records in America, approached Spector with the admittedly audacious notion of remixing some of their recent recordings for the dance floor and, hopefully, beyond. Depeche's most recent single, 'A Question Of Lust', had boasted a peculiarly Spectoresque drum sound and, from a marketing point of view, the marriage certainly seemed workable.

Unfortunately, although Spector certainly set to work on the project (and an Italian Depeche Mode tribute album later insinuated it had one of the resultant tapes, an instrumental rendering of the early hit 'New Life'), he was never to complete it. Accustomed to remixes being delivered within a day, maybe two, Depeche Mode simply didn't have the patience to wait around until Spector himself was satisfied with the mix. The project was scrapped.

Organising the abortive Depeche Mode session was one of the last projects that Donna Sekulidis, Spector's personal secretary, would undertake for him. Later in the year, the pair argued – not for the first time, but certainly for the last. The dispute, according to several sources, was itself insignificant: who owned the typewriter that she had been using for the past ten years? But before it was over, Spector had fired her.

For many of the people whose situations placed them in regular contact with Spector, the departure of Sekulidis was seen as yet another example of his withdrawal from anything remotely approaching the 'real world'. They'd grown so accustomed to her acting as his mouthpiece that they had almost forgotten what Spector's own voice sounded like.

But, once again, he did not withdraw. Sekulidis was replaced with the equally efficient Norma Kemper, and life went on. That July, in fact, he even turned up at his high school graduation class's 30th anniversary reunion, besuited and shaded, and shadowed by two bodyguards. He barely spoke to anybody – even old friends acknowledged that that would have been too much to expect. But he spent the entire evening at the event, he nodded as old classmates passed by and said hello, and he might even have agreed with many peoples' assumption that he attended the event in the hope of returning, however briefly, to a time when he was simply Harvey Spector, unknown, unfettered and unaware of all that the future would pile down upon him. Or maybe he just went for the hell of it, to see what his old classmates were up to and what the school looked like. Sometimes, people can read way too much into a simple situation.

Of course he had doubts. In a rare interview with the *LA Times* in 1991, he recalled 'asking myself, "Do they remember Lenny Bruce as the philosophical genius and great comic mind, or do they remember him as some sick, stupid morphine addict?"' Spector himself was haunted by the fear that he might have the same reputation: was he remembered as a great producer? Or a madman with a firearm fixation? 'Do I have regrets? Sure, lots of them. From people I married to records I could have done, I have a lifetime of regrets.' In the past, he would simply have wallowed in them. Now he intended ridding himself of some of them.

Conscious of the worsening health of manager Marty Machat, Spector had quietly begun considering who he might recruit to his side, should the worse happen. And, when it did – Machat passed away in early 1988 – Spector sprung into action.

As far back as the *Let It Be* sessions, Allen Klein had made no secret of the fact that he wanted to represent Spector. Cynically, one could even say that is why Spector was given the job in the first place and, during the weeks that Spector worked on those tapes, Klein frequently sat in on the session, quietly listening. All these years later, it was not Klein's musical ear that now interested Spector, and would ensure Klein's dream finally came true. It was the business acumen that had not only generated vast sums of money for his clientele, but also ignited a voracious market for the back catalogues that

Klein shrewdly withheld from the market. The pair linked up shortly after Machat's death and Klein immediately swung into action, finally resolving a legal battle that Spector and Leiber and Stoller's Trio Music publishers had kept simmering for years. And, six months later, Spector was back in the headlines, only this time it was for stepping onto the biggest stage he had walked across in years.

1983 saw the launch of the Rock 'n' Roll Hall of Fame, an ambitious project designed to confer the plaudits of the music industry upon the artists and entrepreneurs who had built that industry up in the first place. The notion was not without its critics, of course; primarily those souls who saw the entire concept as another attempt to suck rock's rebel spirit into the self-satisfied halls of mainstream entertainment glitz. In fact, that had happened so long before that the very accusation was all but ripe for induction; the criteria for election demanded that 25 years needed to pass between an artist's first recording and their nomination for the Hall of Fame.

The Hall of Fame held its first induction ceremony in 1986, welcoming the cream of the very first wave of rock 'n' rollers into its midst: Chuck Berry, Elvis Presley, Jerry Lee Lewis and Buddy Holly. 1987 was the turn of the doo-wop and early soul era; 1988 brought the first sign of the 'modern' rock era, as The Beatles, the Beach Boys and Bob Dylan marched in.

Phil Spector had been eligible for inclusion in the 'non-performer' category since the Hall of Fame's first ceremony, in 1986, brought inductions for Alan Freed and Sam Phillips. 1987 honoured Leonard Chess, Ahmet Ertegun, Jerry Wexler and Leiber and Stoller, 1988 celebrated Berry Gordy Jr. If Spector gave any thought whatsoever to the Hall of Fame, then, he no doubt imagined that the next round of inductions, for 1989, would similarly pass by without reference to him.

That, however, was before he hired Allen Klein. Regardless of whether or not ABKCo's considerable weight played any part whatsoever in the nomination process, still the company would be well represented at the 1989 ceremony, as The Rolling Stones received a nod in the Artists category, and Phil Spector was finally acknowledged among the non-performers – Tina Turner announced his induction and, to complete a circle of sorts, Dion DiMucci, too, found himself drawn into the festivities.

Spector attended the ceremony in New York, accompanied by Jack Nitzsche. He did not cut an instantly dazzling shape – recollecting the somewhat rambling speech that Spector had clearly *not* prepared for the ceremony, Pete Townshend, onstage to announce the Stones, later condemned, 'what's awful about [rock 'n' roll] mythology is that when you wheel fucking Phil Spector out on the stage to honour him...you can see that the guy is dead, physically, emotionally and spiritually dead.'

Andrew Loog Oldham, on the other hand, described the evening as 'a gorgeous occasion. I had a sweet time, but what's not to have a sweet time on the night Philip was being honored? Even Phil was very sweet that night.' After the ceremony, Oldham joined Spector and Nitzsche at Foreigner frontman Mick Jones' apartment on Central Park, and remembered 'Phil... telling me off about taking drugs. The pot calling the kettle beige.'

Of course the Rock 'n' Roll Hall of Fame brings little material benefit to its beneficiaries, just a heightened awareness of who they are (or, in some cases, who they were) and a demand, among people who may only just have found that out, to hear something of what they were made of. Unfortunately, for anybody latching onto Phil Spector for the first time – or anyone else, for that matter – that was something of a hopeless task. With the exception of those '70s albums that dribbled out on compact disc, the vast majority of Spector's back catalogue, his 1960s work in particular, had languished out of print since the early 1980s.

Spector had made several attempts to remedy that situation and, shortly before Marty Machut died, he entered into discussions with two labels, the Los Angeles-based oldies specialist Rhino, and Japan's Moon Records, for the production of two separate boxed sets, which would contain three CDs in the United States and five in Japan.

Described as the most ambitious project the then-fledgling Rhino had mustered so far, *The Wall Of Sound: The Essential Phil Spector* was originally announced in June 1987, with a scheduled release date of September. A total of 60 songs would, said Rhino A&R director Gary Stewart, run the gamut of the Philles catalogue, including 'a couple of unreleased cuts, and a lot of things that've never been available in America'.

The Japanese set was even more impressive but, as time passed, the only news about either was that the release dates were forever being pushed back while work continued on track selection and remastering. And, while February 1989 saw the US magazine *Ice* suggest 'it's unlikely that we'll go another entire year without seeing something', it would be close to three years before the Rhino box, now retitled *Back To Mono*, finally saw the light of day, as ABKCo's own, eponymous label took over the project.

Newly remixed by Larry Levine and Allen Klein's son Jody, the box upped the original project's 60 tracks with the inclusion of the 1963 *Christmas Album* (itself a projected Rhino release back in 1987) and, at a stroke, wiped out every other *Wall Of Sound* compilation there had ever been. Released in October 1991, *Back To Mono* sold over 30,000 copies before the end of the year. The Japanese collection, in the meantime, was scrapped altogether.

The Hall of Fame induction and the release of *Back To Mono* effectively ended Phil Spector's story. Indeed, author Mark Ribowsky's best-selling biography *He's A Rebel*, originally published in 1989 and closing with the induction alone, itself leaves the reader with the distinct impression that Phil Spector had already lived his life. He was just 49 years old.

16 End Of A Century?

In 1999, on his compulsively readable The Blacklisted Journalist website, Al Aronowitz wrote of Spector's last decade, 'he has dedicated his life to collecting not firearms but royalties, and he hangs out mostly in the shadowed periphery of the music business...in the darkness circling the round, bright, pinpointing glare of the spotlight. But then, out of the spotlight is where he's always done his best work, operating in the shadows, behind the scenes, pulling the strings like a master puppeteer.

'Is it that Phil doesn't relish scrutiny anymore? He doesn't seem to be the publicity hound he used to be. Once famous for his "Wall of Sound", he's now famous for his "Wall of Silence". And his friends and associates have become bricks in that wall, protecting him from journalists like me who want to know such things as who is the mother of his teen daughter. I've always considered Phil a friend, but everyone close to him clams up when I start to ask personal questions about Phil. And Phil hardly talks to me any more.'

Spector, Janice and the family had moved away from the mansion by now. In 1991, they took up residence in the hills above the suburb of Alhambra, 20 miles outside of LA. Shielded from prying eyes by a grove of Himalayan deodar trees, to which Spector quickly added an electric fence, security cameras and guard dogs, 1700 Grandview Drive was a 33-room replica of an 18th-century Pyrenean chateau (hence its local nickname of the Pyrenees Castle), built in 1926 by a homesick Basque rancher. It was, Spector marvelled, 'a beautiful and enchanting castle in a hick town where there is no place to go that you shouldn't go.' Having rented it since the early 1990s, Spector bought the house outright for $1.1 million in 1998.

Spector and Janice had parted by that time, separating sometime after Phil Jr's passing, although she continued working for him for several years to come; the boys had grown up and fled the nest; his staff was smaller than ever. But, just because he was rarely seen in public, that does not mean he never went out in public. He just refused to advertise his presence when he did, trailing along either with friends or daughter Nicole, and behaving with the dignity and decorum that one perhaps wishes our other celebrity heroes would adopt. The man who was allegedly terrified of crowds wasn't simply willing to take his place in one, he relished it, neither demanding nor expecting special treatment because he was 'a star'.

When journalist and author Mick Brown interviewed him for the *Daily Telegraph* in January 2003, Spector acknowledged that, in the past, his behaviour had not conformed to many people's definition of normalcy and confessed, 'I wasn't well enough to function as a regular part of society, so I didn't. I chose not to.' Not for the first time, he quoted John Lennon. Talking to *Rolling Stone* in 2000, Spector explained how he had identified with the Plastic Ono Band-era song 'Isolation'; now, he made a similar observation using a title from *Imagine*. 'I was "crippled inside". Emotionally. Insane is a hard word. I wasn't insane, but…I have devils inside that fight me.' What was important for Brown, and the world, to understand was the fact that he had long since learned to defeat them.

He was there when The Rolling Stones played the LA Colisseum in 1989, tagging along with Jack Nitzsche to wonder why the media kept asking if this would be the last time, when he knew that, like him, they would never really stop. He was there, too, when old-time Wrecking Crew member Don Randi threw open his Baked Potato nightclub to celebrate the publication of Hal Blaine's *Hal Blaine & The Wrecking Crew* memoir, in 1990, sitting quietly amid the assembled throng, chatting with old acquaintances – Stan Ross, Dave Gold, Larry Levine, Brian Wilson – while Jack Nitzsche poked mischievous fun at Spector's reputation by pointing out that 'the most outrageous thing about him was his "Back to Mono" [badge]'.

Spector joined the Host Committee for the Blues Foundation, the House Of Blues' organisation's own answer to the Hall of Fame, and attended the annual dinner and awards ceremonies that bestowed Lifetime Achievement Awards upon Jerry Wexler in 1995, and Ahmet Ertegun three years later.

He dropped by local clubs and attended Hollywood parties – and he did, occasionally, step out of line. Comedienne Joan Rivers threw a Christmas bash in the late 1990s, at a time when her own manager was dating Spector, and told the *Sun-Herald* newspaper, 'she was having problems with him. She would say, "He held a gun to my head", and, "I woke up and there was a gun in my mouth." And I thought, "Yeah. Right. Uh-huh." And then I gave a Christmas party and she brought Phil and he pulled a gun on [TV news reader] Walter Cronkite's daughter, who's a very respectable young woman. It was amazing, we had to have him escorted out of the place.'

Context, of course, is everything and Spector has never spoken publicly about why he pulled the gun. But if he remained prone to the occasional lapse in social judgement, he was also still eminently capable of making music – and poking fun at his profession as well. In October 1992, Spector was approached by the makers of the American animated series *Ren And Stimpy*, to appear in a planned episode in which Stimpy joins a girl group, The Cellulites, and scores a massive hit with a song called 'The Leg Jelly Jump'. Spector, whose own kids adored the anarchic cartoon, was instantly enamoured, even offering to voice the fiendish Svengali behind the group, the unequivocally named Ernie Vulva. Unfortunately, the network behind the series, Nickelodeon, pulled the plug on the show before the episode was made, and it would be two years before Spector was again in the public eye.

In 1994, Spector returned to the studio for the first time in 15 years, to oversee sessions by Celine Dion, the French-Canadian songstress who had improbably risen from a mid-1980s Eurovision Song Contestant to become one of the biggest singing stars in the world. Working towards her next album, Dion planned to team up with a number of different producers, but Spector had no fear of the competition – nor of Dion's reputation as one of the decade's most cosseted divas.

On 20 June, Spector took over Ocean Way studio in Los Angeles, filling it with his own coterie of friends and musicians. La Dion entered the studio to find a 60-piece orchestra and close to two dozen players awaiting her, including Spector faithfuls Nino Tempo, Dan and David Kessel and Jim Keltner, plus arranger Jimmie Haskell – meeting Spector again, 38 years after he was handed control of The Teddy Bears album. Dion's manager/husband Rene, however, was contrarily informed that he himself was not welcome in the room. Spector eventually relented on that prohibition, but his point was made – he was in charge of the session, and he would brook no interference from anybody else.

Spector could be charm itself, or he could be hostility personified. Never taking his eyes off Dion, he regaled her with red roses, but constantly put down the other producers lined up for the album, insisting that every one of them had stolen all they knew from his own techniques. As for those techniques themselves, he gave Dion a hands-on demonstration of them all. Across two sessions, on 20 June and 23 June, three songs – titled, for the musicians' benefit, by mere numbers alone – were recorded with very little fuss, and all agreed that they would certainly beautify the new album.

Returning to the studio on 30 June, however, attempts to complete a fourth song were almost absurdly protracted. The studio itself had been booked only from 7–11pm, but here it was, four in the morning, and Dion – who was due to shoot a new video later that day – was still awaiting her turn at the microphone. Finally, one of her entourage asked Spector whether he even needed Dion in the studio. The producer responded with such ferocity that all activity halted, and the entire studio turned to stare.

In her official biography, *Celine*, Dion growled, 'I looked at Rene. I knew exactly what he was thinking and what he was going to do. And I agreed with him. I stood up and I walked out of the studio. I then understood that I would never put my feet in that studio again and that I would never work with Phil Spector again.' Spector, apparently, didn't even notice her departure.

Rene joined her a few minutes later. 'He told him that it was over, that I was gone and would not come back. Even if Spector told him he was sorry, Rene didn't care. He told him that he never permitted anybody to treat his friends like that, and that artists, even the greatest, don't have all the rights.' Spector remained unabashed. 'Her husband was jealous,' he said later. 'He didn't like losing control of the decisions.' All the Dion duo had wanted, he told *Entertainment Weekly*, was hit records, no matter how 'contrived', 'repugnant' or even 'Mariah Carey-rejected soundalike' they were.

The results of the sessions have never been released, but Dion herself offered up at least a suggestion of regret for how it all ended when she appeared on American television's *David Letterman Show* on 8 August 1994, performing 'River Deep – Mountain High'.

Although he would not return to the studio any time soon, Spector continued circulating on the Hollywood scene – and beyond. In March 1999, he attended the latest Rock 'n' Roll Hall of Fame bash at the New York Astoria, to watch as Springsteen, McCartney, Billy Joel and George Martin were elected, and enjoy a dinner that *Entertainment Weekly* described as 'such a spirited love-feast that even the mercurial Phil Spector was being playful. Three journalists descended on the legendarily temperamental producer, tape recorders and pens poised. Rather than turn tail, Spector flashed a chicken-eating grin and asked, "Is there gonna be a fight now?"'

Not on that occasion, there wasn't. But another battle was looming. In 1988, as the phenomenal success of the *Dirty Dancing* soundtrack became apparent, and further Ronettes recordings turned up in commercials for Levi jeans and American Express credit cards, Ronnie, Estelle and Nedra, The Ronettes, reformed to lodge a $10 million claim against Spector, seeking damages for breach of contract and loss of earnings, and to lodge a claim of ownership over the 28 original recordings they cut with him – in other words, the complete overturning of the waiver that they had signed in 1963. They also sought to disqualify another agreement that, according to Spector's attorney, had been made following Ronnie's divorce in 1976, in which she relinquished all rights to The Ronettes' records and, apparently, released Spector from any future claims and lawsuits.

The case hung in the air for several years, but precedents were stirring all around. With former music agent Chuck Rubin's New York-based Artists Rights Enforcement Corporation fighting in the performers' corner, the late 1980s and early 1990s saw a flurry of similar law suits launched against record labels, producers and management companies who had profited from such long-ago arrangements and, in 1991, a decision by the United States Sixth Circuit Court of Appeal apparently voided all such short-sightedness by awarding $1.2 million in back royalties to a group of similarly situated performers.

Tagged the 'victimised artists' law, the ruling adopted the stance that many performers did not realise, and certainly were never told, that they were effectively signing away millions of dollars when they took a one-off payment of a few thousand. The counter-argument, of course, is that there was no way that anybody else could have known how much their catalogues would be worth at some future date, and that there are many artists and performers who actually emerged better off for taking the pay-off when it was offered. That consideration, however, is very rarely raised and, even if it had been, it would have made no difference to The Ronettes.

Preparations for the case dragged on interminably. It would be a full decade before it finally came to court in New York on 9 June 1998, by which time, another precedent had stung home. On 7 March 1997, a court ordered Spector to pay Darlene Love $263,000 in back royalties (negotiating for the release of *Back To Mono*, Allen Klein had offered her less than one-tenth of that), and portrayed Spector himself in less than effervescent light as the hearing rattled along.

For his first deposition, delivered by video, Spector appeared wearing a doctor's mask and surgical gloves, and left the jury wondering precisely what kind of man they were dealing with. For his second, in person, he oozed charm, cracked jokes and had the courtroom rolling in the aisles. And at his third, he lost both his temper and, perhaps, lost the jury's sympathy, as he railed furiously against every piece of evidence presented before him.

He was on a considerably more even keel as The Ronettes' case came around. The hearing opened with The Ronettes' attorney, Alexander Peltz, first playing a handful of the group's records to Manhattan Supreme Court Judge Paula Omansky, before assuring her, 'Phil Spector was a boy genius in music, producing, assembling, marketing girl groups. But he was also a genius in greed, vengeance and spite.'

Spector's attorney, Andrew Bart, responded by accusing The Ronettes of trying to rewrite their original Philles deal to include items that might have become common in contemporary contracts, but which simply did not exist three decades earlier – things like compact discs, movie rights and advertisement licenses...whoever could have imagined a credit card company trying to sell itself with a pop song in 1963? Bart concluded by saying Spector would concede to owing, at most, $350,000 in unpaid royalties to the trio.

The law suit dragged on for the next two years, but finally appeared to have been resolved on 16 June 2000, with the award of $2.6 million (plus interest) to The Ronettes – statute of limitation concerns had ultimately restricted the group's claim to royalties dating back only as far as 1981. Judge Omansky threw out the trio's demand for ownership of their original masters, and her ruling included the acknowledgement that 'Spector's contributions to The Ronettes' success cannot be underestimated, as composer of their songs, and as creator of the sound for which The Ronettes' recording hits became famous.' But her verdict nevertheless insisted that, based upon his original contract with the trio, Spector had underpaid them.

Ronnie was ecstatic. 'I worked very, very hard making those records in the '60s. I just didn't know I'd have to wait 37 years to get paid for my efforts. Does this change all the obstacles and restrictions that the defendants put in front of me that have damaged my career, such as not being able to perform my songs on TV [and] being blackballed from the Rock 'n' Roll Hall of Fame? No, it doesn't, but it's a step forward...maybe now I can get back to doing what I love: making records and performing.'

She was still in celebratory mood in a *Rolling Stone* interview in September 2000. 'He had to put the money [owed] in an escrow account. [The deadline to appeal] is practically over, and so is he, if you know what I mean.' Unfortunately, she spoke too soon. Spector did indeed file an appeal and, on 18 October 2002, a New York state appeals court dismissed the earlier verdict, with the ruling that the 1963 contract remained legally binding and afforded Spector the right to license the group's music in any way he saw fit, without entitling them to residuals.

The Ronettes were entitled to royalties from compilations and reissues, of course, and the five-judge panel returned the case to a lower court to calculate that figure. The court also determined that Ronnie herself was entitled to additional payments, as the 1976 agreement turned out not to have relinquished her right to future royalties. It would all add up to what lawyer Ira Greenberg hoped would be 'a reasonable sum of money'. At a fixed royalty rate of 3 per cent, however, it would never come close to the $3 million The Ronettes had just lost.

'The best evidence of what parties to a written agreement intend is what they say in their writing,' wrote Judge Victoria Graffeo as she summed up the 15-year-long battle, while Spector's lawyer, Andrew Bart, celebrated by telling the *New York Daily*, 'the court is sending a clear signal that we're a system of law that regards contracts as things that have to be followed'.

Not everybody celebrated alongside Spector. Hilary Rosen, CEO of the Recording Industry Association of America, told *Billboard* magazine, 'Phil Spector can certainly do voluntarily what our members have done and make fair payments based on The Ronettes' incredible contribution to his career. Not because he has to, but because it is right.' The Recording Artists' Coalition (RAC), too, weighed in, as spokesman Jay Rosenthal complained that the ruling 'will do nothing but embolden those who make a living out of exploiting recording artists'.

Spector had other reasons to be buoyant that autumn. Not only had he won a case that many observers had assumed he was destined to lose, but he had also returned to the recording studio for the first time since the aborted Celine Dion sessions, to work with a new British band, Starsailor.

Rumours had been circulating for a couple of years that he was preparing to step back into the control room – one story linked him with Sean Lennon, the younger of John's two sons, with whom he was said to be recording material that sounded like a cross between Weezer and classic Brian Wilson.

Nothing had come of those tales. But this time was different. Touring the US earlier in the year, Starsailor were astonished when Spector appeared backstage at their show at the LA Palace on 12 January 2002, and invited them back to the Castle.

It was daughter Nicole who made the introductions. 'We ended up having a few drinks,' bassist James Stelfox said. 'She said, "My Dad's a big fan of yours. Would you like to meet him?"' Starsailor frontman James Walsh continued, 'we've heard all these stories about [Spector] being this mad eccentric, and luckily he was really on form.' Their first glimpse of Spector found him resplendent in a curly wig, built-up heels and one of a wardrobe full of identical suits with his initials embroidered on the label. Later, he allowed Walsh to handle the guitar that Yoko gave Spector following Lennon's death. 'That was pretty incredible.' But he also talked with the group about their music, asking if they wanted to record with him.

He'd been a fan of the band since Nicole played him a song from their first album, 'Lullaby', and when the band played a demo of their most recent composition, 'Silence Is Easy', Spector's enthusiasm knew no bounds. 'This should be the fuckin' national anthem! I'm gonna take this to number one.'

Starsailor were not necessarily holding their breath. Back in London, Walsh told XFM radio, 'he hasn't done anything since working with the Ramones, so it [will be] a massive honour to work with him. We'll do one song with him and see how it goes. It might not work, but then again it might.' On another occasion, Walsh cautioned, 'nothing's set in stone. We don't want to be pressured into doing something because he's such a renowned producer. But if it's what's right for the band, it's not something we'd rule out.' Just weeks later, in July, Spector flew to London to meet up with the band at Metropolis Studios.

Immediately, the band's doubts flew. 'It was an amazing experience, first and foremost,' Walsh marvelled. 'To see, for example, the way he could make a string quartet sound like an orchestra. We wanted to make the sound as big and wide screen and as open as possible, while everyone else was trying to make themselves sound small and bluesy. Spector was great at doing that.'

Of course he demanded they work through the night – sessions began at six and ended at four in the morning. Neither had his production methods changed. 'He didn't want to use anything modern, any pro-tools or anything like that. Whatever you recorded, stuck. You couldn't really go back over anything and say "That could sound better or that could sound better."'

'He's just an enigma really,' Walsh told Radio One. 'What was great about him was how down to earth he was, and how he treated this as important as recording with John Lennon and things. That's not to be big-headed or anything, but he was still enthusiastic. It wasn't like – "Oh gosh, I've got to do this band. Why couldn't I have got the Bruce Springsteen album or something?"'

The initial intention was to record just the one number, 'Silence Is Easy', but the session went so well that a second song, 'White Dove', followed, and plans were laid for further sessions at Abbey Road in September. There, however, the relationship fell apart. Interviewed by *The Guardian* newspaper the following August, Walsh recalled Spector's mood shifting day by day, from cheerfully enthusiastic to absolute disinterest, punctuated by moments of dictatorial firmness. 'It gradually became a very strange experience. It was like working with a completely different person, day to day.'

Finally the band made the hardest decision of their career so far – to sack Spector. James Stelfox swung the axe: 'I shot two straight brandies and just said, "Phil, it has been great working with you, but we feel we need to carry on".' Spector recovered his shock within moments. 'I understand. This is your baby. It's your dream. Go realise it.'

Spector offered up his own side of the story to *Esquire*. 'You can't spend three months of your life making an album with guys who play pinball and video games all day. These guys are very good, but they're dumb. There *are* no Rolling Stones anymore. There *are* no Beatles.'

Both of the songs he completed with the band made it onto the next Starsailor album, September 2003s *Silence Is Easy*, with the so majestic title track itself instantly leaping into the UK Top 10, impressing everyone who heard it with a lyric that was nothing less than eerie biography. 'Silence is easy, it just becomes me', after all, could well have summed up Spector's own famed reticence within the circus that had always surrounded him, while the remainder of the chorus implored, 'you don't even know me, you all lie about me, why do you hate me?' And that really hit home for, by the time the record was released, Spector had spent nine months enduring such hatred and lies that any past prejudices to which he'd been exposed seemed absolutely insignificant in comparison.

The tape was still warm from Spector's work with Starsailor when word began flying that he was interested in another new band, the Australian combo, The Vines. Like Starsailor, they were looking to follow up a successful debut album and, in conversation with the *New York Times*, Spector's friend, lawyer Marv Michelson, insisted the producer was 'very bullish' in his enthusiasm for the group.

In the event, the speculation was quashed within days of its arrival on the streets (or, more properly, the internet). But the very fact that Spector's name was being avidly associated with another of the year's most vibrant 'new' acts suggested that a veil of some sort had finally been drawn aside, and he was straining to step back into action.

Bono, ebullient frontman with U2 and all-round saviour of the universe, made overtures towards him, suggesting they try writing a song together. Spector was regularly spotted checking out fresh bands – so regularly that, where once passers-by would have drawn back when they spotted him, fearful that Crazy Phil was on the prowl, nowadays people scarcely even noticed him; or, if they did, thought nothing about saying hello. Sometimes he even said hello back to them. He had quit drinking, and was throwing himself into a veritable social whirl. Friends looked forward to the annual bowling parties he hosted in Montrose. He was spotted at LA Lakers games and, when Nancy Sinatra needed someone to accompany her to a Bruce Springsteen concert, Spector joined her. He was happy, he was calm... in short, he was normal.

And then his entire world was blown apart.

Around 5am on 3 February 2003, Hollywood police received a phone call from an address in Alhambra. A limo driver had just dropped off his employer and a woman, and was still parking the Mercedes, when he heard shots ring out – as many as three or four. But when the police arrived at the house, the Pyrenees Castle, there was just one body to be found, a woman who lay slumped in a white antique chair in the foyer.

The police arrested Phil Spector on the spot, leading him out to the squad car at Taser-point. Other officers remained behind to strip the limousine, search the house, scoop up his computers and round up his guns. At the station, they ran gunshot residue tests, and then left him to sit in a cell until his attorney, Robert Sharp, arrived. With his arraignment set for 30 days hence, on 3 March, Spector was released that afternoon on $1-million bail. When he arrived home and switched on the news, he found he *was* the news.

The previous evening, Spector's first port of call was Dan Tana's, an old-style Italian restaurant on Santa Monica Boulevard that he had frequented since the 1960s. He was not alone; he and a lady friend ordered salad and a sweet cocktail each, and left a $500 tip on a $55 meal. As usual.

Parting with his companion later in the evening, Spector made his way to the House of Blues in West Hollywood. He arrived around 2.30am, heading straight for the VIPs-only Foundation Room, a select corner of the club open to anybody with $2,200 to drop on the annual membership fee.

There he fell into conversation with one of the hostesses, a b-movie actress named Lana Clarkson. She'd only been working at the venue for a month or so, picking up a regular payslip to supplement her somewhat bitty career in acting – straight-to-video horror flicks with names like *Death Stalker* and *Blind Date*. She'd played small parts in *Scarface* and *Fast Times At Ridgemont High*, but she was probably best known for the title role in Roger Corman's *Barbarian Queen*, a film that was widely regarded, if not necessarily acknowledged, as the inspiration for television's *Xena: Warrior Princess*. Later, a Hollywood reporter smiled sadly, 'every producer in town knows a Lana. It was just sad that this one had to die before anyone else knew who she was.'

Spector, too, had undergone some major life changes in recent weeks. Though his marriage to Janice had ended, the couple remained friends, and she continued working for him long after they stopped living together. That arrangement, however, had finally ended just a couple of weeks earlier, in January 2003, and when Spector hit the House of Blues that evening, maybe he was looking for company...or maybe he wasn't.

He found it, though, and when the media swooped on the venue in the days that followed, to interrogate anybody who might have seen the couple together – everyone from the bar staff to singer Rob Halford, who was performing that evening – at least a handful remembered seeing the pair talking, laughing...nothing out of the unusual in the slightest.

A little before five, Spector announced that he was ready to go home. So was Clarkson; as they left, she grabbed a bottle of tequila off the bar, and they walked out to where Spector's limo was waiting. According to Spector, his intention was simply to give the woman a lift home. But she asked if they could detour via the Castle on the way and Spector, to whom such a request really didn't seem that strange, agreed. They went into the house...they got as far as the foyer. And after that...the media went into overdrive. 'Spector Was In Dark Place.' 'Music, Mystery and Murder.' 'The Wall of Unsound Mind.' Photographs of him being led away by the police hit the front pages

– and even his greatest adversaries could not fail to be affected by one of them, a half-profile shot of a heartbreakingly forlorn-looking Spector, looking suddenly so much older than his 62 years, arms locked behind his back, snapped in the back of a police van. Although Spector had been popping up all over the place for the last few years, Crazy Phil had been out of sight for over a decade. The absolute panic and confusion etched upon the face in that photograph brought all the old legends tumbling out of the closet, accompanied by a host of new ones.

Britain's *The Sun* tabloid uncovered a former girlfriend, stand-up comic Barbara Nichols, whom he dated during 1996, who 'told how deranged music legend Phil Spector held a gun to her head after a kinky sex session'. And, no matter how many of Spector's own friends and old associates rushed to his defence, still America's A&E network constructed a *Biography* episode that was so heavily weighted towards the standard mythology that objectivity itself seemed set to go on vacation.

Other tabloids combed Clarkson's own website in search of clues as to her fate, while FoxNews.com reporter Roger Friedman speculated that maybe Spector was 'upset' by the recent news that surviving Beatles Paul McCartney and Ringo Starr were readying a de-Spectorised version of *Let It Be* for release later in the year.

Donté Spector stepped out with his allegations of abuse, and the interview Spector gave to the *Daily Telegraph*'s Mick Brown just weeks before Clarkson's death provided its own share of self-immolating ammunition. 'Tortured Producer Admits "I'm Insane!"'

But Ronnie Spector, interviewed by the American ABC television network, insisted, 'I never thought he would ever kill anybody. He would yell, but he would never hit me.' Darlene Love raced to his defence: 'this is horrible. How could it possibly be true?' Marky Ramone exclaimed, 'Phil to me is no murderer.' Marv Mitchelson affirmed his own '100 per cent' conviction that 'it's not a homicide'.

Even District Attorney spokeswoman Sandi Gibbons acknowledged, 'we haven't seen any evidence yet' and, as the 3 March arraignment approached, it became apparent that they were not going to, as the lead investigator in the case, Los Angeles police Lieutenant Dan Rosenberg, admitted that detectives would not be ready to present their case that soon. 'Once we present the case,' he explained, 'the district attorney will determine what charges will be filed, if any.' But until they presented it, all hands were tied.

Spector's team worked on. His lawyer, Robert Shapiro, was one of the leading lights in the infamous OJ Simpson murder trial in the mid-1990s; he enlisted another veteran of that circus, forensic expert Dr Michael Baden. Arraignment was now scheduled for 1 August 2003.

On 10 March Michelle Blaine, daughter of drummer Hal and one of Spector's closest confidantes in recent years, e-mailed Mitchelson and a few other friends to explain, in Spector's words, that Clarkson's death was 'an accidental suicide'. The e-mail expressed confidence that the investigators would shortly be drawing the same conclusion themselves.

The police struck back immediately. According to LA Sheriff's Captain Frank Merriman, the authorities had already ruled out suicide and remained convinced that the shooting was a crime. 'No one involved in this investigation said that [Spector will be cleared]. My opinion is that somebody is orchestrating this to plant seeds of doubt with potential jurors.'

They were strong words, but Spector remained curiously convincing. In one of the most widely quoted interviews he had ever given, to *Esquire* magazine's Scott Raab, he whispered, 'it's *Anatomy of a Frame-Up*. There is no case. They have no case.' Referring to a high-profile celebrity murder case already gripping the LA media, he insisted, 'this is *not* Bobby Blake'.

What it was…was inexplicable, Spector admitted that. 'She kissed the gun. I have no idea why. I never knew her, never even saw her before that night. I have no idea who she was or what her agenda was.' The gun was not his and, presumably, his own hands were clear of any incriminating residue. They were certainly clear of blood, and the DA's desk remained clear of evidence as the August arraignment date came and went. The police were *still* investigating. 'We're waiting to get all of the reports back from the crime lab,' explained Rosenberg. In a brief hearing conducted by telephone, Spector's $1 million bail was extended until 30 September.

A summer of silence on the investigative front was finally shattered on 19 September, when detectives finally presented their case to the DA – one that would unequivocally dismiss Spector's side of the story. 'We had plenty of evidence…' Frank Merriman said. Blaming the protracted investigation on delays in completing unspecified tests, he affirmed, Clarkson's death was 'not an accident. It's not a suicide. Phil Spector shot her.'

Three days later, the coroner's office confirmed the police's opinion, as Lt Cheryl MacWillie of the Los Angeles County coroner's office told the media that, according to the coroner, Clarkson died of a single gunshot wound 'of the head and neck', and that she was 'shot by another' person. The coroner's full autopsy report was not released by request of prosecutors, while the sense that something was about to happen was increased that same day, as a Superior Court judge refused journalist Carlton Smith's request that the search warrants be unsealed, stating that doing so could result in the 'substantial probability of irreparable damage' to the ongoing investigation.

Suggestions that the DA was ready to move ahead with a prosecution, however, were swiftly dismissed at the next arraignment on 30 September as a Superior Court judge extended his bail yet another month…and again on 31 October, when another extension pushed the delay to 9 January 2004, a full 11 months after Clarkson's death.

In the meantime, Spector refused to let the gossip drag him down. He knew that every eye in the city was on him, that every tongue was wagging, but he continued to go out when he felt like it, carried on going to clubs and restaurants, still hung out in the Foundation Room, still left monster tips at Dan Tana's.

He just didn't do it on his own any longer.

Discography

Releases are listed chronologically by original (usually US) release date. UK releases and all reissues follow immediately after original release information.

Month / Year US = original US release (chart position follows catalogue number)
Month / Year UK = original UK release (chart position follows catalogue number)
Year USR = US reissue (chart position follows catalogue number)
Year UKR = UK reissue (chart position follows catalogue number)
* tracks marked = non-Spector productions (includes releases on related labels:
    Philles, Ember, Warner–Spector, Phil Spector Int'l etc)
** tracks marked = Spector co-productions
[?] tracks marked = unconfirmed involvement

1958-59: THE TEDDY BEARS

SINGLES
08/58 US: To Know Him Is To Love Him / Don't You Worry My Little Pet
    (Doré 503 – No 1)
08/58 UK: To Know Him Is To Love Him / Don't You Worry My Little Pet
    (London HL 8733 – No 2)
1970 UKR: To Know Him Is To Love Him / cut by Jewel Aiken (Contempo)
1979 UKR: To Know Him Is To Love Him / cut by Jody Reynolds
(Lightning LIG 9015 – No 66)
01/59 US: I Don't Need You Anymore / Oh Why
    (Imperial 5562 – No 98; B–side No 91)
01/59 UK: I Don't Need You Anymore / Oh Why (London HLP 8836)
03/59 US: If Only You Knew / You Said Goodbye (Imperial 5581)
03/59 UK: If Only You Knew / You Said Goodbye (London HLP 8889)

04/59 US: Wonderful Lovable You / I Really Do (Doré 520)

06/59 US: Don't Go Away / Seven Lonely Days (Imperial 5594)

ALBUMS

02/59 US: *The Teddy Bears Sing!* (Imperial 9067)

Oh Why / Unchained Melody / My Foolish Heart / You Said Goodbye / True Love / Little Things Mean A Lot / I Don't Need You Anymore / Tammy / Long Ago And Far Away / Don't Go Away / If I Give My Heart To You / Seven Lonely Days

1990s Euro: *The Teddy Bears Sing!* (Doré 503 – bootleg)

as above + To Know Him Is To Love Him / Don't You Worry My Little Pet / Wonderful Lovable You / Say You'll Be Mine / If You Only Knew / If I Gave My Heart To You / To Know Him Is To Love Him (live)

1990s Euro: *My Little Pet* (Trey 20207 – bootleg)

Don't You Worry My Little Pet / To Know Him Is To Love Him / Till You'll Be Mine / Wonderful Loveable You / Oh Why / Unchained Melody / My Foolish Heart / You Said Goodbye / Seven Lonely Days / I Don't Need You Anymore / Tammy / Long Ago And Far Away / Don't Go Away / If I Give My Heart To You / True Love / Little Things Mean A Lot

1959-60: PHIL SPECTOR PRODUCTIONS / PERFORMANCES

SINGLES

03/59 US: **Phil Harvey:** Bumbershoot / Willy Boy (Imperial 5583)

11/59 US: **Spector's Three:** I Really Do / I Know Why (Trey 3001)

05/60 US: **Spector's Three:** Mr Robin / My Heart Stood Still (Trey 3005)

11/60 US: **Ben E King:** Spanish Harlem (co-wrote) / First Taste Of Love (co-wrote) (Atco 6185 – No 10)

01/61 UK: **Ben E King** First Taste Of Love (co-wrote) / Spanish Harlem (co-wrote) (London HLU 9258 – No 27)

NOTE: Other Spector performances for Atlantic / Leiber and Stoller remain unconfirmed. For productions, see over.

1950-65: PHIL SPECTOR PRODUCTIONS

SINGLES

02/60 US: **Greg Connors:** Tears Me Up / Caught In The Act (Trey 3003)

08/60 US: **Kell Osborne:** The Bells Of St Mary's / That's Alright Baby (Trey 3006)

10/60 US: **Billy Storm:** Sure As You're Born / In The Chapel At Midnight (Atlantic 2076)

10/60 UK: **Billy Storm:** Sure As You're Born / In The Chapel At Midnight (London HLK 9236)

11/60 US: **Ray Peterson:** Corinne, Corinna / Be My Girl (Dunes 2002 – No 9)

11/60 UK: **Ray Peterson:** Corinne, Corinna / Be My Girl (London HLX 9246 – No 41)

02/61 US: **Johnny Nash:** Some Of Your Lovin' / A World Of Tears (ABC Paramount 10181 – No 104)

02/61 US: **Billy Storm:** When You Dance / Dear One (Atlantic 2098)

02/61 US: **Paris Sisters:** Be My Boy / I'll Be Crying Tomorrow (Gregmark 2 – No 56)

02/61 US: **Blackwells:** Love Or Money / Big Daddy And The Cat (Jamie 1179)

02/61 UK: **Blackwells:** Love Or Money / Big Daddy And The Cat (London HLW 9334 – No 46)

04/61 US: **The Top Notes:** Heart Of Stone / Basic Things (Atlantic 2097)

05/61 US: **Jean Du Shon** Tired Of Trying / Talk To Me Talk To Me (Atco 6198)

05/61 US: **Billy Storm:** Honey Love* / A Kiss From Your Lips (Atlantic 2112)

05/61 US: **Curtis Lee:** Pretty Little Angel Eyes / Gee How I Wish You Were Here (Dunes 2007 – No 7)

05/61 UK: **Curtis Lee:** Pretty Little Angel Eyes / Gee How I Wish You Were Here (London HLX 9397 – No 47)

06/61 US: **The Top Notes:** Always Late / Twist And Shout (Atlantic 2115)

06/61 UK: **The Top Notes:** Twist And Shout / **April Stevens and Nino Tempo:** Sweet And Lovely (London HLK 9580)

06/61 US: **Johnny Nash:** I Need Somebody To Stand By Me* / A Thousand Miles Away [?] (ABC Paramount 10212)

06/61 US: **Karen Lake:** I'd Like To Miss My Graduation / Air Mail Special Delivery (Big Top 3073)

07/61 US: **Ruth Brown:** Anyone But You / It Tears Me All To Pieces*
(Atlantic 2104)

07/61 US: **Castle Kings:** You Can Get Him Frankenstein / Loch Lomond
(Atlantic 2107)

08/61 US: **Ducanes:** I'm So Happy / Little Did I Know
(Goldisc 3024 – No 109)

08/61 US: **Blackwells:** You Took Advantage Of Me / I (Jamie 1199)

08/61 US: **Gene Pitney:** Every Breath I Take / Mr Moon, Mr Cupid And I
(Musicor 1011 – No 42)

08/61 UK: **Gene Pitney:** Every Breath I Take / Mr Moon, Mr Cupid And I
(HMV POP 937)

09/61 US: **Johnny Nash:** I Lost My Baby / I'm Counting On You [?]
(ABC Paramount 10230)

09/61 US: **Paris Sisters:** I Love How You Love Me / All Through The Night
(Gregmark 6 – No 5)

09/61 UK: **Paris Sisters:** I Love How You Love Me / I'll Be Crying Tomorrow
(Top Rank JAR 588)

09/61 US: **Creations:** The Bells / Shang Shang (Jamie 1197)

10/61 US: **Curtis Lee:** Under The Moon Of Love / Beverly Jane
(Dunes 2008 – No 46)

10/61 UK: **Curtis Lee:** Under The Moon Of Love / Beverly Jane
(London – HLX 9445)

10/61 US: **Ben E King:** Young Boy Blues* (Spector co-wrote) / Here Comes
The Night* (Atco 6207 – No 66)

10/61 UK: **Ben E King:** Here Comes The Night* / Young Boy Blues*
(Spector co-wrote) (London HLK 9457)

11/61 US: **Ray Peterson:** I Could Have Loved You So Well / Why Don't You
Write Me (Dunes 2009 – No 57)

11/61 UK: **Ray Peterson:** I Could Have Loved You So Well / Why Don't You
Write Me (London HLX 9489)

11/61 US: **LaVern Baker:** Hey Memphis / Voodoo Voodoo* (Atlantic 2119)

11/61 UK: **LaVern Baker:** Hey Memphis / Voodoo Voodoo*
(London HLK 9468)

11/61 US: **Sammy Turner:** Falling* / Raincoat In The River (Big Top 3089)

11/61 UK: **Sammy Turner:** Falling* / Raincoat In The River
(London HLXZ 9488)

12/61 US: **Billy Storm:** 3000 Tears / Who'll Keep An Eye On Jane (Gregmark 9)

—/61 US: **Arlene Smith:** Everything* / Good Girls*
(Spectorius 150 – release unconfirmed)

01/62 US: **Joel Scott:** Here I Stand* / You're My Only Love* (Philles 101)

01/62 US: **Paris Sisters:** He Knows I Love Him Too Much / A Lonely Girl's
Prayer (Gregmark 10 – No 34)

02/62 US: **Arlene Smith:** He Knows I Love Him Too Much / Love Love Love
(Big Top 3073)

02/62 US: **Ben E King:** Ecstasy* (Spector co-wrote) / Yes* (Atco 6215 – No 56)

02/62 UK: **Ben E King:** Ecstasy* (Spector co-wrote) / Yes*
(London HLK 9517)

03/62 US: **Gary Crosby:** That's Alright Baby / Who (Gregmark 11)

05/62 US: **Paris Sisters:** Let Me Be The One / What Am I To Do
(Gregmark 12)

05/62 US: **Troy Shondell:** Na-Ne-No / Just Because* (Liberty 55445)

05/62 US: **Connie Francis:** Second Hand Love / Gonna Git That Man*
(MGM 13074 – No 7)

07/62 US: **Bobby Sheen:** How Many Nights / How Can We Be Together
(Liberty 55459)

08/62 US: **Obrey Wilson:** Hey There Mountain / Say It Again
(Liberty 55483)

09/62 US: **Timi Yuro:** What's A Matter Baby / Thirteenth Hour
(Liberty 55469 – remixed)

11/62 US: **Paris Sisters:** Yes I Love You / Once Upon A While Ago
(Gregmark 13)

—/62 US: **Russell Byrd:** Little Bug / Nights Of Mexico (Wand 121)

02/63 US: **Terry Day:** Be A Soldier / I Love You Betty (Columbia 4–43678)

—/65 US: **Equal Employment Opportunities Campaign:** Things Are
Changing (T–4LM 8172–1)

ALBUMS

—/62 US: **Gene Pitney:** *The Many Sides Of Gene Pitney* (Musicor MU
2001) 2 tracks only produced by Spector: Dream For Sale / Every Breath
I Take

11/63 US: **Various Artists:** *KYA's Memories of the Cow Palace* (Autumn
101)* Live recording 28 Sept 1963. Spector credited as arranger and
conductor.

1990s Euro: **Paris Sisters:** *Sing Their Favourites* (A-Side AZ8001 – bootleg)

(7 tracks only prod by Spector) Be My Boy / I Love How You Love Me /
All Through The Night / He Knows I Love Him Too Much / A Lonely
Girl's Prayer / Let Me Be The One / What Am I To Do

1990s Euro: Various Artists: *Twist And Shout – 12 Atlantic Tracks
Produced By Phil Spector* (MMG AMCY 25 – bootleg)

When You Dance – **Billy Storm** / Dear One – **Billy Storm** / Hearts of Stone
– **The Top Notes** / Basic Things – **The Top Notes** / Hey Memphis –
LaVern Baker / Anyone But You – **Ruth Brown** / Honey Love – **Billy
Storm** / A Kiss from Your Lips – **Billy Storm** / Twist and Shout – **The Top
Notes** / Always Late – **The Top Notes** / Tired of Trying – **Jean Du Shon** /
Talk to Me, Talk to Me – **Jean Du Shon**

1961-67: PHILLES RECORDS RELEASES

SINGLES

10/61 US: The Crystals: There's No Other / Oh Yeah, Maybe Baby
(Philles 1001 – No 20)

02/62 UK: The Crystals: There's No Other / Oh Yeah, Maybe Baby
(Parlophone R4867)

1985 USR: The Crystals: There's No Other / **Bob B Soxx:** Not Too Young
To Get Married (Philles / Collectables 3207)

03/62 US: The Crystals: Uptown / What A Nice Way To Turn 17
(Philles 102 – No 13)

1985 USR: The Crystals: Uptown / He's Sure The Boy I Love
(Philles / Collectables 3202)

04/62 US: Al Hazan: Malagüeña* / Chopsticks* (Philles 103)

04/62 US: Steve Douglas And His Merry Men: Lt Colonel Bogey's Parade*
/ Yes Sir, That's My Baby* (Philles 104)

06/62 US: The Crystals: He Hit Me / No-one Ever Tells You
(Philles 105 – withdrawn)

10/62 US: The Crystals: He's A Rebel / I Love You Eddie (Philles 106 – No 1)

10/62 UK: The Crystals: He's A Rebel / I Love You Eddie
(London HLU 9611 – No 19)

1975 UKR: The Crystals: He's A Rebel / I Love You Eddie
(Phil Spector Int'l 2010 002)

1985 USR: The Crystals: He's A Rebel / He Hit Me
(Philles / Collectables 3200)

10/62 US: Bob B Soxx And The Blue Jeans: Zip-A-Dee-Doo-Dah / Flip And Nitty (Philles 107 – No 8)

01/63 UK: Bob B Soxx And The Blue Jeans: Zip-A-Dee-Doo-Dah / Flip And Nitty (London HLU 9646 – No 45)

1975 UKR: Bob B Soxx And The Blue Jeans: Zip-A-Dee-Doo-Dah / Flip And Nitty (Phil Spector Int'l 2010 004 – unissued)

10/62 US: The Alley Cats: Puddin 'n' Tain / Feel So Good* (Philles 108 – No 43)

1985 USR: / The Alley Cats: Puddin 'n' Tain /**The Crystals:** Then He Kissed Me (Philles / Collectables 3201)

12/62 US: The Crystals: He's Sure The Boy I Love / Walking Along (Philles 109 – No 11)

01/63 UK: The Crystals: He's Sure The Boy I Love / Walking Along (London HLU 9661)

01/63 US: Bob B Soxx And The Blue Jeans: Why Do Lovers Break Each Other's Hearts? / Dr Kaplan's Office (Philles 110 – No 38)

03/63 UK: Bob B Soxx And The Blue Jeans: Why Do Lovers Break Each Other's Hearts? / Dr Kaplan's Office (London HLU 9694)

01/63 US: The Crystals: (Let's Dance) The Screw parts 1 and 2 (Philles 111 – DJ only)

04/63 US: Darlene Love: The Boy I'm Gonna Marry / My Heart Beat A Little Faster (Philles 111 – withdrawn)

04/63 US: Darlene Love: The Boy I'm Gonna Marry / Playing For Keeps (Philles 111 – No 39)

04/63 UK: Darlene Love: The Boy I'm Gonna Marry / Playing For Keeps (London HLU 9725)

04/63 US: The Crystals: Da Doo Ron Ron / Git It (Philles 112 – No 3)

04/63 UK: The Crystals: Da Doo Ron Ron / Git It (London HLU 9732 – No 5)

1974 UKR: The Crystals: Da Doo Ron Ron / Then He Kissed Me (Warner-Spector K 19010 – No 15

1976 UKR: The Crystals: Da Doo Ron Ron / Then He Kissed Me (Phil Spector Int'l 2010 011)

1985 USR: The Crystals: Da Doo Ron Ron / All Grown Up (Philles / Collectables 3206)

05/63 US: Bob B Soxx And The Blue Jeans: Not Too Young To Get Married / Annette (Philles 113 – No 63)

07/63 UK: Bob B Soxx And The Blue Jeans: Not Too Young To Get Married / Annette (London HLU 9754)

07/63 US: **Darlene Love:** Wait Til My Bobby Gets Home / Take It From Me
(Philles 114 – No 26)

08/63 UK: **Darlene Love:** Wait Til My Bobby Gets Home / Take It From Me
(London HLU 9765)

07/63 US: **The Crystals:** Then He Kissed Me / Brother Julius
(Philles 115 – No 6)

09/63 UK: **The Crystals:** Then He Kissed Me / Brother Julius
(London HLU 773 – No 2)

1985 USR: **The Crystals:** Then He Kissed Me / **The Alley Cats:** Puddin 'n'
Tain (Philles / Collectables 3201)

08/63 US: **The Ronettes:** Be My Baby / Tedesco and Pitman (Philles 116 – No 2)

10/63 UK: **The Ronettes:** Be My Baby / Tedesco and Pitman
(London HLU 9763 – No 4)

1975 UKR: **The Ronettes:** Be My Baby / Do I Love You
(Phil Spector Int'l 2010 003 – 1975)

11/63 US: **Darlene Love:** A Fine, Fine Boy / Nino and Sonny
(Philles 117 – No 53)

11/63 UK: **Darlene Love:** A Fine, Fine Boy / Marshmallow World
(London HLU 9815)

12/63 US: **The Ronettes:** Baby I Love You / Miss Joan And Mr Sam
(Philles 118 – No 24)

01/64 UK: **The Ronettes:** Baby I Love You / Miss Joan And Mr Sam
(London HLU 9826 – No 11

11/63 US: **Darlene Love:** Christmas (Baby Please Come Home) / Harry And
Milt Meet Hal B (Philles 119 – withdrawn)

1964 USR: **Darlene Love:** Christmas (Baby Please Come Home) / Winter
Wonderland (Philles 125)

1965 USR: **Darlene Love:** Christmas (Baby Please Come Home) / Winter
Blues (Philles 125)

1974 USR: **Darlene Love:** Christmas (Baby Please Come Home) / Winter
Wonderland (Warner Spector 0401)

1974 UKR: **Darlene Love:** Christmas (Baby Please Come Home) / Wait Till
My Bobby Gets Home (Warner-Spector K19011)

01/64 US: **The Crystals:** Little Boy / Harry (from WVA) and Milt
(Philles 119 – No 92)

01/64 UK: **The Crystals:** Little Boy / Uptown
(London HLU 9837 – withdrawn)

01/64 UK: The Crystals: I Wonder / Little Boy (London HLU 9852 – No 36)

04/64 US: The Ronettes: (The Best Part Of) Breaking Up / Big Red
(Philles 120 – No 39)

07/64 UK: The Ronettes: (The Best Part Of) Breaking Up / Big Red
(London HLU 9905 – No 43)

1981 UKR: The Ronettes: (The Best Part Of) Breaking Up / Do I Love You
(Phil Spector Int'l POSP 377)

06/64 US: The Ronettes: Do I Love You / Bebe And Susu (Philles 121 – No 34)

09/64 UK: The Ronettes: Do I Love You / Bebe And Susu
(London HLU 9922 – No 35)

06/64 US: The Crystals: All Grown Up / Irving (Jaggered Sixteenths)
(Philles 122 – No 98)

07/64 UK: The Crystals: All Grown Up / Irving (London HLU 9909)

1977 UKR: The Crystals: All Grown Up / The Twist
(Phil Spector Int'l 2010 020)

09/64 US: Darlene Love: Stumble and Fall /Quiet Guy (Philles 123 w'drawn)

10/64 US: The Ronettes: Walking In The Rain / How Does It Feel?
(Philles 123 – No 23)

11/64 UK: The Ronettes: Walking In The Rain / How Does It Feel?
(London HLU 9931)

1977 UKR: The Ronettes: Walking In The Rain / I Wonder
(Phil Spector Int'l 2010 017)

12/64 US: Righteous Brothers: You've Lost That Lovin' Feelin' / There's A
Woman* (Philles 124 – No 1)

12/64 UK: Righteous Brothers: You've Lost That Lovin' Feelin' / There's A
Woman* (London HLU 9943 – No 1)

1969 UKR: Righteous Brothers: You've Lost That Lovin' Feelin' / There's
A Woman* (London HL 10241)

1977 UKR: Righteous Brothers: You've Lost That Lovin' Feelin' / Rat Race
(Phil Spector Int'l 2010 022)

1990 UKR: Righteous Brothers: You've Lost That Lovin' Feelin' / Ebb Tide
(Polydor PO 116)

01/65 US: The Ronettes (featuring Veronica): Born To Be Together / Blues
For Baby (Philles 126 – No 52)

02/65 US: The Ronettes (featuring Veronica): Born To Be Together / Blues
For Baby (Philles 126)

03/65 US: Righteous Brothers: Just Once In My Life / The Blues*

(Philles 127 – No 9)

04/65 UK: **Righteous Brothers:** Just Once In My Life / The Blues*
(London HL 9962 – withdrawn)

08/66 UKR: **Righteous Brothers:** Just Once In My Life / The Blues*
(London HL 10066)

05/65 US: **The Ronettes (featuring Veronica):** Is This What I Get For Loving
You / Oh I Love You (Philles 128 – No 75)

05/65 UK: **The Ronettes (featuring Veronica):** Is This What I Get For Loving
You / You Baby (London HLU 9976)

06/65 US: **Righteous Brothers:** Hung On You / Unchained Melody [?]
(Philles 129 – No 47 / B-side No 4)

06/65 UK: **Righteous Brothers:** Unchained Melody [?] / Hung On You
(London HL 9975 – No 14)

1990 USR: **Righteous Brothers:** Unchained Melody [?] / Hung On You
(Verve 87–1882)

11/65 US: **Righteous Brothers:** Ebb Tide / For Sentimental Reasons
(Philles 130 – No 5)

12/6 5 UK: **Righteous Brothers:** Ebb Tide / For Sentimental Reasons
(London HL 10011 – No 48)

04/66 US: **Ike and Tina Turner:** River Deep – Mountain High / I'll Keep You
Happy (Philles 131 – No 88)

05/66 UK: **Ike and Tina Turner:** River Deep – Mountain High / I'll Keep You
Happy (London HLU 10046 – No 3)

1969 USR: **Ike and Tina Turner:** River Deep – Mountain High / I'll Keep
You Happy (A&M 1118 – 1969)

1969 UKR: **Ike and Tina Turner:** River Deep – Mountain High / Oh Baby*
(A&M AMS 829 – 1969)

—- UKR: **Ike and Tina Turner:** River Deep – Mountain High / A Love Like
Yours / Save The Last Dance For Me (A&M AMS 7083)

07/76 US: **Righteous Brothers:** White Cliffs Of Dover / She's Mine All
Mine* (Philles 132 – No 21)

10/66 UK: **Righteous Brothers:** White Cliffs Of Dover / Baby She's Mine*
(London HL 10086)

08/66 US: **The Ronettes (featuring Veronica):** I Can Hear Music* / When I
Saw You (Philles 133 – No 100)

10/66 UK: **The Ronettes (featuring Veronica):** I Can Hear Music* / When I
Saw You (London HLU 10087 – withdrawn)

1976 UKR: **The Ronettes:** I Can Hear Music* / How Does It Feel
(Phil Spector Int'l 2010 014)

08/66 US: **Ike And Tina Turner:** A Man Is A Man Is A Man* / Two To
Tango* (Philles 134)

05/67 US: **Ike And Tina Turner:** I'll Never Need More Than This / Cashbox
Blues (Philles 135)

05/67 UK: **Ike And Tina Turner:** I'll Never Need More Than This / Save The
Last Dance For Me (London HLU 10155)

08/67 US: **Ike And Tina Turner:** A Love Like Yours / I Idolize You*
(Philles 136)

08/66 UK: **Ike And Tina Turner:** A Love Like Yours / I Idolize You*
(London HLU 10083)

1970 USR: **Ike And Tina Turner:** A Love Like Yours / Save The Last Dance
For Me (A&M 1170)

EPs

02/64: **UK The Crystals:** Da Doo Ron Ron (London REU 1381 – No 18)

ALBUMS

—/62 US: **The Crystals:** *Twist Uptown* (Philles 4000)

1965 USR: **The Crystals:** *Twist Uptown* (Capitol Record Club T90722)
Uptown / Another Country–Another World / Frankenstein Twist / Oh
Yeah Maybe Baby / Please Hurt Me / There's No Other (Like My Baby)
/ On Broadway / What A Nice Way To Turn Seventeen / No One Ever
Tells You / Gee Whiz Look At His Eyes (Twist) / I Love You Eddie

03/63 US: **The Crystals:** *He's A Rebel* (Philles 4001 – No 131)

—/63 UK: **The Crystals:** *He's A Rebel* (London HAU 8120)
He's A Rebel / Uptown / Another Country–Another Town / Frankenstein
Twist / Oh Yeah Maybe Baby / He's Sure The Boy I Love / There's No
Other (Like My Baby) / On Broadway / What A Nice Way To Turn
Seventeen / No One Ever Tells You / He Hit Me / I Love You Eddie

—/63 US: **Bob B Soxx And The Blue Jeans:** *Zip-A-Dee-Doo-Dah*
(Philles 4002)

—/63 UK: **Bob B Soxx And The Blue Jeans:** *Zip-A-Dee-Doo-Dah*
(London HAU 8121)
Zip-A-De-Doo-Dah / Why Do Lovers Break Each Other's Hearts? / Let
The Good Times Roll / My Heart Beat A Little Bit Faster / Jimmy Baby /

Baby (I Love You) / The White Cliffs of Dover / This Land Is Your Land / Dear (Here Comes My Baby) / I Shook The World / Everything's Gonna Be All Right / Dr Kaplan's Office

—/63 US: **The Crystals:** *The Crystals Sing The Greatest Hits Vol 1* (Philles 4003)

Da Doo Ron Ron / On Broadway / He's A Rebel / Hot Pastrami / There's No Other / The Watusi / Mashed Potato Time / He's Sure The Boy I Love / Uptown / The Twist / Gee Whiz (Look At His Eyes) / Look In My Eyes

—/63 US: **Various Artists:** *Philles Records Presents Today's Hits* (Philles 4004)

Then He Kissed Me – **The Crystals** / Da Doo Ron Ron – **The Crystals** / Oh Yeah Maybe Baby – **The Crystals** / Zip-A-De-Doo-Dah – **Bob B Soxx And The Blue Jeans** / Why Do Lovers Break Each Other's Hearts? – **Bob B Soxx And The Blue Jeans** / Not Too Young To Get Married – **Bob B Soxx And The Blue Jeans** / Be My Baby – **The Ronettes** / Wait 'Til My Bobby Gets Home – **Darlene Love** / (Today I Met) The Boy I'm Gonna Marry – **Darlene Love** / My Heart Beat A Little Bit Faster – **Darlene Love** / Playing For Keeps – **Darlene Love** / Puddin 'n' Tain – **The Alley Cats**

11/63 US: **Various Artists:** *A Christmas Gift For You From Philles Records* (Philles 4005)

11/63 UK: **Various Artists:** *A Christmas Gift For You* (London HAU 8141)

1972 USR: **Various Artists:** *Phil Spector's Christmas Album* (Apple SW 3400)

1972 UKR: **Various Artists:** *Phil Spector's Christmas Album* (Apple APCOR 24 – No 21)

1974 UKR: **Various Artists:** *Phil Spector's Christmas Album* (Warner Brothers K59010)

1975 UKR: **Various Artists:** *Phil Spector's Christmas Album* (Phil Spector Int'l 2307 005)

1977 USR: **Various Artists:** *Phil Spector's Christmas Album* (Warner-Spector SP 9103)

1981 UKR: reissue within box set **Various Artists:** *The Wall Of Sound* (Phil Spector Int'l WOS 001)

1983 UKR: **Various Artists:** *Phil Spector's Christmas Album / Greatest Hits* (Impression —— – No 19)

1987 USR: **Various Artists:** *Phil Spector's Christmas Album* (Chrysalis —— – No 69)

1991 USR: reissue within box set **Various Artists:** *Back To Mono 1958–69* (ABKCo 7118–1)

1991 UKR: reissue within box set **Various Artists:** *Back To Mono 1958–69* (ABKCo 7118–1)

White Christmas – **Darlene Love** / Frosty The Snowman – **The Ronettes** / The Bells Of St Mary – **Bob B Soxx And The Blue Jeans** / Santa Claus Is Comin' To Town – **The Crystals** / Sleigh Ride – **The Ronettes** / (It's A) Marshmallow World – **Darlene Love** / I Saw Mommy Kissing Santa Claus – **The Ronettes** / Rudolph The Red-nosed Reindeer – **The Crystals** / Winter Wonderland – **Darlene Love** / Parade Of The Wooden Soldiers – **The Crystals** / Christmas (Baby Please Come Home) – **Darlene Love** / Here Comes Santa Claus – **Bob B Soxx And The Blue Jeans** / Silent Night – **Phil Spector and Artists**

12/64 US: The Ronettes: *Presenting The Fabulous Ronettes Featuring Veronica* (Philles 4006 – No 96)

12/64 UK: The Ronettes: *Presenting The Fabulous Ronettes Featuring Veronica* (London HAU 8212)

1965 USR: The Ronettes: *Presenting The Fabulous Ronettes Featuring Veronica* (Capitol Record Club ST 90721 – 1965)

1981 UKR: The Ronettes: *Wall Of Sound, Vol 1: The Ronettes Sing Their Greatest Hits* (Phil Spector Int'l 2307 003)

1981 UKR: reissue within box set **Various Artists:** *The Wall Of Sound* (Phil Spector Int'l WOS 001)

Walkin' In The Rain / Do I Love You / So Young / (The Best Part Of) Breakin' Up / I Wonder / What'd I Say / Be My Baby / You Baby / Baby I Love You / How Does It Feel? / When I Saw You / Chapel Of Love

12/64 US: Righteous Brothers: *You've Lost That Lovin' Feelin'* (Philles 4007 – No 4)

01/65 UK: Righteous Brothers: *You've Lost That Lovin' Feelin* (London HA 8226)

1965 USR: Righteous Brothers: *You've Lost That Lovin' Feelin* (Capitol Record Club ST 90692)

1 track only produced by Spector: You've Lost That Lovin' Feelin'

05/65 US: Righteous Brothers: *Just Once In My Life* (Philles 4008 – No 9)

—/65 UK: Righteous Brothers: *Just Once In My Life* (London HA 8245)

2 tracks only prod by Spector: Just Once In My Life / Unchained Melody

11/65 US: Lenny Bruce: *Lenny Bruce Is Out Again* (Philles 4010)

Craphouse / Obscenity / The Law / Marijuana / Midgets / Guys Exposing Themselves / Dating Advice / Guys Don't Cheat On Girls / Get Even / Thank You Masked Man / Orphan Annie

11/65 US: Righteous Brothers: *Back To Back* (Philles 4009 – No 16)

11/65 UK: Righteous Brothers: *Back To Back* (London HA 8278)
4 tracks only produced by Spector: Ebb Tide / Hung On You / For Sentimental Reasons / White Cliffs Of Dover

—/67 US: Ike And Tina Turner: *River Deep – Mountain High* (Philles 4011)

09/66 UK: Ike And Tina Turner: *River Deep – Mountain High*
(London HAU / SHU 8298 – No 27)
(5 tracks only produced by Spector) River Deep – Mountain High / A Love Like Yours (Don't Come Knocking Every Day) / Hold On Baby / Save The Last Dance For Me / Every Day I Have To Cry

1969 USR: Ike And Tina Turner: *River Deep – Mountain High* (revised issue) (A&M SP 4178 – No 102)

1969 UKR: Ike And Tina Turner: *River Deep – Mountain High* (revised issue) (A&M AMLP 8013)

1982 USR: Ike And Tina Turner: *River Deep – Mountain High* (revised issue) (A&M SP 3179)
(5 tracks only produced by Spector) River Deep – Mountain High / A Love Like Yours (Don't Come Knocking Every Day) / Hold On Baby / Save The Last Dance For Me / Every Day I Have To Cry

SELECTED COMPILATIONS AND ARCHIVE RELEASES

SINGLES

1975 UK: The Ronettes: I'm A Woman In Love With You / When I Saw You (Phil Spector Int'l 2010 009)

1975 UK: Various Artists: Frosty The Snowman / Santa Claus Is Coming To Town / White Christmas (Phil Spector Int'l 2010 010)

1976 US: Ronnie Spector: Paradise / When I Saw You (Warner–Spector 0409)

1982 US The Crystals: Rudolph The Red-nosed Reindeer / **The Ronettes:** I Saw Her Mommy Kissing Santa Claus (Pavilion 03333)

1987 UK Various Artists: Christmas Mix (Sleigh Ride / Winter Wonderland / White Christmas / Christmas (Baby Please Come Home) (Chrysalis CHS 3202)

ALBUMS

1972 US: Various Artists: *The Phil Spector Spectacular* (Philles 100 – white label promo / possibly planned Apple release)

You've Lost That Lovin' Feelin' – **Righteous Brothers** / Then He Kissed Me – **The Crystals** / Zip-A-De-Doo-Dah – **Bob B Soxx And The Blue Jeans** / Walkin' In The Rain – **The Ronettes** / Wait 'Til My Bobby Gets Home – **Darlene Love** / Baby I Love You – **The Ronettes** / Da Doo Ron Ron – **The Crystals** / Uptown – **The Crystals** + 8 unknown titles

1975 UK: Bob B Soxx And The Blue Jeans: *Phil Spector Wall Of Sound, Vol 2* (Phil Spector Int'l 2307 004)

1981 UKR: reissue within box set **Various Artists:** *The Wall Of Sound* (Phil Spector Int'l WOS 001)

Not Too Young To Get Married / Why Do Lovers Break Each Other's Hearts? / Let The Good Time Roll / My Heart Beat A Little Faster / Baby (I Love You) / Dr Kaplan's Office / Zip-A-Dee-Doo-Dah / The White Cliffs Of Dover / This Land Is Your Land / Dear (Here Comes My Baby) / I Shook The World / Everything's Gonna Be Alright

1975 UK: The Crystals: *Phil Spector Wall Of Sound, Vol 3: The Crystals Sing Their Greatest Hits* (Phil Spector Int'l 2307 006)

1981 UKR: reissue within box set **various artists:** *The Wall Of Sound* (Phil Spector Int'l WOS 001)

He's A Rebel / Uptown / There's No Other (Like My Baby) / Oh Yeah Maybe Baby / Please Hurt Me / Mashed Potato Time / Another Country – Another World / He's Sure The Boy I Love / Then He Kissed Me / On Broadway / What A Nice Way To Turn Seventeen / He Hit Me (And It Felt Like A Kiss) / I Love You Eddie / Look In My Eyes / No One Ever Tells You / Da Doo Ron Ron

1976 UK: Various Artists: *Phil Spector Wall Of Sound, Vol 4: Yesterday's Hits Today* (Phil Spector Int'l 2307 007)

Baby I Love You – **The Ronettes** / Uptown – **The Crystals** / (Today I Met) The Boy I'm Gonna Marry – **Darlene Love** / Why Do Lovers Break Each Other's Hearts? – **Bob B Soxx And The Blue Jeans** / I Can Hear Music – **The Ronettes** / Puddin 'n' Tain – **The Alley Cats** / Is This What I Get For Loving You – **The Ronettes** / Then He Kissed Me – **The Crystals** / (The Best Part Of) Breaking Up – **The Ronettes** / All Grown Up – **The Crystals** / A Fine Fine Boy – **Darlene Love** / Little Boy – **The Crystals** / Born To Be Together – **The Ronettes** / Wait Till My Bobby Gets Home – **Darlene Love**

1976 UK: **Various Artists:** *Phil Spector Wall Of Sound, Vol 5: Rare Masters, Vol 1* (Phil Spector Int'l 2307 008)

Paradise – **The Ronettes (featuring Veronica)** / Run Run Run Runaway – **Darlene Love** / Why Don't They Let Us Fall In Love – **Veronica** / Soldier Baby (Of Mine) – **The Ronettes** / All Grown Up – **The Crystals** / (He's A) Quiet Guy – **Darlene Love** / Torpedo Rock – **Phil Spector Wall Of Sound Orchestra** / Home Of The Brave – **Bonnie And The Treasures** / Why Can't A Boy And Girl Just Stay In Love? – **April Stevens** / Stumble And Fall – **Darlene Love** / Heartbreaker – **The Crystals** / Strange Love – **Darlene Love** / (I'm A) Woman In Love – **The Ronettes**

1976 UK: **Various Artists:** *Phil Spector Wall Of Sound, Vol 6: Rare Masters, Vol 2* (Phil Spector Int'l 2307 009)

Everything Under The Sun – **The Ronettes** / I Wish I Never Saw The Sunshine – **The Ronettes** / This Could Be The Night – **Modern Folk Quartet** / Act Naturally – **Betty Willis** / Take It From Me – **Darlene Love** / But You Don't Love Me – **Bob B Soxx And The Blue Jeans** / A Long Way To Be Happy – **Darlene Love** / Keep On Dancing – **The Ronettes** / Here I Sit – **The Ronettes** / Hold Me Tight – **The Treasures** / The Walk – **Bob B Soxx And The Blue Jeans** / Playing For Keeps – **Darlene Love** / If I Had A Hammer – **Betty Willis** / Johnny (Baby Please Come Home) – **Darlene Love**

1976 UK: **Various Artists:** *Phil Spector's 20 Greatest Hits* (Phil Spector Int'l 2307 012)

09/77 UKR: **Various Artists:** *Echoes Of The 60s* (Phil Spector Int.2307 013 No 10)

River Deep – Mountain High – **Ike and Tina Turner** / Then He Kissed Me – **The Crystals** / Be My Baby – **The Ronettes** / Why Do Lovers Break Each Other's Hearts? – **Bob B Soxx And The Blue Jeans** / Proud Mary – **The Checkmates Ltd** / (Today I Met) The Boy I'm Gonna Marry – **Darlene Love** / Zip-A-Dee-Doo-Dah – **Bob B Soxx And The Blue Jeans** / (The Best Part Of) Breakin' Up – **The Ronettes** / You've Lost That Lovin' Feelin' – **Righteous Brothers** / Da Doo Ron Ron – **The Crystals** / He's A Rebel – **The Crystals** / Not Too Young To Get Married – **Bob B Soxx And The Blue Jeans** / Uptown – **The Crystals** / Unchained Melody – **Righteous Brothers** / Walking In The Rain – **The Ronettes** / A Love Like Yours – **Nilsson and Cher** / He's Sure The Boy I Love – **The Crystals** / Ebb Tide – **Righteous Brothers** / Wait Till My Bobby Gets Home – **Darlene Love** / Baby I Love You – **The Ronettes**

—/77 US: **Various Artists:** *Phil Spector's Greatest Hits*
(Warner-Spector 2SP – 9104)

—/77 USR: **Various Artists:** *Lakeshore Music Presents Rock & Roll Forever*
(Warner Special Products OP 2508)
Be My Baby – **The Ronettes** / Da Doo Ron Ron – **The Crystals** / You've
Lost That Lovin' Feelin' – The **Righteous Brothers** / Then He Kissed Me –
The Crystals / Baby I Love You – **The Ronettes** / Walkin' In The Rain –
The Ronettes / He's A Rebel – **The Crystals** / Uptown – **The Crystals** / Zip-
A-De-Doo-Dah – **Bob B Soxx And The Blue Jeans** / Not Too Young To
Get Married – **Bob B Soxx And The Blue Jeans** / (Today I Met) The Boy
I'm Gonna Marry – **Darlene Love** / Wait 'Til My Bobby Gets Home –
Darlene Love / To Know Him Is To Love Him – **The Teddy Bears** / Pretty
Little Angel Eyes – **Curtis Lee** / I Love How You Love Me – **Paris Sisters** /
Every Breath I Take – **Gene Pitney** / Under The Moon Of Love – **Curtis
Lee** (alternate version) / He's Sure the Boy I Love – **The Crystals** (alternate
version) / Spanish Harlem – **Ben E King** / Unchained Melody – **The
Righteous Brothers** / River Deep – Mountain High – **Ike And Tina Turner**
/ Just Once In My Life – **The Righteous Brothers** / Black Pearl – **Sonny
Charles And The Checkmates Ltd** / Ebb Tide – **The Righteous Brothers**

1981 UK: **The Righteous Brothers:** *Masters: The Greatest Hits*
(Polydor 2335 229)

1981 UKR: reissue within box set **Various Artists:** *The Wall Of Sound* (Phil
Spector Int'l WOS 001)
You've Lost That Lovin' Feelin' / The White Cliffs Of Dover / Georgia On
My Mind / (I Love You) For Sentimental Reasons / You'll Never Walk
Alone / Just Once In My Life / Unchained Melody / See That Girl / Ebb
Tide / Guess Who? / Hung On You / The Great Pretender

1981 UK: **The Ronettes:** *The Greatest Hits, Volume II*
(Polydor 2335 233)
reissue within box set **Various Artists:** *The Wall Of Sound* (Phil
Spector Int'l WOS 001)
I Can Hear Music / Is This What I Get For Loving You / Born To Be
Together / Paradise / Soldier Baby (Of Mine) / (I'm A) Woman In Love /
/ Everything Under The Sun / I Wish I Never Saw The Sunshine / Keep
On Dancing / Here I Sit / Why Don't They Let Us Fall In Love / Lovers

1981 UK: **Darlene Love:** *Masters* (Polydor 2335 236)

1981 UKR: reissue within box set **Various Artists:** *The Wall Of Sound*

(Phil Spector Int'l WOS 001)

Run Run Run Runaway / (He's A) Quiet Guy / Stumble And Fall / Strange Love / Take It From Me / A Long Way To Be Happy / Playing For Keeps / Johnny (Baby Please Come Home) / (Today I Met) The Boy I'm Gonna Marry / A Fine Fine Boy / Wait Till My Bobby Gets Home / Lord If You're A Woman / I Love Him Like I Love My Very Life

1981 UK: **Various Artists:** *Phil Spector Masters* (Polydor 2335 237)

1981 UKR: reissue within box set **Various Artists:** *The Wall Of Sound* (Phil Spector Int'l WOS 001)

River Deep – Mountain High – **Ike And Tina Turner** / Baby Let's Stick Together – **Dion** / Torpedo Rock – **Phil Spector Wall of Sound Orchestra** / Home Of The Brave – **Bonnie And The Treasures** / Why Can't A Boy And A Girl Just Stay In Love – **April Stevens** / This Could Be The Night – **Modern Folk Quartet** / Puddin' 'n' Tain – **The Alley Cats** / Act Naturally – **Betty Willis** / But You Don't Love Me – **Bob B Soxx And the Blue Jeans** / Hold Me Tight – **The Treasures** / The Walk – **Bob B Soxx And The Blue Jeans** / If I Had A Hammer – **Betty Willis** / All Grown Up – **The Crystals** / Little Boy – **The Crystals**

1964-65: ROLLING STONES SESSIONS

SINGLES

01/64 UK: **Rolling Stones:** Not Fade Away* / Little By Little* [Spector percussion] (Decca F11845 – No 3)

02/65 US: **Rolling Stones:** The Last Time* / Play With Fire* [Spector bass] (London 9741 – No 9 / B-side No 96)

02/65 UK: **Rolling Stones:** The Last Time* / Play With Fire* [Spector bass] (Decca F12104 – No 1)

ALBUMS

06/64 US: **Rolling Stones:** *England's Newest Hitmakers* (London 375 – No 11)

04/64 UK: **Rolling Stones:** *The Rolling Stones* (Decca LK 4605) (Spector percussion on 2 tracks) Can I Get A Witness / Now I Got A Witness

1964-65: ASSOCIATED LABELS

SINGLES

—/64 US: **Bonnie Jo Mason:** I Love You Ringo / Beatle Blues (Annette 1000)

—/64 US: **Gene Toone And The Blazers:** You're My Baby / Jose (Annette 1001)

—/64 US: **Harvey And Doc With The Dwellers:** Oh Baby / Uncle Kev (Annette 1002)

—/64 US: **Veronica:** So Young / Larry L (Phil Spector 1)

—/64 US: **Veronica:** Why Don't They Let Us Fall In Love? / Chubby Danny D (Phil Spector 2)

—/64 US: **The Treasures:** Hold Me Tight / Pete Meets Vinnie (Shirley 500)

08/65 US: **Bonnie And The Treasures:** Home Of The Brave* / Our Song* (Phi–Dan 5005 – No 77)

—/65 UK: **Bonnie And The Treasures:** Home Of The Brave* / Our Song* (London HLU 9998)

1977 UKR: **Bonnie And The Treasures:** Home of the Brave* / Our Song* (Phil Spector Int'l 2010 021)

—/65 US: **Florence DeVore:** Kiss Me Now* / We're Not Old Enough* (Phi–Dan 5000)

—/65 US: **Betty Willis:** Act Naturally* / Soul* (Phi–Dan 5001)

—/65 US: **Al de Lory:** Yesterday* / Traffic Jam* (Phi–Dan 5006)

—/65 UK: **Al de Lory:** Yesterday* / Traffic Jam* (London HLU 9999)

—/65 US: **George McCannon III:** You Can't Grow Peaches On A Cherry Tree* / Seven Million People* (Phi–Dan 5007)

—/65 US: **Lovelites:** (When) I Get Scared* / Malady* (Phi–Dan 5008)

—/65 US: **The Ikettes:** Whatcha Gonna Do* / Down Down* (Phi–Dan 5009)

—/65 UK: **The Ikettes:** Whatcha Gonna Do* / Down Down* (London HLU 10081)

—/65 US: **Sugar Plums:** Lovers Wonderland* / Sugar Plums Blues* (Phi–Dan 5010)

ALBUMS

1966 US: **Barney Kessell:** *On Fire** (Emerald ELP–1201)

1977 UKR: **Barney Kessell:** *Slow Burn** (Phil Spector Int'l 2307011 011 – 1977)

Slow Burn / Just In Time / The Shadow Of Your Smile (Love Theme From *The Sandpiper*) / Recado Bossa Nova (Gift Of Love) / Sweet Baby / Who Can I Turn To (When Nobody Needs Me) / One Mint Julep

1969: A&M LABEL PRODUCTIONS

SINGLES

02/69 US: **The Checkmates Ltd:** Baby Don't You Get Crazy / Spanish Harlem (A&M 1006 – unreleased)

03/69 US: **The Checkmates Ltd:** Love Is All I Have To Give / Never Should Have Tried* (A&M 1039 – No 65)

03/69 UK: **The Checkmates Ltd:** Love Is All I Have To Give / Never Should Have Tried* (A&M AMS 747)

03/69 US: **The Ronettes feat the Voice of Veronica:** You Came You Saw You Conquered / Oh I Love You (A&M 1040 – No 108)

03/69 UK: **The Ronettes feat the Voice of Veronica:** You Came You Saw You Conquered / I Can Hear Music* (A&M AMS 748)

05/69 US: **Sonny Charles And The Checkmates Ltd:** Black Pearl / Lazy Susan* (A&M 1053 – No 13)

05/69 UK: **Sonny Charles And The Checkmates Ltd:** Black Pearl / Lazy Susan* (A&M AMS 752)

10/69 US: **Sonny Charles And The Checkmates Ltd:** Proud Mary / Spanish Harlem (A&M 1127)

10/69 US: **Sonny Charles And The Checkmates Ltd:** Proud Mary / Do You Love Your Baby* (A&M 1130 – No 69)

10/69 UK: **Sonny Charles And The Checkmates Ltd:** Proud Mary / Do You Love Your Baby* (A&M AMS 769 – No 30)

11/69 UK: **Sonny Charles And The Checkmates Ltd:** I Keep Forgetting / Do You Love Your Baby* (A&M AMS 780)

11/69 UK: **Ike And Tina Turner:** Everyday I Have To Cry / Make 'Em Wait (A&M AMS 783)

ALBUMS

10/69 US: **The Checkmates Ltd featuring Sonny Charles:** *Love Is All We Have To Give* (A&M 4183 – No 178)

01/9 UK: **The Checkmates Ltd featuring Sonny Charles:** *Love Is All We Have To Give* (A&M AMLS 943)

1977 UKR: The Checkmates Ltd (Phil Spector Int'l 2307 010 – (unissued) Proud Mary / Spanish Harlem / Black Pearl / I Keep Forgettin' / Love Is All I Have To Give / The Hair Anthology Suite: Ain't Got No – I Got Life (Prelude–Theme–Postlude) – Let The Sunshine (Overture) (Prelude) – Aquarius (Prelude–Theme) – Let The Sunshine In – Ain't Got No (Finale) (Prelude–Postlude)

1970-75: APPLE RECORDS (AND ASSOCIATED) PRODUCTIONS

SINGLES

02/70 US: Plastic Ono Band: Instant Karma (US mix)** / Who Has Seen The Wind?* (Apple 1818 – No 3)

02/70 UK: Plastic Ono Band: Instant Karma** (UK mix)/ Who Has Seen The Wind?* (Apple 1003 – No 5)

05/70 US: The Beatles: The Long And Winding Road / For You Blue (Apple 2832 – No 1)

11/70 US: George Harrison: My Sweet Lord** / Isn't It A Pity** (Apple 2995 – No 1)

01/71 UK: George Harrison: My Sweet Lord** / What Is Life** (Apple R5884 – No 1)

12/70 US: John Lennon and the Plastic Ono Band: Mother** / Why** (Apple 1827 – No 31)

11/70 US: Derek And The Dominoes: Tell The Truth / Roll It Over (Atco 6780 – withdrawn)

11/70 UK: Derek And The Dominoes: Tell The Truth / Roll It Over (Polydor 2058 057 – withdrawn)

02/71 US: George Harrison: What is Life** / Apple Scruffs** (Apple 1828 – No 9)

03/71 US: John Lennon and the Plastic Ono Band: Power To The People** / Touch Me* (Apple 1830 – No 11)

03/71 UK: John Lennon and the Plastic Ono Band: Power To The People** / Open Your Box* (Apple R5892 – No 7)

04/71 US: Ronnie Spector: Try Some Buy Some** / Tandoori Chicken** (Apple 1832)

04/71 UK: Ronnie Spector: Try Some Buy Some** / Tandoori Chicken** (Apple 33)

04/71 UK: Yoko Ono: Mind Train* / Listen, The Snow Is Falling**

(Apple 41)

07/71 US: **Bill Elliott and the Elastic Oz Band:** God Save Us** / Do The Oz*
(Apple 1835)

07/71 UK: **Bill Elliott and the Elastic Oz Band:** God Save Us** / Do The Oz*
(Apple 36)

07/71 US: **George Harrison:** Bangla-Desh** / Deep Blue**
(Apple 1836 – No 21 / B-side No 95)

07/71 UK: **George Harrison:** Bangla-Desh** / Deep Blue**
(Apple 5912 – No 10)

10/71 US: **John Lennon:** Imagine** / It's So Hard** (Apple 1840 – No 3)

10/75 UK: **John Lennon:** Imagine** / Working Class Hero**
(Apple R6009 – No 6)

11/71 US: **John Lennon and Yoko Ono:** Happy Xmas (War Is Over)** /
Listen, The Snow Is Falling** (Apple 1843)

11/72 UK: **John Lennon and Yoko Ono:** Happy Xmas (War Is Over)** /
Listen, The Snow Is Falling** (Apple R5970 – No 4)

04/72 US: **John Lennon and Yoko Ono:** Woman Is The Nigger Of The
World** / Sisters O Sisters** (Apple 1848 – No 77)

ALBUMS

05/70 US: **The Beatles:** *Let It Be* (Apple 34001 – No 1)

05/70 UK: **The Beatles:** *Let It Be* (Apple PXS 1 / PCS 7096 – No 1)

11/70 US: **George Harrison:** *All Things Must Pass*** (Apple 639 – No 1)

11/70 UK: **George Harrison:** *All Things Must Pass*** (Apple 639 – No 4)
I'd Have You Anytime / My Sweet Lord / Wah Wah / Isn't It A Pity? /
What Is Life / If Not For You / Behind That Locked Door / Let It Down
/ Run Of The Mill / Beware Of Darkness / Apple Scruffs / Ballad Of Sir
Frankie Crisp / Awaiting On You All / All Things Must Pass / I Dig Love
/ Art Of Dying / Isn't It A Pity? (version two) / Hear Me Lord / It's
Johnny's Birthday / Plug Me In / I Remember Jeep / Thanks For The
Pepperoni / Out Of The Blue

2000 US: **George Harrison:** *All Things Must Pass*
(Capitol CDP 7243 5 30474 2 9) as above + bonus tracks: I Live For You
/ Beware Of Darkness (demo) / Let It Down (demo) / What Is Life
(backing track) / My Sweet Lord (2000)

12/70 US: **John Lennon:** *John Lennon / Plastic Ono Band***
(Apple 3372 – No 6)

12/70 UK: John Lennon: *John Lennon / Plastic Ono Band* * *
(Apple PCS 7124 – No 11)
Mother / Hold On / I Found Out / Working Class Hero / Isolation /
Remember / Love / Well Well Well / Look At Me / God / My Mummy's Dead

2000 US: John Lennon: *John Lennon / Plastic Ono Band* * * (digitally
remastered and remixed) (Capitol 2435–28740–2)
as above + bonus tracks: Power To The People / Do The Oz

09/71 US: John Lennon: *Imagine* * * (Apple 3379 – No 1)

09/71 UK: John Lennon: *Imagine* * * (Apple PAS 10004 – No 1)

2000 US: John Lennon: *Imagine* * * (digitally remastered and remixed)
(Capitol 2435–24858–2)
Imagine / Crippled Inside / Jealous Guy / It's So Hard / I Don't Wanna be
A Soldier Mama / Gimme Some Truth / Oh My Love / How Do You
Sleep? / How? / Oh Yoko

12/71 US: George Harrison and Others: *The Concert For Bangla-Desh* * *
(Apple 3385 – No 2)

12/71 UK: George Harrison and Others: *The Concert For Bangla-Desh* * *
(Apple 3385 – No 1)

06/72 US: John Lennon and Yoko Ono: *Sometime In New York City* * *
(Apple 3392 – No 48)

06/72 UK: John Lennon and Yoko Ono: *Sometime In New York City* * *
(Apple PCSP 716 – No 11)
Woman Is The Nigger Of The World / Sisters O Sisters / Born In A Prison
/ New York City / Sunday Bloody Sunday / The Luck Of The Irish / John
Sinclair / Angela / We're All Water + live disc

05/73 US: George Harrison: *Living In The Material World* * * (Apple 3410)

05/73 UK: George Harrison: *Living In The Material World* * *
(Apple PAS 10006– No 2) 1 track only co-prod by Spector / Harrison: Try
Some Buy Some

02/75 US: John Lennon: *Sings The Great Rock 'n' Roll Hits (Roots)*
(Adam VIII 8018 – withdrawn)
6 tracks only prod by Spector: Angel Baby (edited version) / Be My Baby
/ Bony Moronie / Just Because / You Can't Catch Me / Sweet Little Sixteen

02/75 US: John Lennon: *Rock 'n' Roll* (Apple 3419 – No 6)

02/75 UK: John Lennon: *Rock 'n' Roll* (Apple PCS 7169 – No 6)
4 tracks only prod by Spector: Bony Moronie / Just Because / You Can't
Catch Me / Sweet Little Sixteen

10/86 US: **John Lennon:** *Menlove Avenue* (Capitol 12533 – No 127)

10/86 UK: **John Lennon:** *Menlove Avenue*

out-takes compilation: 4 tracks only prod by Spector: Here We Go Again / Angel Baby (full-length version) / Since My Baby Left Me / To Know Her Is To Love Her

1974-79: WARNER-SPECTOR/PHIL SPECTOR INTERNATIONAL

SINGLES

—/74 US: **Cher:** A Woman's Story / Baby I Love You (Warner-Spector 0400)

03/76 UK: **Cher:** A Woman's Story / Baby I Love You
(Phil Spector Int'l 2010 013)

—/74 US: **Cher and Nilsson:** A Love Like Yours / (Just Enough To Keep Me) Hanging On* (Warner-Spector 0402)

07/75 UK: **Cher and Nilsson:** A Love Like Yours / (Just Enough To Keep Me) Hanging On* (Phil Spector Int'l 2010 006)

—/74 US: **Dion:** Make The Woman Love Me / Running Close Behind You* (Warner-Spector 0403)

06/75 UK: **Dion:** Make The Woman Love Me / Running Close Behind You* (Phil Spector Int'l 2010 005)

05/75 US: **Jerri Bo Keno:** Here It Comes / I Don't Know Why
(Warner-Spector 0406)

05/75 UK: **Jerri Bo Keno:** Here It Comes / I Don't Know Why
(Phil Spector Int'l 2010 001)

08/75 US: **Calhoon:** Dance Dance Dance* / Rain 2000 (Warner-Spector 0405)

08/75 UK: **Calhoon:** Dance Dance Dance* / Rain 2000
(Phil Spector Int'l 2010 007)

02/76 US: **Dion:** Born To Be With You / Running Close Behind*
(Big Tree-Spector 16063)

02/76 UK: **Dion:** Born To Be With You / Good Lovin' Man
(Phil Spector Int'l 2010 012)

04/76 US: **Calhoon:** Soul Man parts 1 and 2* (Warner-Spector 0407)

04/76 UK: **Calhoon:** Soul Man parts 1 and 2* (Phil Spector Int'l 2010 015)

06/76 UK: **Mark Stein:** The Long And Winding Road* / Best Years Of My Life* (Phil Spector Int'l 2010 008)

07/76 US: **Danny Potter:** Standing In The Sunshine* / Red Bluff* (Warner-Spector 0408)

07/76 UK: Danny Potter: Standing In The Sunshine* / Red Bluff*
(Phil Spector Int'l 2010 016)

08/76 UK: Dion: Baby Let's Stick Together / New York City Song*
(Phil Spector Int'l 2010 018)

01/77 US: Darlene Love: Lord, If You're A Woman / Stumble and Fall
(Warner-Spector 0410)

01/77 UK: Darlene Love: Lord, If You're A Woman / Johnny*
(Phil Spector Int'l 2010 019)

ALBUMS

1974: US: Lenny Bruce: *The Law, Language And Lenny Bruce*
(Warner-Spector – 9101)

08/75: UK: Lenny Bruce: *The Law, Language And Lenny Bruce*
(Phil Spector Int'l 2307 001)
The Law / Tits And Ass / Ballbreakers / Chicken / Language / Ruby / Get
Even / Religion / How The Negro And Jew Got Into Show Business /
Crime And Punishment / Goering was a Transvestite / Eichmann (rec
live 1965)

10/75 UK: Dion: *Born To Be With You* (Polydor 2307 022)

1981 UKR: reissue within box set **Various Artists:** *The Wall Of Sound*
(Phil Spector Int'l WOS 001)
6 tracks only prod by Spector: Born To Be With You / Make The Woman
Love Me / (He's Got) The Whole World In His Hands / Only You Know
/ In And Out Of The Shadows / Good Lovin' Man

2001 UK: Dion: *Born To Be With You* (Ace CDCHD 793)
as above + Baby Let's Stick Together (plus 1976 *Streetheart* LP)

SELECTED COMPILATIONS & ARCHIVE RELEASES

1980 UK: Various Artists: *Phil Spector 74 / 79* (Phil Spector Int'l 2307 015)
Make The Woman Love Me – **Dion** / Here It Comes (And Here I Go) –
Jerri Bo Keno / A Love Like Yours (Don't Come Knocking Every Day) –
Nilsson and Cher / Baby Let's Stick Together – **Dion** / Lord If You're A
Woman – **Darlene Love** / A Woman's Story – **Cher** / Give It To Me – **Kim
Fowley** * / Baby I Love You – **Cher** / I Love Him Like I Love My Very
Life – **Darlene Love** / Born To Be With You – **Dion**

1981: UK: Various Artists: *The Wall Of Sound* (Phil Spector Int'l WOS 001)

9 LP boxed set containing: *Born To Be With You* – **Dion** / *The Ronettes Sing Their Greatest Hits* – **The Ronettes** / *Bob B Soxx And The Blue Jeans* – **Bob B Soxx And The Blue Jeans** / *Phil Spector's Christmas Album* – **Various Artists** / *The Crystals Sing Their Greatest Hits* – **The Crystals** / *The Greatest Hits* – **Righteous Brothers** / *The Greatest Hits Volume II* – **The Ronettes** / *Darlene Love Masters* – **Darlene Love** / *Phil Spector Masters* – **Various Artists**

1977-DATE: PHIL SPECTOR PRODUCTIONS

SINGLES

12/77 **UK: Leonard Cohen:** Memories / Don't Go Home With Your Hard-on (CBS 5882)

03/78 **US: Leonard Cohen:** Iodine / True Love Leaves No Traces (Warners 8527)

03/78 **UK: Leonard Cohen:** True Love Leaves No Traces / I Left A Woman Waiting (CBS 6095)

—/79 **US: Ramones:** Rock 'n' Roll High School* (Spector remix) / Do You Wanna Dance* [live] (Sire 1051)

01/80 **US: Ramones:** Baby I Love You / High Risk Insurance (Sire 49182)

01/80 **UK: Ramones:** Baby I Love You / High Risk Insurance (Sire 4031 – No 8)

04/80 **US: Ramones:** Do You Remember Rock 'n' Roll Radio / Let's Go (Sire 49261)

04/80 **UK: Ramones:** Do You Remember Rock 'n' Roll Radio / I Want You Around* (Spector remix) (Sire 4037 – No 67)

06/81 **US: Yoko Ono:** No No No** / Will You Touch Me**(Geffen 49802)

09/2003 **UK: Starsailor:** Silence Is Easy / Could You Be Mine* / She Understands* (EMI CDEM 625)

09/2003 **UK: Starsailor:** Silence Is Easy / Could You Be Mine* / Good Souls (live)* / behind the scenes interview – DVD single (EMI DVDEM 625)

ALBUMS

11/77 **US: Leonard Cohen:** *Death Of A Ladies Man* (Warners 3125)

11/77 **UK: Leonard Cohen:** *Death Of A Ladies Man* (CBS 86042 – No 35) True Love Leaves No Traces / Iodine / Paper Thin Hotel / I Left A Woman Waiting / Don't Go Home With Your Hard-on / Fingerprints / Death Of A Ladies Man

01/80 **US: Ramones:** *End Of The Century* (Sire 6067 – No 44)

01/80 UK: **Ramones:** *End Of The Century* (Sire SRK 6077 – No 14)
Do You Remember Rock 'n' Roll Radio / I'm Affected / Danny Says / Chinese Rock / The Return Of Jackie and Judy / Let's Go / Baby I Love You / I Can't Make It On Time / This Ain't Havana / Rock 'n' Roll High School / All The Way / High Risk Insurance

2002 US: **Ramones:** *End Of The Century* (Rhino R2 78155)
as above + I Want You Around (Spector remix) and bonus demos

06/81 US: **Yoko Ono:** *Season Of Glass*** (Geffen 2004 – No 49)

06/81 UK: **Yoko Ono:** *Season Of Glass*** (Geffen K99164 – No 47)

09/2003 UK: **Starsailor:** *Silence Is Easy* (EMI 5900072)
Produced 2 tracks: Silence Is Easy / White Dove

SELECTED MISCELLANEOUS COMPILATIONS & ARCHIVE RELEASES

1991 US / UK: **Various Artists:** *Back To Mono 1958–69* (ABKCo 7118–1)
The Alley Cats: Puddin 'n' Tain; **Bob B Soxx And The Blue Jeans:** Zip-A-Dee-Doo-Dah / Why Do Lovers Break Each Other's Hearts? / Not Too Young To Get Married / The Bells Of St Mary's / Here Comes Santa Claus; **Sonny Charles And The Checkmates:** Black Pearl / Love Is All I Have To Give; **The Crystals:** There's No Other (Like My Baby) / Uptown / He Hit Me (And It Felt Like A Kiss) / He's A Rebel / He's Sure The Boy I love /Da Doo Ron Ron / Heartbreaker / All Grown Up / Then He Kissed Me / Girls Can Tell / Little Boy / Santa Claus Is Coming To Town / Rudolph The Red-nosed Reindeer / Parade Of The Wooden Soldiers; **Ben E King:** Spanish Harlem; **Curtis Lee:** Pretty Little Angel Eyes / Under The Moon Of Love; **Darlene Love:** (Today I Met) The Boy I'm Gonna Marry / Chapel Of Love / Wait Till My Bobby Gets Home / A Fine, Fine Boy / Strange Love / Stumble And Fall / Long Way To Be Happy / White Christmas/ Marshmallow World / Winter Wonderland / Christmas (Baby Please Come Home); **Modern Folk Quartet:** This Could Be The Night; **Paris Sisters:** I Love How You Love Me; **Ray Peterson:** Corrine, Corrina; **Gene Pitney:** Every Breath I Take; **Righteous Brothers:** You've Lost That Lovin' Feelin' / Just Once In My life / Unchained Melody / (I Love You) For Sentimental Reasons /Ebb Tide; **The Ronettes:** Baby I Love You / I Wonder (The Best Part Of) Breakin' Up / Soldier Baby Of Mine / When I Saw You / Do I Love You / Keep On Dancing / You, Baby / A Woman In Love (With You) / Walking In The Rain / Born To Be Together / Is This What I Get For Loving

You? / Paradise / I Wish I Never Saw The Sunshine / You Came You Saw You Conquered / Frosty The Snowman / Sleigh Ride / I Saw Mommy Kissing Santa Claus; **Phil Spector and Artists:** Silent Night; **The Teddy Bears:** To Know Him Is To Love Him; **The Treasures:** Hold Me Tight; **Ike & Tina Turner:** River Deep – Mountain High / I'll Never Need More Than This / A Love Like Yours (Don't Come Knockin' Everyday) / Save The Last Dance For Me; **Veronica:** Why Don't They Let Us Fall In Love / So Young

1990s Euro: **Various Artists:** *Masterpiece Volume One* (A-Side Records AZ 5023 – bootleg)

Mr Robin – **Spectors Three** / Another Country Another World – **Bobby Day** / Bumbershoot – **Phil Harvey** / Where Can You Be – **Tony and Joe** / Cryin' Fool – **Jo Mann** / If You Only Knew – **The Teddy Bears** / Don't You Worry My Little Pet – **Art and Dotty Todd** / Some of Your Lovin' – **Emil O'Conner** / Dream for Sale – **Gene Pitney** / Ecstasy – **Ben E King** / Second Hand Love – **Connie Francis** / World of Tears – **Johnny Nash** / I Love You Betty – **Terry Day** / That's All Right Baby – **Gary Crosby** / To Know Him Is To Love Him – **Lesley Gore** / Be My Girl – **Ray Peterson** / Yes I Love You – **Paris Sisters** / Hey Little Girl – **Ray Sharpe** / That's What Girls Are For – **Timothy Hay** / Oh I Love You – **The Ronettes** / Spanish Harlem – **Santo and Johnny**

1990s Euro: **Various Artists:** *Masterpiece Volume Two* (A-Side Records AZ 5029 – bootleg)

Willy Boy – **Phil Harvey** / Oh Why – **The Teddy Bears** / I Really Do – **Spectors Three** / I Know Why – **Spectors Three** / Little Did I Know – **Ducanes** / That's All Right Baby – **Kell Osborn** / I'll Be Crying Tomorrow – **Paris Sisters** / Why Can't A Boy And Girl Just Stay In Love – **Noreen Corcoran** / I'll Keep You Happy – **Ike and Tina Turner** / (Let's Dance) The Screw Parts 1 and 2 – **The Crystals** / Young Boy Blues – **Ben E King** / You Can Get Him Frankenstein – **Castle Kings** / Some of Your Lovin' – **Johnny Nash** / Oh Baby! – **Harvey and Doc and the Dwellers** / I Just Go Wild Inside – **Barons** / There's a Woman – **Righteous Brothers** / Dear (Here Comes My Baby) – **Toni James** / Oui Les Filles – **Les Gams** / To Know You Is To Love You – **Peter and Gordon** / It's That Kind of Day – **Phil Spector** / Dr Kaplan's Office – **Phil Spector**

1990s Euro: **Various Artists:** *Masterpiece Volume Three* (A-Side Records AZ 5033 – bootleg)

Ringo I Love You – **Bonnie Jo Mason** / Raincoat In the Rain – **Sammy**

Turner / He Knows I Love Him Too Much – **Arlene Smith** / How Many Nights – **Bobby Sheen** / One Thousand Miles Away – **Johnny Nash** / Once Upon a While Ago – **Paris Sisters** / Na Ne No – **Troy Shondell** / Twist and Shout – **The Top Notes** / Air Mail Special Delivery – **Karen Lake** / Why Don't You Write Me – **Ray Peterson** / Nights of Mexico – **Russell Byrd** / You Took Advantage of Me – **Blackwells** / The Bells – **Creations** / Be a Soldier – **Terry Day** / My Heart Stood Still – **Spectors Three** / Gee How I Wish You Were Here – **Ray Peterson** / Hey There Mountain – **Obrey Wilson** / You're My Baby – **Gene Toone and the Blazers** / Wonderful Lovable You – **The Teddy Bears** / He's Sure the Boy I Love – **The Crystals** / Hot Pastrami – **Crystals** / Git It – **Phil Spector**

1990s **Euro: Various Artists:** *Phil Spector's Flips and Rarities* (PS 001 – bootleg)

I Idolize You – **Ike And Tina Turner** / Black Pearl – **Sonny Charles And The Checkmates** / Dream For Sale – **Gene Pitney** / Some Of Your Loving – **Johnny Nash** / World Of Tears – **Johnny Nash** / When You Dance – **Billy Storm** / Spanish Harlem – **Santo And Johnny** / Mr Robin – **Spectors Three** / Some Of Your Lovin – **Emil O Conner** / I Love You Betty – **Terry Day** / That's All Right Baby – **Gary Crosby** / Yes I Love You – **Paris Sisters** / That's What Girls Are For – **Timothy Hay** / Where Can You Be – **Tony And Joe** / Raincoat In The River – **Sammy Turner** / To Know Him Is To Love Him – **Lesley Gore** / Be My Girl – **Ray Peterson** / Unchained Melody – **Blackwells** / Oh Why – **The Teddy Bears** / Home Of The Brave – **Bonnie And The Treasures** / Why Can't A Boy And Girl Just Stay In Love – **April Stevens** / Why Don't They Let Us Fall In Love – **Veronica** / The Screw – **The Crystals** / Bumbershoot – **Phil Harvey** / Woman In Love – **The Ronettes** / Quiet Guy – **Darlene Love** / Here It Comes And Here I Go – **Jeri Bo Keno/** Puddin 'n' Tain – **The Alley Cats** / Dream For Sale – **Joey Paige** / I'm So Happy – **Ducanes**

MISCELLANEOUS

The following indexes Phil Spector production, co-compositions and performances referenced in other discographies, but either untraced or unreleased at the time of writing.

1961? **Ray Sharpe:** Hey Little Girl (Garex – cat no unavailable)
co-written by Spector / Barrett

1962 Little Eva: Uptown
Unreleased out-take

1962? Jo Mann: Cryin' Fool (other details unavailable)
Spector / Phillips composition

1962? Tony and Joe: Where Can You Be (other details unavailable)
Spector composition originally demoed by The Teddy Bears

1963 Noreen Corcoran: Why Can't A Girl And Boy Just Stay In Love (label / cat no unavailable)
co-written by Spector / Nino Tempo

1963–65 The Crystals: I'm A Woman In Love / It's My Party / Mary Ann
Unreleased out-takes

1963–65 The Ronettes: Baby Let's Be Lovers / Home Of The Brave / I Can Hear Music / Please Don't Hurt My Little Sister
Unreleased out-takes

1964 The Rolling Stones: Andrew's Blues / Spector And Pitney Came Too
Unreleased out-takes.

1965 Harry Nilsson: It's Over
Rumoured out-take

1966 Ike and Tina Turner: Everything Under The Sun
Unreleased out-take

1969 The Ronettes: Love Me Like You're Gonna Lose Me
Unreleased A&M recording

1969 Mortimer: Two Of Us
Apple acetate widely rumoured to have some Spector connection. However, it was recorded in April 1969, predating his arrival on the scene by eight months.

1971 Ronnie Spector: You / Loverley Laddy Day
Out-takes from 'Try Some Buy Some' session, subsequently included within *Complete Apple Singles* bootleg box set.

1975 Dion: They Call Me Mr Prestone
Only title known from rumoured album's worth of out-takes.

1987 Molly Ringwald: The Best Part Of Breaking Up
According to Mark Ribowsky's *He's A Rebel* biography, this performance was produced by Spector utilising an original Philles-era backing track.

1995 Celine Dion: four songs
Unreleased out-takes

Compositions

NOTE: Composer credits are taken from original record labels wherever possible, and, in some instances, may not correspond with subsequent releases and documentation.

Song titles are followed by original release: 'A' / 'B' denotes A- or B-side; LP denotes album track; BTM / RM / PSM denotes unreleased cut subsequently released on compilations *Back To Mono*, *Rare Masters* or *Phil Spector Masters*.

Pete Andreoli / Vincent Poncia Jr / Phil Spector
Best Part Of The Breakin' Up (The Ronettes 'A')
Do I Love You (The Ronettes 'B')
He's A Quiet Guy (Darlene Love 'B')
How Does It Feel (The Ronettes 'B')
I Go Wild Inside
Mary Ann (Crystals Out-Take)
Ringo I Love You (Bonnie Jo Mason 'A')
Soldier Baby Of Mine (The Ronettes BTM)
Strange Love (Darlene Love RM)
Stumble And Fall (Darlene Love 'B')
Wild Flower
You're My Baby (Gene Toone 'A')
Richard Barrett / Phil Spector
Hey Little Girl (Ray Sharpe 'A')
Jeff Barry / Phil Spector
Here It Comes And Here I Go (Jerri Bo Keno 'A')
Jeff Barry / Ellie Greenwich / Phil Spector
All Grown Up (Crystals 'B')

Baby I Love You (The Ronettes 'A')
Be My Baby (The Ronettes 'A')
Chapel Of Love (Darlene Love BTM)
Christmas (Baby Please Come Home) (Darlene Love 'A')
Da Doo Ron Ron (The Crystals 'A')
Don't Take Your Love Away From Me
Fine Fine Boy (Darlene Love 'A')
Gee The Moon Is Shining Bright
Girls Can Tell (The Crystals BTM)
Gonna Have A Party Tonight
He Loves Me I Can Tell
Heartbreaker (The Crystals RM)
I Can Hear Music (The Ronettes 'A')
I'll Never Need More Than This (Ike and Tina Turner 'A')
I Want You To Be My Boyfriend
I Wish I Never Saw The Sun Shine (The Ronettes RM)
I Wonder (The Crystals 'A')
Keep On Dancing (The Ronettes RM)
Little Boy (The Crystals PSM)
Not Too Young To Get Married (Bob B Soxx 'A')
River Deep – Mountain High (Ike and Tina Turner 'A')
Run Run Runaway (Darlene Love RM)
Then He Kissed Me (The Crystals 'A')
Wait Till My Bobby Gets Home (Darlene Love 'A')
Why Don't They Let Us Fall In Love (Veronica 'A')

Leroy R Bates / Phil Spector

There 's No Other Like My Baby (The Crystals 'A')

Leonard Cohen / Phil Spector

Death Of A Ladies Man
Don't Go Home With Your Hard-on
Fingerprints
I Left A Woman Waiting
Iodine
Memories
Paper Thin Hotel
True Love Leaves No Traces
(All from Cohen LP *Death Of A Ladies Man*)

Dion DiMucci / Phil Spector
    Good Lovin' Man (with A Bernstein / K Discofarno)
    (He's Got) The Whole World In His Hands
    (both from Dion LP *Born To Be With You*)

Ahmet Ertegun / E Adlum / Phil Spector
    You Can Get Him Frankenstein (Castle Kings 'A')

Gerry Goffin / Phil Spector
    In And Out Of The Shadows (Dion LP *Born To Be With You*)
    Leaving The One You Love
    Only You Know (Dion LP *Born To Be With You*)

Gerry Goffin / Carole King / Phil Spector
    Hung On You (Righteous Bros 'A')
    Is This What I Get For Loving You (The Ronettes 'A')
    Just Once In My Life (Righteous Bros 'A')
    No One Ever Tells You (Crystals LP *Twist Uptown*)

Ellie Greenwich / Tony Powers / Phil Spector
    (Today I Met) The Boy I'm Gonna Marry (Darlene Love 'A')
    Why Do Lovers Break Each Other's Hearts? (Bob B Soxx 'A')

George Harrison / Phil Spector
    Tandoori Chicken (Ronnie Spector 'B')

Robert Hatfield / Bill Medley / Phil Spector
    There's A Woman (Righteous Bros 'B')

Hank Hunter / Phil Spector
    I Love You Betty (Terry Day 'A')
    I Love You Eddie (Crystals 'B')
    Oh Yeah Maybe Baby (Crystals 'B')
    Second Hand Love (Connie Francis 'A')

Jerry Leiber / Phil Spector
    Spanish Harlem (Ben E King 'A')

John Lennon / Phil Spector
    Here We Go Again (Lennon LP *Menlove Avenue*)

Barry Mann / Cynthia Weil / Phil Spector
    Born To Be Together (The Ronettes 'A')
    Just For You Baby
    Walking In The Rain (The Ronettes 'A')
    I'm A Woman In Love With You (The Ronettes 'A')
    You Baby (The Ronettes 'B')

You've Lost That Lovin' Feelin' (Righteous Bros 'A')

Harry Nilsson / Phil Spector

Here I Sit (The Ronettes RM)

Paradise (Ronnie Spector 'A')

This Could Be The Night (Modern Folk Quartet BTM)

Nanker Phelge / Phil Spector

Little By Little (The Rolling Stones 'B')

Terry Phillips / Phil Spector

Cryin' Fool (Jo Mann 'A'?)

Dream For Sale (Gene Pitney LP *Many Sides Of*)

Hands Of A Fool (+ **Eugene A Rowley**)

Some Of Your Lovin (Johnny Nash 'A')

Wishful Thinking

World Of Tears (Johnny Nash 'B')

Doc Pomus / Phil Spector

Another Country Another World (Crystals LP *Twist Uptown*)

Ecstasy (Ben E King 'A')

First Taste Of Love (Ben E King 'B')

Laugh Right In My Face

Runaround (Gene McDaniels CD Compilation *The Best Of Gene McDaniels*)

What Am I To Do (Paris Sisters 'B')

Young Boy Blues (Ben E King 'A')

Cory Sands (Shirley Spector) / Phil Spector

A Lonely Girl's Prayer (Paris Sisters 'B')

All Because Of You

Annette (Bob B Soxx 'B')

Be My Boy (Paris Sisters 'A')

Be My Girl (Ray Peterson 'B')

I'll Be Crying Tomorrow (Paris Sisters 'B')

Little Did I Know (Ducanes 'B')

Too Good To Be True

Philip Spector

Bebe And Susu (The Ronettes 'B')

Blues For Baby (The Ronettes 'B')

Bumbershoot (Phil Harvey 'A')

But You Don't Love Me (Bob B Soxx RM)

Chubby Danny D (Veronica 'B')
Dear (Bob B Soxx LP *Zip A Dee Doo Dah*)
Don't Go Away (The Teddy Bears 'A')
Don't You Worry My Little Pet (The Teddy Bears 'B')
Dr Kaplan's Office (Bob B Soxx 'B')
Everything's Gonna Be Alright (Bob B Soxx LP *Zip-A-Dee-Doo-Dah*)
Flip And Nitty (Bob B Soxx 'B')
Harry And Milt Meet Hal B (Darlene Love 'B')
I Don't Need You Anymore (The Teddy Bears 'A')
I Know Why (Spector's Three 'B')
I'll Keep You Happy (Ike and Tina Turner 'B')
I Really Do (The Teddy Bears 'B')
If You Only Knew The Love I Have (The Teddy Bears 'A')
Lucy In London
Miss Joan And Mr Sam
My Love's A Growin' For You
Oh I Love You (The Ronettes 'B')
Oh Why (The Teddy Bears 'B')
Playing For Keeps (Darlene Love 'B')
Silent Night (LP *A Christmas Gift For You*)
Stand By Him (working demo of 'Paradise' – Nilsson / Spector)
Take It From Me (Darlene Love 'B')
Tedesco And Pitman (The Ronettes 'B')
That's Alright Baby (Kell Osborne 'B')
The Screw (Crystals 'A')
The Walk (Bob B Soxx RM)
Things Are Changing (Equal Opportunities promo)
Till You'll Be Mine (*The Teddy Bears* LP)
To Know Him Is To Love Him (The Teddy Bears 'A')
Torpedo Rock (Phil Spector Wall of Sound Orchestra RM)
Walkin' Along (The Crystals 'B')
When I Saw You (The Ronettes 'B')
Where Can You Be (Tony and Joe 'A'?)
Who Wants Your Lovin'
Willy Boy (Phil Harvey 'B')
Wonderful Loveable You (The Teddy Bears 'a')
You Said Goodbye (The Teddy Bears 'B')

Bobby Stevens / Phil Spector
  Love Is All I Have To Give (Checkmates 'A')
Nino Tempo / Phil Spector
  A Woman's Story (+ **Carol Lo Tempio**) (Cher 'A')
  Why Can't A Boy And Girl Just Stay In Love (Noreen Corcoran 'A')
Kathie Venet / Phil Spector
  Mister Robin (Spector's Three 'A')
Brian Wilson / Phil Spector
  Don't Hurt My Little Sister (The Ronettes out-take)
  Things Are Changing (Public service jingle)
Toni Wine / Irwin Levine / Phil Spector
  Black Pearl (Checkmates 'A')
  I Loved You Like I Loved
  You Came You Saw You Conquered (The Ronettes 'A')

GREAT SPECTOR COVERS

A selection of 20 cover versions of songs associated with Phil Spector:

  Baby I Love You – **Dave Edmunds** (1973)
  Best Part Of The Breakin Up – **The Teasers** (1982)
  Black Pearl – **Horace Faith** (1970)
  Born To Be Together – **PP Arnold** (1970)
  Born To Be With You – **Dave Edmunds** (1973)
  Da Doo Ron Ron – **Grumble** (1972)
  First Taste Of Love – **Wayne Fontana And The Mindbenders** (1964)
  I Love How You Love Me – **Paul and Barry Ryan** (1966)
  Is This What I Get For Loving You Baby – **Marianne Faithfull** (1966)
  Memories – **Black-Eyed Susans** (1993)
  Pretty Little Angel Eyes – **Showaddywaddy** (1978)
  River Deep – Mountain High – **Supremes and Four Tops** (1971)
  Spanish Harlem – **Jimmy Justice** (1962)
  This Could Be The Night – **David Cassidy** (1975)
  To Know Him Is To Love Him – **Steeleye Span** (1974)
  Try Some Buy Some – **David Bowie** (2003)
  Under The Moon Of Love – **Showaddywaddy** (1976)
  Uptown – **Little Eva** (1962)
  You Came, You Saw, You Conquered – **The Pearls** (1972)
  You've Lost That Lovin' Feelin' – **Cilla Black** (1965)

Sources And Bibliography

A full list of sources (absenting those, of course, who asked not to be named) appears below, together with a bibliographical directory of the many books and magazine articles that helped shape the chronological flow and content of the narrative. As I quickly learned which works actually had something to say on the subject, and which could be thrown, barely opened, to the pigs outside my window, it goes without saying that all the titles quoted are recommended to all readers.

PERSONAL INTERVIEWS AND CONTACTS (1985 TO DATE)

Tony Ashton
Sonny Bono
Leonard Cohen
Donovan
Geoff Goddard
George Harrison
Jimmie Haskell
Nicky Hopkins
Tony King
Harry Nilsson
Jack Nitzsche
Doc Pomus
Dee Dee Ramone
Joey Ramone
Ronnie Spector
Bill Wyman

BOOKS AND MEMOIRS

Blaine, Hal and Mr Nonzai: *Hal Blaine & The Wrecking Crew* (Mixbooks, 1990)

Bono, Sonny: *And The Beat Goes On* (Simon & Schuster, 1991)

DiMucci, Dion and Seay, Davin: *The Wanderer* (Beech Tree, 1988)

Finnis, Rob: *The Phil Spector Story* (Rock On, 1975)

Fitzpatrick, John J and Fogerty, James E: *Collecting Phil Spector* (Spectacle Press, 1991)

Germain, Georges-Hébert: *Celine* (LibreExpression, 1997)

Goodman, Fred: *Mansion On The Hill* (Times Books, 1997)

Jackson, La Toya: *La Toya – Growing Up In The Jackson Family* (Dutton, 1991)

Leng, Simon: *The Music Of George Harrison: While My Guitar Gently Weeps* (Firefly 2003)

Lewisohn, Mark: *The Beatles Recording Sessions* (Harmony 1988)

Love, Darlene: *My Name Is Love* (Morrow, 1998)

Miles, Barry: *Paul McCartney – Many Years From Now* (Henry Holt, 1997)

Oldham, Andrew Loog: *Stoned* (Secker & Warburg, 2000)

Oldham, Andrew Loog: *2Stoned* (Secker & Warburg, 2002)

Ramone, Dee Dee with Kofman, Veronica: *Lobotomy: Surviving The Ramones* (Thundersmouth, 1997)

Ribowsky, Mark: *He's A Rebel – Phil Spector* (Dutton, 1989)

Spector, Ronnie with Waldron, Vince: *Be My Baby* (Harmony, 1990)

Tobler, John and Grundy, Stuart: *The Record Producers* (BBC, 1982)

True, Everett: *Hey Ho Let's Go: The Story Of The Ramones* (Omnibus 2002)

Turner, Ike with Cawthorne, Nigel: *Taking Back My Name* (Virgin, 1999)

Turner, Tina with Loder, Kurt: *I Tina* (Morrow 1986)

Williams, Richard: *Out Of His Head: The Sound Of Phil Spector* (Dutton, 1972; revised Omnibus 2003)

MAGAZINE ARTICLES

Aronowitz, Al: *Column 47:* 'A Legendary Night: Phil Spector's Fuck You Fuck You Fuck You Party' (*The Blacklisted Journalist*, 1 July 1999)

Brown, Mick: interview with Phil Spector (*Daily Telegraph*, 6 February 2003)

Carr, Roy: interview with Phil Spector (*New Musical Express*, 6 March, 20 March 1976)

DeCurtis, Anthony: 'To Know Him Is To Love Him: Phil Spector reflects on John Lennon and more' (*Rolling Stone*, 9 November 2000)

Garfield, Simon: 'Stalking Spector' (*Observer*, 27 July 2003)

Kubernik, Harvey: 'Jack Nitzsche Remembers The Wall of Sound' (*Goldmine*, 17 June 1988)

Puterbaugh, Parker: 'Reconstructing Producer Phil Spector's Legendary Style' (*Rolling Stone*, 23 August 1990)

Raab, Scott: 'Be My, Be My Baby' (*Esquire*, July 2003)

Shaw, Greg: 'Phil Spector: To Know Him Is To Love Him' (*The History Of Rock*, 1982)

Wenner, Jan: interview with Phil Spector (*Rolling Stone*, 1 November 1969)

GENERAL PUBLICATIONS

Circus, Goldmine, Hit Parader, Let It Rock, Melody Maker, New Musical Express, Record Collector, Zig Zag

INTERNET SITES

www.carolkaye.com (official homepage of former Wall of Sound sessioneer)

www.ronniespector.com (official homepage)

www.spectropop.com

www.spectormurdercase.com (detailed and up-to-date summary of events)

Index